LIFE VISION

Workbook

B2

Upper Intermediate

Vicky Butt and Rachel Godfrey

CONTENTS

INTRODUCTION p.4	LESSON 0.1	LESSON 0.2	LESSON 0.3	LESSON 0.4
	Vocabulary: Injuries and treatment **Grammar:** Present tenses	**Vocabulary:** Nature **Grammar:** Past tenses	**Vocabulary:** Work and study **Grammar:** Future tenses	**Vocabulary:** Travel and tourism **Grammar:** Relative clauses

UNIT	VOCABULARY 1	GRAMMAR 1	LISTENING	VOCABULARY 2
1 Live and learn p.8	The road to success **Vocabulary:** Skills and natural talents ▶ Vlog	Past perfect simple and past perfect continuous ▶ Grammar animation	You and art **Strategy:** Using key words to identify the main point **Vocabulary:** Phrasal verbs	The best age **Vocabulary:** Life stages and learning
	Review p.17 **How to learn vocabulary** p.96			
2 Highs and lows p.18	It drives me crazy! **Vocabulary:** Feelings ▶ Vlog	Modal verbs: advice, obligation and necessity; possibility, probability and certainty ▶ Grammar animation	Taking control of your life **Strategy:** Recognising paraphrasing **Vocabulary:** Being more in control	Well-being **Vocabulary:** Well-being
	Review p.27 **Exam skills** p.28 **Listening** Multiple-choice task **Use of English** Word formation task			
3 An active life p.30	Let's keep fit **Vocabulary:** Doing exercise ▶ Vlog	Advanced and qualifying comparatives ▶ Grammar animation	Sports products **Strategy:** Distinguishing facts and speculation **Vocabulary:** Origins of sport	Transferable skills **Vocabulary:** Transferable skills
	Review p.39 **How to learn vocabulary** p.98			
4 A place like home p.40	Alternative living spaces **Vocabulary:** Living spaces ▶ Vlog	Future continuous, future perfect simple and future perfect continuous ▶ Grammar animation	GEOCAST – urban teenagers **Strategy:** Understanding discourse markers **Vocabulary:** Work	Nomads **Vocabulary:** Home and community
	Review p.49 **Exam skills** p.50 **Listening** Multiple-choice task **Use of English** Multiple-choice cloze task			
5 Technology p.52	What gadget couldn't you live without? **Vocabulary:** Technology ▶ Vlog	Second and third conditionals; conjunctions: alternatives to *if* ▶ Grammar animation	Artificial intelligence **Strategy:** Distinguishing between supporting and contrasting information **Vocabulary:** Streaming	Technology and the environment **Vocabulary:** Technology and the environment
	Review p.61 **How to learn vocabulary** p.100			
6 Money matters p.62	No-spend challenge **Vocabulary:** Spending money **Pronunciation:** Compound nouns ▶ Vlog	The passive: all tenses; verbs with two objects in the passive ▶ Grammar animation	Consumerism **Strategy:** Drawing conclusions from what we hear **Vocabulary:** Minimalism	Social commerce **Vocabulary:** Online shopping
	Review p.71 **Exam skills** p.72 **Listening** Multiple-matching task **Use of English** Key-word transformation task			
7 All about art p.74	That sounds amazing! **Vocabulary:** Different art forms ▶ Vlog	Reported speech ▶ Grammar animation	Concerts **Strategy:** Recognising the new meaning of a known word **Vocabulary:** Film and music	Updated masterpieces **Vocabulary:** Interpreting art
	Review p.83 **How to learn vocabulary** p.102			
8 Local and global citizenship p.84	Lending a helping hand **Vocabulary:** Volunteering in the community ▶ Vlog	Verb patterns ▶ Grammar animation	Volunteering **Strategy:** Recognising features of informal English **Vocabulary:** Informal phrases **Pronunciation:** Connected speech	Crisis mapping **Vocabulary:** Responding to a humanitarian crisis
	Review p.93 **Exam skills** p.94 **Listening** Multiple-choice task **Use of English** Open cloze task			

VOCABULARY BOOSTER	p.104
FUNCTIONS BANK	p.112
WRITING BANK	p.114
WORD LIST	p.120

GRAMMAR 2	READING	GLOBAL SKILLS	SPEAKING	WRITING
Used to, would, be / get used to ▶ Grammar animation Pronunciation: used to	Connectivism: A Theory of Learning for a Digital Age Strategy: Understanding new words and phrases Vocabulary: Phrases with get	Emotional intelligence Vocabulary: Emotions	A social exchange Strategy: Being able to backtrack and reformulate to correct errors or slips Phrasebook: Restating your ideas	An article Strategy: Using comment adverbs to make your writing more interesting Phrasebook: Comment adverbs
Past modal verbs ▶ Grammar animation	Quick thinking? Life-saving! Strategy: Previewing and predicting Vocabulary: Collocations	Building resilience Vocabulary: Challenging situations	Comparing photos Strategy: Using adjectives Phrasebook: Talking about photos Pronunciation: Contrastive stress	An opinion essay Strategy: Planning what to include Phrasebook: Opinion essays

Reading Multiple-choice task Speaking Discussion task Writing Story How to learn vocabulary p.97

| Articles and quantifiers
▶ Grammar animation | Autism and sport
Strategy: Understanding referencing
Vocabulary: Disability in sport | Managing your reaction
Vocabulary: Handling disagreements | A discussion
Strategy: Managing the conversation
Phrasebook: Discussing ideas
Pronunciation: Sentence stress | A report
Strategy: Using impersonal language
Phrasebook: Impersonal language |
| Future time clauses; first conditional
▶ Grammar animation | Brain drain migration
Strategy: Recognising the writer's point of view
Vocabulary: Extreme weather | Identifying and analysing trends
Vocabulary: Describing trends in graphs and diagrams | A stimulus-based discussion
Strategy: Speculating about the future; co-operating and contributing
Phrasebook: Commenting on someone's opinion
Pronunciation: Chunking | A formal email of enquiry
Strategy: Using formal register
Phrasebook: Enquiring |

Reading Meaning through context Speaking Researching topics Writing Checking for errors How to learn vocabulary p.99

| Mixed conditionals
▶ Grammar animation | Classroom learning vs screen learning
Strategy: Using topic sentences
Vocabulary: Social media | Your digital footprint
Vocabulary: Online activity | Giving a presentation
Strategy: Organising a presentation
Phrasebook: Signposting a presentation
Pronunciation: Linking | An app review
Strategy: Using modifying adverbs
Phrasebook: Reviewing an app |
| The passive: advanced forms
▶ Grammar animation | Virtual mirror
Strategy: Recognising functional language to identify purpose
Vocabulary: Fashion | The importance of the small print
Vocabulary: Consumer rights | Asserting your rights as a customer
Strategy: Register
Phrasebook: Consumer issues
Vocabulary: Faulty items | A for and against essay
Strategy: Ordering points into a coherent argument
Phrasebook: For and against essays |

Reading Missing sentences task Speaking Comparing photos Writing Formal emails How to learn vocabulary p.101

| Reporting verbs
▶ Grammar animation
Pronunciation: -ed endings | Statues
Strategy: Using the introduction and conclusion to understand the gist
Vocabulary: Travel idioms | Understanding copyright and plagiarism
Vocabulary: Copyright and plagiarism | Selecting an option
Strategy: Using a range of vocabulary to avoid repetition
Phrasebook: Discussing options; making a decision | A formal letter
Strategy: Using persuasive language
Phrasebook: Persuasive language |
| Participle clauses
▶ Grammar animation | Future-proofing the world … by leaving it
Strategy: Recognising fact, opinion and speculation
Vocabulary: Scientific intervention | Disagreeing diplomatically
Vocabulary: Differences of opinion | A debate
Strategy: Listening actively
Phrasebook: Engaging with ideas | A discursive essay
Strategy: Using nominalisation |

Reading 'True, False or Doesn't Say' tasks Speaking Making decisions role play Writing Informal emails How to learn vocabulary p.103

0.1 INTRODUCTION

Use present tenses and talk about injuries and treatment.

GRAMMAR BOOSTER SB P128

1 Choose the correct answer: A, B or C.
  1 Have you ever had a ___ injury like a broken arm?
    A emergency B severe C sprained
  2 I needed ___ when I fell and cut my leg.
    A a bump B first aid C a sprained ankle
  3 A woman ___ in the street and I had to call an ambulance.
    A collapsed B sprained C recovered
  4 James was ___ for about five minutes.
    A emergency B specialist C unconscious
  5 Taryn got a ___ on the head playing rugby. It wasn't too bad, and she kept playing, but she had a headache in the evening.
    A bump B bruise C sprain
  6 It isn't bleeding, but you've probably got ___ there. It'll show in the next few days.
    A a severe injury B a bruise C first aid
  7 He's hurt his back and it's going to take him a few weeks to ___.
    A recover B collapse C be unconscious
  8 I got a ___ when I was playing hockey.
    A first aid B sprained ankle C specialist
  9 Carl loves his job with the ___ because he never knows what's going to happen when he goes out to work.
    A specialist B first aid C emergency services
  10 She's going to Paris next week to see an eye ___.
    A bruise B service C specialist

2 Who or what are they talking about? Use words in Ex 1.
  1 'I know what to do if someone's cut themselves or hits their head.' ___
  2 'Look at it! It's yellow, purple and green!' ___
  3 'She studied general medicine at university, but then decided to focus on heart health.' ___
  4 'I can't walk on it!' ___
  5 'It's going to take her a very long time to recover from it.' ___
  6 'Fire, police or ambulance?' ___

3 Match rules 1–5 to sentences A–E.
  1 We use the present simple for facts and permanent situations. ___
  2 We use the present simple for habits and routines. ___
  3 We use the present simple for timetables and schedules. ___
  4 We use the present continuous for things happening now or around now. ___
  5 We use the present continuous to describe annoying or repeated behaviour. ___

  A The next fitness class starts at 4.45.
  B Damian's making a good recovery.
  C Your heart beats about 100,000 times a day.
  D Anita's always talking about her health!
  E Maryam works as a tennis coach at the weekends.

4 Choose the correct alternative.
  1 The human brain **contains** / **is containing** a large amount of water.
  2 What's the matter? What **happens** / **is happening**?
  3 The match **starts** / **is starting** at half past two.
  4 A I can't find my keys.
    B Oh no, not again! You **always lose** / **'re always losing** your keys!
  5 We **study** / **are studying** the history of medicine at the moment.
  6 Jasmine **sees** / **is seeing** a specialist every two years.

5 Complete the dialogue with the correct form of the verbs in brackets. Use contractions where possible.

Anya What [1]_____ (Lily / do) these days?
Milo She's at university. She [2]_____ (study) to be an ambulance worker.
Anya Oh, really? My uncle [3]_____ (work) for the ambulance service. He really [4]_____ (enjoy) it. He [5]_____ (always / tell) me I should think about it as a career because I'm good with people and I [6]_____ (love) driving. It's a bit annoying, really – I have to keep reminding him that I [7]_____ (not / like) the sight of blood!
Milo Ha! I'm the same!
Anya So, when [8]_____ (Lily's course / finish)?
Milo Next summer. She and her friend [9]_____ (think) about working in Australia for a year after that.

6 Answer the questions so they are true for you.
  1 Would you like to work for the ambulance service? Why? / Why not?
  2 Would you like to work for one of the other emergency services? If so, which one and why? If not, why not?

4 Introduction

GRAMMAR BOOSTER SB P129

Use past tenses and talk about nature.

0.2 INTRODUCTION

1 Tick (✓) the correct meaning.
  1 I'd never heard of an air plant until Soroush gave me one.
    A I heard about air plants and then Soroush gave me one. ☐
    B The first time I heard about air plants was when Soroush gave me one. ☐
  2 The trees have grown.
    A I don't know when the trees grew, but they look different now. ☐
    B I know when the trees started and stopped growing. ☐
  3 We've been learning about plants.
    A We learned about plants at an unspecified time in the past. ☐
    B We started learning about plants some time ago and we're still learning about them now. ☐
  4 We were doing some work in the garden when it started raining.
    A The rain started, but we did some work in the garden. ☐
    B While we worked in the garden, the rain started. ☐
  5 I gave them some flowers.
    A This finished event is part of a narrative. ☐
    B This finished event has some connection to now. ☐
  6 I've given them some flowers.
    A This finished event is part of a narrative. ☐
    B This finished event has some connection to now. ☐

2 Choose the correct alternative.
  1 Jack doesn't live here now. He **has moved** / **had moved** / **has been moving** to the countryside.
  2 It **was snowing** / **has been snowing** / **had snowed** all night. I wonder when it will stop!
  3 I saw Sami at the park. He **was sitting** / **sat** / **has sat** on the grass with some friends.
  4 The room looked completely different because we **have put** / **had been putting** / **had put** about ten houseplants in it.
  5 We **had learned** / **learned** / **have learned** about the rainforest last year.
  6 He **visited** / **had visited** / **has visited** the rainforest three times and he's going again next year.

3 Complete the blog post with the correct form of the verbs in brackets. More than one answer may be possible.

BLOG > new posts

Sleeping in the trees

You ¹_____ (probably / climb) trees when you were a child, but ²_____ (you / ever / sleep) in a tree? Last summer, I ³_____ (have) my first tree-sleeping experience, and I loved it!
I ⁴_____ (travel) around Italy and I ⁵_____ (stay) one night in a tent seven metres off the ground in a tree in the beautiful forest of Gorgonero, Sicily. I ⁶_____ (camp) all my life, but I ⁷_____ (never / spend) the night in a tree before! I ⁸_____ (sleep) really well, and when I ⁹_____ (wake up) up the next morning, birds ¹⁰_____ (singing) all around me. It was really special!

💬 Comment

4 Match the words below to the definitions.

biofuels   carbon dioxide   houseplants
leaves   modify   monitor   natural habitat
oxygen   roots   rural   transform   tropical

  1 connected with areas of the world which are warm all year round, such as Brazil, Malaysia and Kenya _____
  2 plants kept in indoor spaces like houses, offices and classrooms _____
  3 connected with the countryside, not the city _____
  4 a gas that people and animals can't live without _____
  5 the green parts of a plant _____
  6 watch and check something over a period of time _____
  7 change something slightly, especially in order to make it more suitable for a particular purpose _____
  8 a gas that plants need _____
  9 the place where a particular type of animal or plant is normally found _____
  10 the parts of a plant which are underground _____
  11 to change the structure of something completely _____
  12 alternative sources of energy made from plant or animal sources and used in engines _____

5 Complete the texts with the correct form of the words in Ex 4.

The ¹_____ of a plant take up water from the ground. The ²_____ of a plant produce food for the plant. They create sugars from sunlight, water and ³_____, and they release ⁴_____ into the air.

Scientists have been researching the use of seaweed (plants which grow in the sea) in the production of ⁵_____. This could ⁶_____ the energy industry, as seaweed doesn't need land or fresh water to grow.

6 Complete the sentences with your own ideas using narrative tenses.
  1 When I woke up this morning, _____.
  2 I _____ a few times recently.
  3 Yesterday, I _____ and then I _____.
  4 Yesterday, I _____ because _____.

Introduction 5

0.3 INTRODUCTION
Use future tenses and talk about work and study.

GRAMMAR BOOSTER SB P130

1 Choose the correct alternative.
  1 A company recruits **people** / **jobs**.
  2 People do placements to **get work experience** / **help a company or other organisation**.
  3 Applicants for a job usually **want** / **have** the job.
  4 Coursework **never** / **often** contributes to a student's final grade.
  5 People **are** / **aren't** paid to do voluntary work.
  6 A student loan helps students to **find a good course** / **pay for their course**.
  7 A module is **part of a course** / **a course**.
  8 People who have full-time jobs **have a lot of** / **don't have much** free time.
  9 A personal statement is something you **say at an interview** / **write on an application form**.
  10 TV presenters **are** / **aren't** usually well paid.
  11 Trainees have **a lot of** / **a little, some or no** experience.
  12 A curriculum is formed of **subjects** / **teachers** included in a particular course.

2 Complete the sentences with the underlined words in Ex 1.
  1 We do a lot of _____ and then two exams at the end of the year.
  2 She's a _____ news reporter. She's learning fast, but she isn't an expert yet.
  3 I couldn't afford to do the course without a _____.
  4 He's doing the _____ work to gain experience, not money.
  5 Do you know how many other _____ there were for the job?
  6 It's an interesting _____. It has _____ in American poetry and 19th-century Japanese literature.
  7 The theme park _____ ride attendants and tour guides every summer.
  8 I've got a _____ with a clothing company next summer.

3 Match uses 1–8 to sentences A–H.
  1 a prediction based on what we think ___
  2 a decision made at the time of speaking ___
  3 a promise or offer ___
  4 a plan or intention ___
  5 a prediction based on what we see ___
  6 an event in a scheduled timetable ___
  7 a future arrangement ___
  8 an action in progress at a time in the future ___

  A I'll help you.
  B This time next week, we'll be sitting on the beach.
  C Their train arrives at 7.15.
  D I'm going to apply for the job.
  E I'll have the fish, please.
  F He'll need something to eat.
  G We're playing tennis later.
  H This form is going to take ages to fill in.

4 Choose the correct answer: A, B or C.
  1 I ___ you tomorrow, I promise.
    A 'm calling   B 'm going to call   C 'll call
  2 A Have you decided?
    B No, I don't know what I ___!
    A 'm going to do   B 'll be doing   C 'll do
  3 A Do you want to come to my house after lunch?
    B Thanks, but I ___ Soraya at two.
    A 'll meet   B am going to meet   C 'm meeting
  4 A Someone's at the door!
    B I ___ it!
    A 'm going to get   B 'll get   C 'll be getting
  5 Don't go near that tree. Look, it ___!
    A 's going to fall   B will fall   C will be falling

5 Complete the emails with the future forms below. There are three future forms you do not need.

| do   'll be helping   'll do   'll help   'll write
| 'm doing   'm going to call   'm not doing
| starts   will start   won't see

From: Daniel
To: Victor

Hi Victor,
I hope you're having a good holiday. I'm just writing to say you ¹_____ me at college when everyone goes back next week because I ²_____ a four-week placement with a law company. They had recruited someone else, but that person can't take the place, so they've offered it to me. The work ³_____ next Tuesday. I ⁴_____ and tell you how my first day goes!
Daniel
PS Do you want to meet up on Saturday at about eleven?

From: Victor
To: Daniel

Hi,
That's great news! I'm sure you ⁵_____ really well. I still haven't heard anything from the company I applied to, but I ⁶_____ them later today and ask them what's happening. Meeting at the weekend sounds good, but at eleven on Saturday morning I ⁷_____ my grandma with her shopping. I ⁸_____ anything in the afternoon, though. Are you free then?
Take care,
Victor

6 Complete the sentences so they are true for you.
  1 I _____ next week.
  2 This time tomorrow, I _____
  3 I'm never going to _____

GRAMMAR BOOSTER SB P131 — Use relative clauses and talk about travel and tourism.

0.4 INTRODUCTION

1 Does each sentence contain a defining relative clause (*D*), giving essential information, or a non-defining relative clause (*ND*), giving extra non-essential information?
1 We went to the Harbin International Ice and Snow Sculpture Festival, which takes place in China every winter. ____
2 There was a café where we sat every evening and watched people go by. ____
3 Where's the map I bought? ____
4 The Plitvice Lakes, which are famous for their beautiful colours, are in a large national park in Croatia. ____
5 This is Ade, who I often travel with. ____
6 I've got a friend who has visited every continent in the world. ____

2 Choose the correct alternative.
1 We need someone **who / which** knows the area.
2 Late March to early April is the time **which / when** the cherry trees in Japan are in flower.
3 We took a bus **who / that** stopped in lots of pretty villages.
4 Is that the campsite **where / which** you stayed?
5 I had an email from Martha **Smith who / Smith, who** I met on holiday.
6 There are two cities **where I want / I want** to visit.
7 There were some tourists on the beach **whose / that** voices were very loud!
8 The room, **that / which** has beautiful views of the island, is on the third floor.

3 Join the sentences with defining or non-defining relative clauses. Only use a pronoun where necessary.
1 We met a man. He had walked from Paris to Berlin.
  We met a _____ from Paris to Berlin.
2 I've found a great beach. We can swim there.
  I've found a great _____ swim.
3 We walked across Karamagara Bridge. It is one of the oldest bridges in the world.
  We walked across Karamagara _____ _____ oldest bridges in the world.
4 They're staying in the hotel. It opened last month.
  They're staying in _____ last month.
5 You sent a postcard from Italy. I've finally got it!
  I've finally _____ sent from Italy!
6 Ollie Parker is cycling across the USA. His sister is in my class.
  Ollie Parker _____ _____ across the USA.
7 I'll speak to my friend. His parents live there.
  I'll speak to my friend _____ there.
8 You don't want to tell me about your holiday. Is there a reason?
  Is there _____ to tell me about your holiday?

4 What are they talking about? Match the words below to the quotes.

| all-inclusive   get away   go trekking   holidaymakers   make a booking   memorable   mountain biking   package holiday   resort |

1 'I'll never forget it!' something _____
2 'The price includes the flight, coach and the accommodation.' _____.
3 'The price includes the flight, the accommodation and also the food, drink and entertainment at the hotel.' _____ holiday
4 'I want to go on holiday somewhere completely different!' _____
5 'I'd like to reserve a table for seven o'clock.' _____
6 'We cycled down the volcano.' _____
7 'Tourists love coming here!' _____
8 'Most of them come here in summer and stay in hotels near the beach.' _____
9 'You will walk in the mountains for about seven hours every day.' _____

5 Complete the blog post with words in Ex 4 and relative pronouns (*who*, *which*, etc.).

FOODIEBLOG
HOME ABOUT BLOG CONTACT

Food tourism

I first became a 'food tourist' when I was on a ¹_____ holiday in South Korea three years ago. The holiday was ²_____, so everything was already paid for. Sounds good, I know. But the trouble was, every day we ate at the hotel restaurant and chose from a menu ³_____ was full of international food like pizza and burgers. Towards the end of my holiday, I realised I hadn't eaten any Korean food at all. I spoke to someone at the hotel, and they kindly helped me ⁴_____ on a food tour, ⁵_____ was basically a tour of different cafés, restaurants and food markets in the local area to try the local food. I had a brilliant guide, Yu-Jun, ⁶_____ knew all the best places to go. Now, whenever I ⁷_____, I always go on at least one food tour. I have discovered so many interesting kinds of food this way and met a lot of really nice people too. The most ⁸_____ experience was when my guide in Paris took me to his grandmother's home, ⁹_____ I ate traditional home-cooked French food.

6 Complete the sentences so they are true for you. Use relative clauses and include some vocabulary from the lesson.
1 I've got a friend _____.
2 I'd love to visit the place _____.
3 Summer is the season _____.
4 My favourite food is _____.

Introduction 7

1.1 VOCABULARY
Talk about skills and natural talents.

1 Live and learn

1 a What can you remember about the vlog? Complete the summary with the correct form of the phrases below.

> attempt to   be a boost to her confidence
> be capable of   be motivated   gain experience
> hopeless   inspire   master   overcome the problem
> put the theory into practice

Yasmin passed her motorbike theory test first time, which ¹_____. However, now that she's on the bike, she's finding it difficult to ²_____. She ³_____ do a U-turn and rode straight into a hedge. She doesn't think she'll ever ⁴_____ learning, and feels ⁵_____. Zaki says she needs more lessons to ⁶_____.
Meeting his deaf neighbour, Sam, ⁷_____ Joe to learn sign language. Although Joe ⁸_____ at first, he got frustrated because he kept forgetting the signs. He ⁹_____ by staying calm and identifying the problem. He videoed Sam making signs and then watched them every day, and was able to ¹⁰_____ about 20 new signs a week.

b ▶ 🔊 **1.01** Watch or listen again and check.

2 Complete the sentences with prepositions.
1 They aren't capable _____ sailing a boat on their own.
2 I'm hopeless _____ drawing and painting!
3 It took James a long time to put theory _____ practice when he was learning to code.
4 You need to focus your attention _____ the music when you're dancing.
5 It didn't take her long to pick _____ the basics when she first learned to ski.
6 Being told they're doing a good job by a teacher or boss can be a real boost _____ someone's confidence.

3 Complete the sentences. Use between two and five words, including the words in brackets.
1 You could be a professional tennis player one day. (potential)
You _____ a professional tennis player one day.
2 Playing chess well is hard, but you can learn the simplest and most important things quickly. (basics)
Playing chess well is hard, but you can _____ quickly.
3 Passing the exam made me feel more confident. (boost)
Passing the exam _____ confidence.
4 Seeing my grandmother's business made me want to set up my own. (me)
My grandmother _____ to set up a business.
5 She concentrated on improving her pronunciation. (attention)
She _____ improving her pronunciation.
6 My friend's dream is to open a restaurant. (dream)
My friend wants to _____ of opening a restaurant.
7 I learn a lot from 'how-to' internet videos. (tutorials)
_____ teaches me a lot.

4 **REAL ENGLISH** Complete the dialogue.
A Are you ¹g_____ a_____ with building your website? You were feeling a bit fed up last time we spoke, like everything ²w_____ g_____ d_____.
B Oh, things are going much better now, thanks. My friend Helen spent some time helping me, and that's ³m_____ a_____ t_____ d_____. It's starting to look really good.
A Erm … Your friend's a website designer, isn't she? That's ⁴a_____ a p_____!
B I know, I'm very lucky. And she's brilliant! Design ⁵c_____ n_____ to her. She's a great teacher too. She didn't do the work for me; she showed me how to do things so that I could try things out for myself. So that's what I've been doing. It's quite fun, actually.
A Well, it sounds like you're really ⁶g_____ t_____ f_____ o_____ the software.
B Yes, I am. I feel much more confident.

5 **VOCABULARY BOOSTER** Now practise **Skills and natural talents** vocabulary on page 104.

8 Unit 1

1.2 GRAMMAR

Grammar animation
GRAMMAR BOOSTER P132

Use the past perfect simple and continuous to talk about talented young people.

1 Read the biography and choose the correct alternative. Sometimes both answers are correct.

The first female international chess grandmaster

In 1978, at the age of 37, chess player Nona Gaprindashvili was awarded the title of International Grandmaster by the International Chess Federation. No woman before her **¹had obtained / had been obtaining** this title.

Nona **²had played / had been playing** chess since she was five years old, when her older brother taught her to play.

Her first big breakthrough came when she was twelve. A chess instructor **³had recognised / had been recognising** Nona's talent and persuaded her parents to let her move to Tbilisi, the capital city of Georgia, to train. She **⁴had lived / had been living** in Zugdidi, 330 km to the west of Tbilisi, so this was a big move for her.

By the time she was 30, Nona **⁵had won / had been winning** many women's chess tournaments. She **⁶had also competed / had also been competing** in men's tournaments since her early twenties, and won several.

Nona's achievements in the male-dominated world of competitive chess continue to offer an inspiring story for young women today.

2 Complete the sentences with the phrases below.

| had been having   had been meeting   had been playing
| had been watching   had had   had known   had run
| had watched   hadn't met

1 Darius wasn't keen to go to the cinema because he _____ videos on his phone all afternoon.
2 Jake was resting on the grass because he _____ a 10 km marathon.
3 I _____ about Tom's sister for a long time, but I _____ her until last week.
4 She missed the match because she _____ problems with her back for several weeks.
5 I'm sorry I didn't chat for very long yesterday, but I _____ new people all morning.
6 When we saw Leyla, she was exhausted because she _____ tennis for over an hour and a half.
7 She _____ the potential to be a great gymnast, but she chose to become a writer instead.
8 I knew what to do because I _____ about ten online tutorials!

3 Complete the text with the past perfect simple or past perfect continuous form of the verbs in brackets.

OPERA STAR AMIRA

In 2013, at the age of nine, Amira Willighagen won the TV talent show *Holland's Got Talent*. She ¹_____ (not have) a single singing lesson in her life. Instead, she ²_____ (teach) herself to sing opera by watching online tutorials.

Amira ³_____ (listen) to classical music all her life, as her mother played the violin and her father played the piano. Her brother Fincent was also a pianist.

Fincent ⁴_____ (prepare) for a performance, and one day he and Amira decided they wanted to perform together. Amira couldn't play an instrument, but she liked singing. She ⁵_____ (be) particularly interested in opera singing since she ⁶_____ (hear) the Italian opera singer Luciano Pavarotti sing when she was seven. She looked online for material, and soon she ⁷_____ (master) the art of opera singing.

After her success on *Holland's Got Talent*, Amira went on to perform in Europe, America, Africa and Asia. In 2019, she gave several concerts in South Africa, where she ⁸_____ (live) with her mother and brother since 2018.

Amira has released several albums and, more recently, has performed live shows online.

4 Complete the second sentence so that it has the same meaning as the first two. Use the past perfect simple or past perfect continuous and the words and phrases in CAPITALS.

1 We were waiting for ages. You arrived. WHEN
We _____.
2 I was hopeless at tennis. Then I had lessons. BEFORE
I _____.
3 Mo mastered Italian. He returned home. BY THE TIME
_____.
4 She wasn't skateboarding long. She entered a national competition. BEFORE
She _____.
5 Sam first attempted to pass his driving test when he was eighteen. He was still trying. SINCE
Sam _____.
6 We overcame the problem. Then Magda offered to help us. BUT BY THEN
Magda _____.

5 Complete the sentences so they are true for you. Use the past perfect simple or past perfect continuous form of the verbs below, or use different verbs.

| learn   live   meet   not learn   not meet
| not travel   play   travel   visit

1 Before I was five, _____.
2 When I was ten, _____.
3 By the time I was fifteen, _____.

Unit 1   9

1.3 LISTENING

Use key words to identify the main points in a radio interview.

1 What can you remember about autodidacts from the Student's Book? Complete the phrasal verbs in the sentences with the correct form of the verbs below.

| catch   come   drop   figure   go (x2)   live   pick

1 Each time Kató Lomb read an English book for the first time, she _____ out the meanings of a lot of new words from context. When she read the book a second time and _____ across unknown words, she looked them up.
2 Jane Austen _____ up her writing skills by spending a long time in her father's library.
3 Vincent van Gogh was an art dealer for a year, but he lost his job because he didn't _____ up to expectations. He had a lot to _____ up on when he became an artist at the age of 27.
4 After graduating from one of the best engineering colleges in France, Gustave Eiffel _____ on to build hundreds of bridges and other structures.
5 When Katherine Johnson first worked for NASA, she had to _____ through the calculations of flight tests and add up the numbers.
6 James Cameron _____ out of university before completing his degree in physics.

2 Complete the questionnaire.

You and art

1 Have you ever been to an art gallery?
A No, never.
B Yes, a few times.
C Yes, loads of times. I love all kinds of art!

2 Are you good at painting and drawing?
A No, I'm hopeless!
B I'm not bad.
C Yes, people tell me I am.

3 What's your response to this picture?
A It's very good, but I'd rather look at a photo, to be honest.
B It's amazing that it's so lifelike!
C I absolutely love it!

4 What about this one?
A I'm not sure. It's a bit weird.
B I prefer more lifelike portraits.
C I like it! It's different and interesting.

STRATEGY Using key words to identify the main point

It is sometimes helpful to make a note of key words while you are listening to a recording. After listening, you can use these words to write a sentence summarising the gist of each part of the recording. These sentences will help you distinguish between the different parts of the recording and identify the main points.

3 🔊 1.02 Read the strategy above. Listen to a radio interview with artist Hasan Arslan and make a note of the key words for each of the topics below.
1 Hasan's artwork: _____
2 Hasan's art teacher at school: _____
3 João Carvalho's artwork: _____
4 Ema Klučovská's artwork: _____
5 How Hasan learned to paint: _____
6 Hasan and the public: _____

4 🔊 1.02 Listen again. Are the sentences true (T), false (F) or not given (NG)? Use your notes from Ex 3 to help you.
1 Hasan paints traditional portraits of famous people. T / F / NG
2 He had been copying photos of famous people until his art teacher told him not to. T / F / NG
3 Hasan's art teacher thought Hasan had the potential to become a famous artist. T / F / NG
4 João Carvalho and Ema Klučovská have different drawing styles. T / F / NG
5 The first paints that Hasan owned were a gift from someone. T / F / NG
6 The first person to buy one of Hasan's paintings had liked and shared his work on social media. T / F / NG

5 🔊 1.02 Listen again and complete the sentences with between one and three words.
1 Hasan paints pictures of famous people, in particular _____.
2 Drawing _____ Hasan when he was a child.
3 Hasan is amazed by how _____ the monsters Ema draws are. They could be real.
4 Ema started drawing when she was _____.
5 Hasan quickly _____ of using paint when he was a child.
6 Hasan had the opportunity to exhibit in a _____ thanks to a friend.

6 Write a short paragraph about your art skills. What do you find easy / difficult? Do you enjoy art lessons? Why? / Why not? How often do you draw or paint? Would you prefer to be able to draw like João Carvalho or Ema Klučovská? Why?

Talk about the ages we do things best.

1.4 VOCABULARY

1 Complete the table with the words and phrases below.

> adolescence   adulthood   in your late teens
> mature   middle age   retirement
> the older generation

| childhood (age 0–9) |
| 1 _____ (age 10–19) |
| age 17–19 2 _____ |
| young 3 _____ (age 20–39) |
| 4 _____ (age 45–60) |
| 5 _____ |
| 6 _____ (age 60+) |
| 7 _____ |

2 Match 1–7 to A–G to make collocations.

1 acquire ___   A mental arithmetic
2 absorb ___   B names
3 be ___   C someone
4 distract ___   D a second language
5 do ___   E wise
6 have ___   F information
7 recall ___   G an extensive vocabulary

3 Choose the correct alternative.

How music can BOOST your brain power

Children who learn a musical instrument are better at maths and have a more [1] _____ vocabulary than children who don't, according to recent research.

Studies have also shown that learning a musical instrument at a young age makes it easier to [2] _____ a second language. This capacity continues into [3] _____, so it is a gift for life.

Music training isn't just for kids. Kathryn took up the guitar at the age of 44 when she realised she needed something to focus on. 'I had always been very easily [4] _____ by things, but it wasn't until I was [5] _____ that I realised how much this was a problem that affected my work. Learning the guitar has really improved my concentration.'

The older [6] _____ can benefit too. Leon started piano lessons when he was 72 and in [7] _____. 'I'd been listening to music all my life, but I'd never thought of learning an instrument,' says Leon. 'I'm really enjoying it and it's been a real boost to my confidence. I highly recommend it!'

Can you play a musical instrument? If not, it might be [8] _____ to start thinking about it!

1 A expensive   B extensive   C expansive
2 A absorb   B gain   C acquire
3 A retirement   B adolescence   C adulthood
4 A distracted   B mature   C wise
5 A in middle age   B my teens   C the older generation
6 A age   B generation   C teens
7 A retirement   B adulthood   C middle age
8 A mature   B late   C wise

4 Complete the dialogues with the correct form of the words and phrases from this lesson.

1 A Can you add up those numbers for me?
  B Have you got a calculator? I'm not great at _____!
2 A I recognise that woman's face, but I can't think what she's called.
  B Same here! I'm hopeless at _____!
3 A I've heard it said that _____ goes on longer these days.
  B Yes, I suppose because people are starting work and getting married later than they did in the past.
4 A I worry about getting older.
  B Well, the good thing about getting more _____ is that you get more confident!
5 A How did Edward learn all those capital cities so quickly?
  B Children his age _____ really quickly and easily, I guess!
6 A Hannah! Look at this!
  B Stop _____ me! I'm trying to study!
7 A Your cousin's younger than you, isn't she?
  B Yes, but she isn't a child anymore. She's in her _____ now.
8 A I'm beginning to think I might need glasses for work.
  B I guess that's normal _____. You are 50 now!

5 Think about your friends and family and answer the questions.

1 Who is in their late teens? _____
2 Who is in middle age? _____
3 Who is in retirement? _____
4 Who is the wisest person you know? _____

6 **VOCABULARY BOOSTER** Now practise **The ages we do things best** vocabulary on page 104.

1.5 GRAMMAR

Use *used to*, *would* and *be / get used to* to reminisce about the past.

▶ Grammar animation
GRAMMAR BOOSTER P133

1 Match sentences 1–12 to A–E.
1 We would try to put theory into practice. ___
2 I used to be hopeless at swimming! ___
3 Sara's used to getting up early. ___
4 You used to hate cooked carrots! ___
5 Mrs Manning retired five years ago. ___
6 He'll have to get used to doing homework after school. ___
7 I didn't use to want to grow up. ___
8 My best friend used to distract me in class. ___
9 The teacher would sometimes give us a mental arithmetic test. ___
10 They're getting used to cycling to school. ___
11 We used our coding skills to overcome the problem. ___
12 Did Maria use to recall things easily? ___

A a past habit
B a past state
C a finished past action
D being familiar with something
E becoming familiar with something

2 🔊 **1.03** Listen to Tom and Zahra talking about their childhood memories. How many games do they talk about?

3 🔊 **1.03** Listen again and choose the correct alternative.
1 Tom **used to / didn't use to** enjoy the lessons much at primary school.
2 Tom **used to / didn't use to** enjoy breaktime.
3 When Tom started school, he **was / wasn't** used to playing games with other children.
4 Zahra **would always / didn't use to** run around with her friends at breaktime.
5 Zahra played the cup game **more than once / once**.
6 Zahra **is used to teaching / used to teach** other people the cup game.

4 a PRONUNCIATION Choose the correct pronunciation of *use(d)* in the sentences: A or B.
1 We used to walk home together.
   A /'juːst/   B /juːzd/
2 Max used Luke's phone.
   A /'juːst/   B /juːzd/
3 I'm not used to working hard!
   A /'juːst/   B /juːzd/
4 They didn't use to be friends.
   A /'juːst/   B /juːzd/
5 Have you ever used a hairdryer?
   A /'juːst/   B /juːzd/

b 🔊 **1.04** Listen, check and repeat.

5 Complete the dialogue with *be / get used to*, *used to* or *would* and the correct form of the verbs in brackets. If *used to* and *would* are both possible, use *would*.

Lily ¹_____ (go) on holiday every year?
Kai Yes. Some of my friends ²_____ (travel) abroad in summer, but my family could never afford to, so we ³_____ (pack up) the car and go camping in the countryside. Unfortunately, it often rained and we ⁴_____ (wake up) in the morning and stuff had got wet in the night. That was pretty miserable, but I ⁵_____ (love) playing in rivers with my sisters – things like that. I'm glad I camped a lot as a child. It means when I go to a music festival or something, I ⁶_____ (sleep) in a tent, which isn't true for a lot of my friends! How about you? What did you do in the summer holidays?

Lily My parents always worked in the summer holidays, so I'd go and stay with my grandparents. I always ⁷_____ (be) homesick at first, but then I soon ⁸_____ (be) there, and by the end of the summer I didn't want to go home. It was especially good in my early teens because I ⁹_____ (belong) to a beach volleyball club there and I ¹⁰_____ (see) the same friends there every summer.

6 Correct the mistake in each sentence.
1 I didn't use to speaking on the phone because I always message my friends! _____
2 My parents would give me a bike on my tenth birthday. _____
3 Are you getting used to live here now? _____
4 I would be afraid of the dark when I was young. _____
5 When I was eleven, I used to start a new school. _____
6 I would know all the words to that song, but I've forgotten them now. _____

7 Complete the sentences with *would*, *used to* or *didn't use to* so they are true for you. Use the verbs below and/or your own ideas.

| be   eat   go   hate   live   love   play   sing

1 When I was a child, I _____
2 As a child, I _____
3 When I first started school, I wasn't _____
4 When I was in my early teens, I _____.
5 My friends and I _____
6 As a teenager, I had to get _____
7 I don't think I'll ever get _____

Understand new words in a blog post about learning.

1.6 READING

1 What can you remember about the Student's Book text? Are the sentences true (T) or false (F)?
  1 The Socs are working class and the Greasers are upper class. ___
  2 Ponyboy is a Greaser. ___
  3 Everyone in Ponyboy's gang likes books and movies. ___
  4 Ponyboy believes he makes good decisions because he's clever. ___
  5 He was worried when he noticed a red car following him. ___
  6 Some people had attacked him once before. ___

2 Think about your answer to the questions.
  - How has the way people taught and learned changed in the last 20 years?
  - What resources did people use to use?
  - What do they use now?

3 Read the text quickly. Complete the text with sentences A–F.
  A The first is Shelly Terrell, who regularly uses technology to connect her students to the world, and also to connect teachers, worldwide.
  B Teaching in a connected way is not completely new.
  C If we accept these eight principles, what does this mean for teaching?
  D I'd like to share what I have learned about connectivism, and what it means for English-language teaching.
  E The ability to learn is more important than what is known.
  F The digital learner can learn anywhere, anytime, 24/7.

STRATEGY Understanding new words and phrases

When you come across a new word or phrase, there are several things you can do to try to guess its meaning.
1 Focus on the context. Read the sentence containing the word or phrase and look for clues to the meaning.
2 Look at each part of the word or phrase. You may recognise one part, which may help you guess the rest.
3 Think about your own language. There may be a word that is similar to the new word or phrase.

4 🔊 **1.05** Read the strategy above. Read the text again and find the highlighted words or phrases in the text that mean …
  1 strong beliefs that influence how you behave _____
  2 working with another person or a group to produce something _____
  3 central, essential _____
  4 enormous changes _____
  5 develop quickly and become successful _____
  6 changed _____
  7 any online material such as pictures, sounds, videos and text _____
  8 advanced, original, using new methods _____
  9 variety, difference _____

5 In what ways are you a connectivist learner? What else could you do? Consider the points below.

  collaborating with other people
  connecting with other people   creating content
  diversity of opinions   seeing connections between things
  using technology

Connectivism: A Theory of Learning for a Digital Age

In this post, Thomas Baker, an English-language teacher in Chile, introduces the idea of digital connectivism and its impact on teachers and students.

Connectivism has been called 'A Learning Theory for the Digital Age.' [1]___

Connectivism is defined as 'a model of learning that acknowledges the tectonic shifts in society where learning is no longer an internal, individualistic activity. How people work and function is altered when new tools are used … Connectivism provides insight into learning skills and tasks needed for learners to flourish in a digital era.' (Siemens, 2005).

For me, this means learning has changed in three ways. Firstly, *what we learn with* has changed. Learners use digital tools to create content rather than just being passive consumers of knowledge.

Secondly, *how we learn* has changed. It isn't an individual activity. Learning takes place through collaborating with other people.

Thirdly, *where we learn* has changed. [2]___

These are the eight principles of connectivism:
1 Learning and knowledge rests in diversity of opinions.
2 Learning is a process of connecting.
3 Learning exists within technology.
4 [3]___
5 Developing and maintaining connections is needed for continual learning.
6 The ability to see connections between things is a core skill.
7 Accurate, up-to-date knowledge is the aim of all connectivist learning.
8 Making decisions is a learning process. What we know today may change tomorrow. The right decision today may be the wrong decision tomorrow.

[4]___ I'll answer this by giving three examples of great teachers who are 'connected'.

[5]___ Her video, *Why We Connect*, explains her views. The second is David Deubelbeiss. David wrote and self-published an innovative coursebook for digital learners called *We Teach | We Learn*. He calls his approach Student Created Content, where 'the student is a social participant in their own learning and creation.' As a third example, I use my blog to connect to other teachers worldwide.

To conclude, connectivism offers English-language teachers a way of teaching that recognises and responds thoughtfully to the digital age our students live in. [6]___ However, we now have the possibility of teaching in a connectivist way that's based on theory as well as practice.

Unit 1   13

1.7 GLOBAL SKILLS

Understand and discuss how to use emotional intelligence.

1 What can you remember about the Student's Book text? Complete the text about emotional intelligence.

Five ways to improve your emotional intelligence

Here are some tips on how to improve your emotional intelligence.

- Recognise your ¹s_____ o_____ m_____ when things go wrong. It's better to be patient than to ²l_____ y_____ t_____ and blame others.

- Use your ³j_____ to decide how to use your emotions. Even anger, which is sometimes seen as negative, can be ⁴j_____ in certain situations.

- If you know what you want, you can be polite but also ⁵a_____ when you need to do (or not do) something.

- Try to see things from other people's ⁶p_____. It will help you understand their actions and decisions better.

- Dealing with ⁷c_____ when people are unhappy with you and apologising when you make a mistake can be difficult, but they are important social skills which will help ⁸m_____ r_____.

2 🔊 1.06 Listen to Part 1 of a presentation about emotional intelligence and study. Choose the correct alternative.

1 Cognitive intelligence is connected with **feelings / thoughts**.
2 Emotional intelligence (EI) is **only slightly less / much more** important than cognitive intelligence for academic performance.
3 Emotional intelligence is **similar to / not the same thing as** having a hard-working attitude towards your studies.
4 We can try to **avoid negative emotions / stop negative emotions from affecting our learning**.

3 🔊 1.07 Listen to Part 2 of the presentation. Number the topics in the order you hear them.

A learning from problems ___
B relationships with others ___
C stress management ___
D seeing things from a different point of view ___
E negative emotions ___
F knowing how you're feeling ___

4 🔊 1.08 Listen to the whole presentation again and add between one and three words to each piece of advice.

✓ Do	✗ Don't
… have a ¹_____ attitude towards your studies.	… just focus on ²_____ intelligence.
… pay attention to ³_____ intelligence.	… let negative emotions ⁴_____ your learning.
… find ways to manage stress that ⁵_____.	… try to push away uncomfortable feelings.
… accept negative feelings and ⁶_____ your emotions.	… expect everything to ⁷_____.
… accept that you will sometimes get things wrong.	… see negative feedback as ⁸_____.
… practise thinking about other people's ⁹_____ in subjects like history and literature.	… expect working with other people to be easy.
… build and maintain strong relationships with other people.	… be afraid ¹⁰_____.

5 Read the problems and respond with advice from the table in Ex 4. Sometimes more than one answer is possible.

1 I feel horrible because I was hoping to do really well in my geography test, and I only got 27%.
_____
_____

2 I'd like to ask my classmate George to put more effort into the project we're working on, but I'm worried I might upset him.
_____
_____

3 I'm anxious about exams. I sometimes go running with my friends because they say it relaxes them, but I don't enjoy it.
_____
_____

4 Some classmates have told me I talk too much. I feel terrible about it.
_____
_____

6 MEDIATION Your friend has emailed you for advice. She was excited about working on a project for a science competition with her classmates Marina and Emma, but they keep arguing. She is not sure exactly how she feels about this, but she is thinking about dropping out of the project. Reply to her email using ideas from the presentation.

Restate your ideas in a social exchange.

1.8 SPEAKING

1 Read and complete the questionnaire.

What kind of student are you?

Mark your answers with a cross (X) on the line.

Attitude to study

A How hard-working are you as a student?
Very hard-working. — I could do better.

B How motivated are you to do well in your studies?
Very motivated. — Not very motivated.

Aspects of study

C How easy do you find figuring out the meanings of unknown words, in your language and in English?
It's easy. — It's difficult.

D How do you feel about studying novels and poems?
I love it. — I don't really enjoy it.

Working with others

E How do you feel about working together with your classmates?
I love it. — I prefer working alone.

F How easy do you find it to be assertive?
It's easy. — It's difficult.

Getting things wrong

G How do you feel when a teacher points out mistakes in your work?
It's OK. — I don't like it.

H When was the last time you apologised to someone at school or college?
Recently. — A long time ago.

2 🔊 1.09 Listen to four people answering four of the questions in Ex 1. Which question does each student answer? Write the letter.
1 ___   2 ___   3 ___   4 ___

> **STRATEGY** Being able to backtrack and reformulate to correct errors or slips
>
> It is normal to make mistakes when you are speaking. The important thing is to recognise the mistakes so that you can go back and correct them.

3 🔊 1.09 Read the strategy above. Listen again and choose the correct alternative.
1 Speaker 1 said something wrong about **himself / other people**.
2 Speaker 2 said something wrong about **herself / someone else**.
3 Speaker 3 didn't express himself **politely / well** at first.
4 Speaker 4 made a **vocabulary / grammar** slip.

4 🔊 1.10 Complete the extracts. Then listen and check.

Dialogue 1
Lucas I like it. Everyone else in the class seems to find it really boring. No, that isn't true actually. ¹W_____ I m_____ w_____ some of my classmates seem to switch off a bit when we're doing it.

Dialogue 2
Priti Sorry, ²t_____ d_____ c_____ o_____ r_____. I didn't mean to sound like I just want to make money. I do enjoy studying too.

Dialogue 3
Senyo It was OK – it wasn't a big deal. But I hate apologising!
Daisy Really?
Senyo Well, no, ³l_____ m_____ r_____ t_____. I find it difficult when people say I've upset them or made them angry. I guess I'm just not very good at dealing with criticism.

Dialogue 4
Erin It's OK. We often have to work on preparations together in ICT, and I enjoy that. Wait, ⁴t_____ c_____ o_____ w_____. I mean presentations. We have to prepare presentations in pairs or groups of three.

5 Order the words to make sentences.
1 say / let / that / me / again
_____
2 meant / isn't / that / what / say / to / I
_____
3 try / that / time / more / me / one / let
_____
4 is / to / I'm / what / trying / say / …
_____
5 way / put / let / me / another / that
_____

6 Look again at the phrases in Ex 5. When do we use each? Write 1–5.
A to admit you didn't say the right thing ___
B to repeat what you were saying ___ ___
C to clarify what you meant to say ___ ___

7 Choose a different question from Ex 1. Write a dialogue of two people discussing the question. Include an error and a slip that the speakers backtrack and reformulate.

Unit 1   15

1.9 WRITING
Write an article and use comment adverbs.

1 Look at the photos. Think about your answers to the questions.
1. Which of these activities have you attempted?
2. Are you better at doing puzzles, dancing or making things?
3. Do you know anyone who's good at any of the activities in the photos, or similar activities?

2 Read the task and the article. Match paragraphs 1–4 to questions A–D.

> A magazine has asked students to write an article about an interesting hobby that they or anyone they know does. Write an article in which you say what the hobby is, say how you / they got into it, give some facts about the activity and say why you / they enjoy doing it.

Which paragraph …
- **A** provides information about the activity? ___
- **B** tells a story? ___
- **C** gives an opinion about the activity? ___
- **D** asks a question to grab the reader's attention? ___

My speedcubing friend Aziz

① How quickly can you solve a Rubik's Cube? I guarantee you aren't as fast as my friend Aziz, who can do one in less than 30 seconds. ¹_____, he's entered lots of **speedcubing** competitions and won quite a few of them.

② Aziz first got into Rubik's Cubes when I shared a video of a famous record-breaking speedcuber with him. I'd been amazed at how fast the guy could do it. He took about five seconds, as I recall. The next time I saw Aziz, he'd bought himself a Cube and he couldn't put it down. He'd been watching online tutorials and was quickly putting into practice what he'd learned. ²_____, I thought it might be something I could master too, but ³_____ that wasn't to be the case. My brain just didn't seem to work the way Aziz's did. Anyway, I soon got used to the sight of him completely focused on turning all those coloured squares into place. I should have known it would be like this. He'd always enjoyed recognising patterns and figuring things out, and used to do way better than me in maths and computer science.

③ ⁴_____, the squares of a Rubik's Cube can sit in 43,252,003,274,489,856,000 different combinations! No wonder playing the Rubik's Cube can improve problem-solving skills and concentration, according to research. Aziz doesn't do it for any of those reasons, though. He just loves the fun and challenge of it.

④ As for me and Rubik's Cubes, well, I still have a go from time to time, but let's just say I need a bit more practice before I get as fast as Aziz!

speedcubing (n) the activity of solving the Rubik's Cube as quickly as possible

---

> **STRATEGY** Using comment adverbs to make your writing more interesting
>
> Comment adverbs are words which add information about the writer's opinion of events. They normally come at the beginning of a sentence. When you write an article, you can make your writing more interesting by using comment adverbs.

3 Read the strategy above. Complete the article with the comment adverbs below.

| amazingly   initially   (not) surprisingly   unfortunately

4 Choose the correct alternative.
1. Do you know what I mean by origami? **Obviously / Basically / Not surprisingly**, it involves folding paper into forms like plants and animals.
2. The first time I tried ice skating, I kept falling over. **Consequently / Amazingly / Interestingly**, I was covered in bruises the next day.
3. I'm joining a gymnastics class. I'm a complete beginner, but **unfortunately / consequently / hopefully**, I'll soon pick up the basics.
4. You'll need somewhere spacious to do yoga. **Ideally / Initially / Admittedly**, it should also be warm and quiet.
5. I'm a huge fan of horse riding. **Hopefully / Personally / Surprisingly**, I think everyone should try it at some point in their life.
6. Researching your family tree can be fascinating. **Interestingly / Ideally / Obviously**, it isn't very sociable, but it can lead to some interesting conversations with your relatives.

5 You are going to write your own article in answer to the task in Ex 2. Plan your article. Think about …
- an activity that you or someone you know has learned to do.
- whether you / they learned how to do the activity from a person or a website.
- how quickly you / they progressed in learning how to do the activity.
- why you / they enjoy the activity.

6 Write the article for the magazine based on your answers in Ex 5. Write four paragraphs and include at least four comment adverbs.

7 ✓ **CHECK YOUR WORK** Did you …
- think of an engaging title?
- use a semi-informal conversational style?
- write four paragraphs?
- express an opinion in the final paragraph?
- use at least four comment adverbs?
- check your spelling, grammar and punctuation?

16   Unit 1

1.10 REVIEW

Grammar

1 Complete the sentences with the past perfect simple or past perfect continuous form of the verbs in brackets.
1. I apologised because I _____ (lose) my temper.
2. Carlos was tired that morning because he _____ (not / sleep) well the night before.
3. I _____ (have) a really interesting conversation with Yasmin when you arrived, and I didn't want to stop.
4. It was easy to ask Anya for help as we _____ (work) on a history project together since the beginning of term.
5. Daria _____ (love) dancing since she was very young.
6. By the time Finn was 35, he _____ (perform) classical music for 20 years.
7. I _____ (try) to speak to Lucy all morning, but she wasn't answering her phone.
8. By the end of the week, he _____ (run) 100 km.

2 Complete the second sentence so that it means the same as the first. You must include the word or phrase in CAPITALS.
1. My dad used to read me a story at bedtime. WOULD
   My dad _____ me a story at bedtime.
2. It feels strange to have short hair! USED
   I _____ short hair!
3. They lived there from 2013 to 2020. USED
   They _____ .
4. When did speaking English start to feel familiar? GET
   When did you _____ English?
5. The teacher always asked me to read aloud. WOULD
   The teacher _____ me to read aloud.
6. There wasn't a cinema here. BE
   There _____ a cinema here.
7. Wearing glasses is beginning to feel familiar. USED
   I _____ glasses.
8. We went and picked mushrooms every autumn. USED
   We _____ mushrooms every autumn.

Vocabulary

3 Complete the sentences.
1. What skill would you like to m_____r? Driving? Surfing? Dancing?
2. Kiara has the p_____l to do really well in her exams.
3. With more practice, you'll soon gain e_____e.
4. You need to f_____s your attention on the details.
5. I a_____d to learn Chinese, but it was really hard and I didn't make much progress.
6. It's a difficult situation, but I'm sure we can find a way to o_____e the problem.
7. I'm h_____s at singing! I've got a terrible voice!
8. I was really m_____d to do well at the beginning, but then I lost interest.

4 Choose the correct alternative.
1. Are you any good at mental **vocabulary / arithmetic**?
2. Luckily, I find it quite easy to **recall / acquire** names.
3. I often ask my grandma for advice because she's very **wise / extensive**.
4. Walking and water aerobics are ideal forms of exercise for people who are **in their late teens / more mature**.
5. **Acquiring / Absorbing** a second language is easier when you're younger.
6. People often think the older **generation / retirement** hold more traditional views, but is this true?
7. Children are good at **distracting / absorbing** information.
8. You'll probably grow a lot in a short space of time during **adolescence / adulthood**.

Cumulative review

5 Complete the article with the words and phrases below.

basics	boost	fulfil	got used to	had been looking
had watched	late	middle age	theory
used to	was capable of	would often go

'I learned to ski when I was 47.'

I ¹_____ think you had to learn to ski when you were young or you would never learn to ski at all, but my experience changed that. I learned to ski in ²_____, when I was 47. Not long after that, I was able to ³_____ my dream of skiing in the mountains in Switzerland before I was 50. My first three lessons were at a dry ski slope, so without any snow. I ⁴_____ forward to the lessons, and I wasn't disappointed. The teacher was excellent. She explained a few things at the beginning, but we were soon on our skis to put the ⁵_____ into practice. I picked up the ⁶_____ fairly quickly, perhaps because I ⁷_____ a few short online tutorials, and I soon realised I ⁸_____ achieving much more than I had imagined. A few weeks later, my grown-up son, Ryan, and I flew to Switzerland, where I ⁹_____ skiing on real snow! I loved it. Ryan ¹⁰_____ skiing with his grandparents when he was in his ¹¹_____ teens, so he's an excellent skier. It was a real ¹²_____ to my confidence when he commented on how well I was doing. We had a great holiday, and I can't wait to go again.

REFLECT Think about the following questions.
1. Which lesson in this unit was your favourite? Why?
2. Which of the grammar points did you find most difficult? Why?
3. How can you practise understanding new words and phrases in reading texts?
4. What three things can you do to improve your emotional intelligence?

2.1 VOCABULARY
Talk about feelings and other people's behaviour.

Highs and lows

1 a What can you remember about the vlog? Choose the correct answer: A, B or C.
   1 Zaki's dad was ___ because Zaki had left the lights on when he came home.
      A furious   B puzzled   C offended
   2 Zaki and his dad ___.
      A both felt miserable all day
      B drove each other crazy
      C talked over the problem
   3 Zaki thinks it's normal to feel ___ by the things that people do and to want to complain about them.
      A irritated and frustrated
      B resentful and miserable
      C puzzled and offended
   4 Daisy's friend sings along to music when she's wearing headphones and this ___.
      A makes Daisy feel puzzled
      B gets on Daisy's nerves
      C calms Daisy down
   5 Daisy ___ with her friend after they'd had an argument.
      A fell out   B made up   C felt frustrated
   6 Joe is starting to feel ___ about the way his parents keep trying to tell him how to live his life.
      A furious   B astonished   C resentful
   7 Yasmin ___ when her uncle called her a snowflake.
      A was offended   B was miserable   C calmed down

   b ▶ 2.01 Watch or listen again and check.

2 🔊 2.02 Listen and match speakers 1–8 to questions A–H. Which speaker …
   A feels astonished? ___
   B has fallen out with someone? ___
   C feels offended? ___
   D feels puzzled? ___
   E has made up with someone? ___
   F feels irritated? ___
   G needs to calm down? ___
   H feels frustrated? ___

3 Complete the second sentence so that it means the same as the first. You must include the word in brackets.
   1 You need to discuss it. (OVER)
      You need to _____.
   2 I hope you resolve your argument with Flora soon. (MAKE)
      I hope you _____ Flora soon.
   3 Try to relax before you take action. (DOWN)
      Try to _____ before you take action.
   4 That noise is really irritating me. (NERVES)
      That noise is really _____.
   5 Olly's had an argument with Laura. (OUT)
      Olly's _____ Laura.
   6 I can't stand the way you're always checking your phone. (DRIVES)
      The way you're always checking your phone _____.

4 Complete the dialogues with words and phrases that mean the same as the definitions in brackets.
   Pria Omar hasn't messaged me since yesterday. I'm really ¹_____ (confused). I don't know if he's ²_____ (annoyed because he thinks I've said something rude) or something.
   Lou Maybe there's a problem with his phone.
   Pria Yeah, but I can see that he's read my messages. Actually, it's really ³_____ (irritating me).
   Lou I can see how ⁴_____ (annoyed because there's nothing you can do to change the situation) you are!

   Tyler What's the matter? You look ⁵_____ (really sad).
   Izzy I am. Jack's ⁶_____ (really angry) with me because I told Elliot something he'd asked me not to tell anyone.
   Tyler Oh, Izzy. I'm sure he'll ⁷_____ (stop feeling angry) soon. You've ⁸_____ (had arguments) before, haven't you?

5 **REAL ENGLISH** Complete the dialogues with the phrases below.

   | a big deal   blew my top   doing my head in
   | give it a rest   lost for words   tell me about it

   Ade That car alarm's so noisy! It's ¹_____!
   Kate ²_____! It woke me up at 4 a.m.!
   Meg I ³_____ when I realised my sister had been reading my private diary.
   Finn She read your diary? I'm ⁴_____.
   Kaya You've been talking about your job interview all week. Can you ⁵_____ now?
   Josh Sorry, but it's ⁶_____ for me!

6 **VOCABULARY BOOSTER** Now practise **Feelings and other people's behaviour** vocabulary on page 105.

18 Unit 2

2.2 GRAMMAR

Grammar animation
GRAMMAR BOOSTER P134

Use modal verbs to talk about advice, obligation and necessity; and possibility, probability and certainty.

1 Complete the sentences with the verbs below and the correct form of the verbs in brackets.

| aren't supposed to   can   may |
| needn't   ought to   won't be able to |

1 You _____ (talk) about it if you don't want to. We can just sit here together quietly for a bit.
2 Unfortunately, he _____ (play) in the match tomorrow because he isn't well.
3 We _____ (go) to that new pizza place sometime. It looks really good.
4 You _____ (find) that there aren't any buses, in which case you'll have to take a taxi.
5 We _____ (speak) during the lessons, but the teacher often lets us chat quietly.
6 My little sister _____ (be) really funny sometimes.

2 Match sentences 1–9 to A–I.
1 This bookshop **might** / **could** close one day. ___
2 Joe **must** be tired after that 20 km walk. ___
3 We **need to** leave now. ___
4 We **mustn't** run with the ball. ___
5 It **can** get really hot here in summer. ___
6 You **don't have to** wait for me. ___
7 You **ought to** tell her how you feel. ___
8 You **should** feel better tomorrow. ___
9 My phone **has to** be here somewhere! ___

A saying that something is likely to happen
B talking about a very strong possibility or certainty
C talking about general truths
D expressing an obligation
E saying that something isn't allowed
F giving advice
G expressing a lack of obligation or necessity
H talking about the possibility of something happening now or in the future
I saying that we think something is true now

3 Complete the sentences with modal verbs. Sometimes more than one answer is possible.
1 People _____ be so annoying!
2 You _____ look at your phone when someone's talking to you. It isn't very polite.
3 He _____ be offended because I asked him which school he went to. I didn't realise he was nineteen.
4 We'll _____ talk it over when we meet tomorrow.
5 The bus _____ come soon. It's nearly eight o'clock.
6 We _____ wear jewellery to school, but people often do, and the teachers don't seem to mind.
7 You _____ clean up. I can do it later.
8 I hear Sam's had his bike stolen. He _____ be furious! I know I would be.

4 Read the article and choose the correct answer: A, B or C.

HEALTH NEWS

LIVING WITH MISOPHONIA

Does the sound of people eating or clicking their pen over and over again get on your nerves? If so, you ¹_____ have misophonia.
For people with misophonia, small sounds like eating, breathing and yawning ²_____ be very upsetting. 'The sound of my family eating drives me crazy,' says Hannah, 17. 'I ³_____ sit there at the dinner table feeling really, really irritated. And then I think, "I love my family, so I ⁴_____ be feeling like this" and that makes me feel even worse!'
A psychologist says, 'If you have misophonia, you ⁵_____ blame yourself or feel guilty about it. It isn't your fault. It's just the way some people's brains work. In fact, a recent survey indicates the number of people in the population with misophonia ⁶_____ be as high as 15%.
So, what ⁷_____ you do if you suffer from misophonia? Headphones or earplugs ⁸_____ be useful for blocking out troubling noises. Or you ⁹_____ try talking about your problem with your loved ones, explaining that it's your problem, not theirs. You never know – they ¹⁰_____ have misophonia too!

1 A need to   B can   C might
2 A have to   B can   C aren't supposed to
3 A have to   B mustn't   C might
4 A may not   B needn't   C shouldn't
5 A won't be able to B ought to   C mustn't
6 A has to   B could   C should
7 A should   B may   C do you have to
8 A need to   B ought to   C can
9 A must   B could   C need to
10 A are supposed to B must   C may

5 Follow the instructions. Use a variety of modal verbs.
1 Write a strict rule in your school or home.
   _____
2 Write an informal rule in your school or home.
   _____
3 Think about next weekend. Write a possible event.
   _____
4 Write a general truth about people.
   People _____.
5 Write a piece of advice about friendship.
   _____

Unit 2

2.3 LISTENING
Recognise and understand paraphrasing.

1 What can you remember about the advice for taking control of your life from the Student's Book? Complete the text with the phrases below.

| adapt to circumstances
| do something positive   maintain your focus
| take control of the situation
| take responsibility for your actions

Taking control of your life is an ambitious goal, but breaking it down into smaller targets can help.

1 Be clear about what is important to you. If you _____, you will be able to ignore people who are negative about your goals.

2 At the same time, remember that things change. It's important to be flexible so that you can _____ if they do.

3 Don't wait for change to happen. Take action and _____ that will make a difference.

4 Things can go wrong. If they do and you're at fault, face the truth and _____.

5 Finally, remember that if something is stressing you out, getting organised and planning how to manage your time will often help you _____.

2 Read the situations. What could the people do?
1 Mo and Victor want to decorate their living room. Mo wants to paint the walls dark blue. Victor thinks light blue would be much better.
2 Fatima and Maria like going to the cinema together. Fatima likes action movies. Maria likes romantic comedies.

3 🔊 **2.03** Listen to a presentation and choose the best summary: A, B, C or D.
A Compromising in different ways and to different extents can benefit all our relationships.
B You should be as assertive as possible when compromising so that you don't end up feeling resentful.
C Some people find it really difficult to know when to say 'no' and when to give in to what other people want, but it isn't impossible to learn.
D When you really listen carefully to what the other person wants, you'll be able to reach a compromise much more easily.

compromise (v) reach agreement in a way that means both sides have changed what they're asking for
give in (phr v) agree completely to what someone wants

STRATEGY Recognising paraphrasing
Speakers often use different vocabulary to express similar ideas in order to avoid repeating what was said or written previously. You may hear familiar ideas expressed in an unfamiliar way. To help you understand, try to listen for words or phrases with a similar meaning to those used to express the idea in an earlier context.

4 🔊 **2.03** Read the strategy above. Listen again and tick (✓) the statements which match what the speaker says: A, B or both.
1 A Most of us find compromising difficult. ☐
  B With effort, we can improve our ability to compromise. ☐
2 A Disagreements are fairly common in all relationships. ☐
  B We should try to reduce the number of disagreements we have with other people. ☐
3 A Some forms of compromise are more difficult than others. ☐
  B Different situations require different kinds of compromise. ☐
4 A Arguments can make us focus very strongly on what we want, need and believe. ☐
  B We can get very angry when we feel that others don't understand the way we see things. ☐
5 A Always try to compromise as little as possible. ☐
  B Sometimes we have to compromise more than other times. ☐
6 A We don't always need to compromise when someone demands something of us. ☐
  B It's important for people to know where our limits are. ☐

5 Complete the paraphrasing sentences with the correct form of the words and phrases below. Use a dictionary if necessary.

| alternate   be clear   be flexible   be grateful   find
| go your way   not be straightforward   say 'no'

1 *That's meeting in the middle. In other situations, we might agree to take turns.*
Compromising can mean either _____ a happy medium or _____.
2 *The examples I've just given are quite easy to resolve, but things don't always play out so easily.*
What can we do when reaching agreement _____?
3 *You don't have to win every battle.*
Things can't _____ every time.
4 *Compromising doesn't have to mean giving up everything you believe in.*
You can _____ to meet the other person's needs, while _____ about your feelings.
5 *You don't always need to give in.*
Sometimes, you just need to _____.
6 *When you reach a compromise you're happy with, it's good to let the other person know how much the conversation has meant to you.*
_____ creates a positive feeling.

6 **MEDIATION** Your friend Seb has written to you for advice. He and his friend Alex meet at the park every Saturday afternoon for a few hours. Seb does not want to upset Alex, but sometimes he would like to do other things on Saturday afternoons, and with other people. Write a short email to Seb, using ideas from the presentation in your own words and your own ideas.

20 Unit 2

Talk about ways to improve your well-being.

2.4 VOCABULARY

1 Match the sentence halves.
1 If you're feeling hopeless, you need to **develop** ___
2 My sister never stops: she's always **on the** ___
3 Some people seem to **thrive on** ___
4 There are lots of things you can do to look after your **mental** ___
5 If you keep thinking about the past or worrying about the future, try to **be** ___
6 Just relax and **chill** ___
7 Take a break when you feel that life is **getting on** ___
8 Learning a new skill can help **build** ___

A mindful.
B self-confidence.
C stress.
D health.
E go.
F a positive mindset.
G top of you.
H out.

2 Read the online magazine interview and choose the correct alternative.

Gaming almost broke me

For most people, gaming is a fun way of [1]**being on the go / chilling out / thriving on stress**, but for a few it can become something much more serious. We spoke to Zak Laurence, 22, about his gaming [2]**addiction / downtime / self-confidence** and how he recovered from it.

Q How did you first get into gaming?
A Like a lot of people, it was how I enjoyed my [3]**well-being / regrets / downtime**. It started out as something I did with friends, then I gradually spent more and more time playing on my own. Once, I played a game for 30 hours without eating or leaving my room.

Q Wow. You were [4]**on the go / being mindful / building self-confidence** for all that time! Didn't you just get tired of it after a while?
A No, it's strange. Some gamers [5]**reach burnout / thrive on stress / develop a positive mindset** and stop playing, but not me. I just kept playing more and more.

Q So, what changed?
A I realised my [6]**addiction / anxiety / mental health** was suffering. I was suffering from depression and [7]**anxiety / self-confidence / regret**.

Q That sounds difficult. But you eventually turned things around.
A Yes, I found some useful advice online, and connected with others who had found themselves in the same situation. I started getting out of the house more, and gradually things improved. In fact, the whole experience of quitting has actually [8]**been mindful / got on top of me / built my self-confidence**, so that's a real plus.

3 What are they talking about? Match the words and phrases below to the sentences.

| addiction anxiety burnout depression downtime regrets self-confidence well-being |

1 'It was wrong of me to shout at them. And why didn't I apologise afterwards?' _____
2 'I was miserable for months, not just a few days.' _____
3 'I feel great physically and mentally.' _____
4 'I couldn't stop feeling worried, even though I didn't always know what it was about.' _____
5 'I realised I didn't just want coffee – I needed it.' _____
6 'I know I'm successful, but I still don't really believe I can do things.' _____
7 'I just kept going and going despite the stress I was feeling, but in the end, it was just all too much for me and I had to stop and recover.' _____
8 'This is when I relax and think about very little!' _____

4 Complete the texts with the correct form of words and phrases from the lesson.

My [1]_____ had been suffering for some time – I'd been feeling miserable and worried. I was involved in lots of online group chats, and I thought they were good for me, but I gradually realised that it was actually receiving all this [2]_____ from morning till night that was the cause of my [3]_____ and anxiety.

Are you always [4]_____? Would you like to slow down? This course helps you relax by teaching you how to [5]_____ and be aware of things in the present moment.

If you're someone who [6]_____ because you find challenging situations exciting, be careful. You may reach [7]_____, where you feel mentally and emotionally exhausted.

I've had a long and interesting life and I don't have any [8]_____. Every experience I've had has taught me something! My parents helped me to [9]_____ from a young age, so I always try to focus on the good bits even when bad things happen.

5 Write a sentence to answer each question.
1 How do you chill out with friends?
2 How do you spend downtime on your own?
3 How do you look after your well-being?
4 What do you do when things get on top of you?

6 **VOCABULARY BOOSTER** Now practise **Ways to improve your well-being** vocabulary on page 105.

Unit 2   21

2.5 GRAMMAR
Use perfect modal verbs to talk about past events.

▶ Grammar animation
GRAMMAR BOOSTER P135

1 Choose the correct meaning. Tick (✓) A or B.
  1 Jayden may not have seen you.
    A Perhaps he didn't see you. ☐
    B I'm sure he didn't see you. ☐
  2 We needn't have taken so much food with us.
    A We didn't take a lot of food with us. ☐
    B We took a lot of food with us, but it was unnecessary. ☐
  3 He shouldn't have sold the painting.
    A It's possible that he didn't sell the painting. ☐
    B Selling the painting was the wrong thing to do. ☐
  4 They were supposed to have arrived two hours ago.
    A We expected them to arrive two hours ago, but they haven't arrived yet. ☐
    B I'm sure they arrived two hours ago. ☐
  5 He didn't need to go to the bank.
    A He went to the bank. ☐
    B We don't know if he went to the bank. We only know that it wasn't necessary. ☐
  6 You could have waited for me!
    A You didn't wait and I'm unhappy about that. ☐
    B I'm happy that you were able to wait for me. ☐

2 Match sentences 1–6 to responses A–F.
  1 I bought you these flowers to say thank you. ___
  2 Nasser seems to have made up with Ellie. ___
  3 The people behind me at the cinema talked all the way through the film. ___
  4 I've just done my maths homework. ___
  5 Why didn't they come to the meeting? ___
  6 I hope you don't mind, but I borrowed your bike. ___

  A You ought to have asked me first.
  B They might have forgotten.
  C You must have felt really irritated!
  D Oh, wow, you needn't have done that!
  E They must have talked things over.
  F Weren't you supposed to do that yesterday?

3 🔊 2.04 Listen to the six dialogues and choose the correct alternative.
  1 Olly **ought not to have heard** / **can't have heard** / **didn't need to hear** us talking.
  2 Anita **didn't need to get up** / **wasn't supposed to get up** / **needn't have got up** early.
  3 Daisy **must have taken** / **should have taken** / **needn't have taken** the backpack.
  4 They **were supposed to call** / **might not have called** / **ought to have called** the police.
  5 She **didn't need to worry** / **needn't have worried** / **might not have worried**.
  6 Simran **was supposed to go** / **didn't need to go** / **may have gone** to the training session.

4 Complete the sentences with the modal verbs below and the correct form of the verbs in brackets.

| could   didn't need to   must   needn't
| not be supposed to   should

  1 He was so rude to you! You _____ (be) furious!
  2 I _____ (bother) to water the garden because it rained an hour later.
  3 It's eight o'clock. Misha's train _____ (arrive) by now. It's usually on time.
  4 The kitchen was a complete mess when I got home. You _____ (clean) the whole room, but you _____ (do) the washing-up!
  5 A What's that cake? Is it for me!?
    B Oh! You _____ (see) that until tomorrow! Oh, well. Happy birthday for tomorrow!

5 Complete the texts with perfect modal verbs from the lesson. Use the correct form of the verbs in brackets. Sometimes more than one answer is possible.

💬 **Chat room** ···

Have you ever made a small mistake that had big consequences? Tell us what happened.

Bella My friend asked me if I liked his new haircut. I told him I didn't, and he got really offended. We didn't speak for months. Clearly, I ¹_____ (say) what I actually thought! Seriously though, I know I ²_____ (behave) better, and I really ³_____ (say) sorry as soon as I realised I'd upset him.

Isla I went for a walk in the forest near my house, and I got lost. I thought I ⁴_____ (take) a map because I'd been there before with my parents. It all looked completely unfamiliar, though, so I ⁵_____ (pay) much attention. My phone had run out of charge and it was starting to get dark. Fortunately, I met some other walkers and they told me which way to go. Otherwise I ⁶_____ (have to) stay there overnight!

6 Write three sentences about yourself and people you know, using perfect modals from this lesson. For example, think about …
  • a speculation about what a friend or family member has done.
  • a logical deduction about what a friend or family member has done.
  • something you haven't done, or something you've done wrong.

  My sister might have had a maths test this morning.
  My mum must have had her lunch.
  I should have gone to bed earlier last night.

  1 _____
  2 _____
  3 _____

Preview and predict the content of a text.

2.6 READING

1 What can you remember about the Student's Book text? Complete the text with the words below.

| account challenge commitment instincts options

Pilots 'Sully' Sullenberger and Jeffrey 'Jeff' Skiles faced a [1]_____ that tested them to the limit when their plane's engines stopped just after taking off from LaGuardia Airport. Sully had made a [2]_____ to ensure the safety of everyone on board and was determined to achieve it. He evaluated the [3]_____ for landing safely and chose to land on the Hudson River. He'd never landed on water before, but he trusted his [4]_____. After the event, investigators questioned whether Sully should have returned to LaGuardia, but they didn't take [5]_____ of the fact that Sully and Jeff needed time to figure out what had happened and what they needed to do.

2 Read the headline and look at the photos. When is quick thinking important, and when is slow thinking more appropriate? What happened to the twins?

QUICK THINKING? LIFE-SAVING!

STRATEGY Previewing and predicting

Before you read a text in English, use information you already know about the subject to predict the content. This will make it easier to understand the text. Read the title and subheadings, and look at any photos. Check how many paragraphs there are. Read the first few words of each paragraph and try to predict what information each paragraph might contain and the words or phrases the writer might use.

3 Read the strategy above. Look at the subheadings and the first few words of each paragraph and predict which paragraph (A, B, C, D or E) answers each of the questions below.
 1 What happens if we use quick thinking at the wrong time? ___
 2 How badly hurt was Melissa? ___
 3 When does slow thinking help us? ___
 4 How did Georgia save her sister's life? ___
 5 What is quick thinking? ___

4 🔊 2.05 Read the article and answer the questions in Ex 3.

5 Read the article again and choose the correct alternative.
 1 Georgia hit the crocodile because **she was furious** / **her sister was scared** / **it was an automatic response**.
 2 The writer suggests you **might** / **should** / **needn't** have felt scared when you saw the photo of the crocodile.
 3 Quick thinking **keeps us safe** / **is something we have to work hard at** / **is an example of System 2 thinking**.
 4 What is true about System 2 thinking is that **it's easy** / **we will always answer maths questions correctly if we use it** / **we have to choose to do it**.
 5 We sometimes get things wrong when using quick thinking because we **take action without feeling emotions** / **don't see situations as they really are** / **don't believe our actions will help**.
 6 The twins **couldn't have got** / **could have got** / **might get** ill from the water in the lagoon.

Ⓐ Crocodile attack!

When a crocodile pulled Melissa Laurie underwater, her twin Georgia had to act fast to save her sister's life. So she did the only thing she could do – she punched it on the nose.

The 28-year-old British twins had been travelling and volunteering in Mexico. Both experienced divers, the sisters were swimming in a lagoon when Georgia realised Melissa had disappeared. Then, she saw her unconscious body and near it, a crocodile.

'She just started hitting it,' said the twins' other sister later. 'She'd heard that with some animals, that's what you've got to do. She said her adrenaline kicked in and she knew what to do.'

Ⓑ Fast thinking for survival

In that moment, Georgia used quick thinking. Our brains process information in two ways: quick thinking and slow thinking. If you had a strong response to the photo of the crocodile, that was your brain using quick thinking. You didn't ask your brain to do it. It just happened. Psychologists call this System 1 thinking. It's fast, emotional and automatic, and our brains use it to help us survive when we sense danger.

Ⓒ Taking your time to figure things out

In contrast, System 2 thinking is slow and careful. We use it to solve problems, like this sum: 42 x 57. Did you try to work out the answer? You may or may not have done, because we make a choice to use System 2 thinking. If you got the answer right (it's at the bottom of the page), you must have applied mental effort and concentration, which System 2 thinking requires.

Ⓓ The dangers of quick thinking

Georgia was right to use quick thinking in the lagoon. It can have its disadvantages, though. A present situation may remind us of a past experience, for example, making us jump to the wrong conclusion about what we need to do. This can lead to bad decision-making.

Ⓔ Recovering from the attack

So, what happened to the twins? Both sisters had to take medicine because doctors were worried about the water they had been swimming in. Doctors were also concerned about what bacteria may have been passed on to Melissa from the crocodile's mouth and teeth. Melissa had to spend time in hospital because she'd suffered a lot of injuries, but she made a full recovery.

lagoon (n) a large area of salt water separated from the sea
adrenaline (n) the hormone (chemical) that prepares your body to fight or run away when you face danger

Answer: 42 x 57 = 2,394

2.7 GLOBAL SKILLS

Look at different ways to cope with challenging situations.

1 What can you remember about the advice for coping with challenging situations from the Student's Book? Complete the text.

How to cope when things don't go our way

There's truth in the saying, 'It's not what happens, but how you cope with it.'

Challenges and ¹s_____s are part of life. Quite simply, they're ²u_____e. However, we can all learn to ³b_____ d r_____e in order to cope with them. Here's some advice to help you.

In fact, we can start by looking after ourselves before things go wrong. One way you can do this is by ⁴s_____g y_____f with people who support and encourage your ⁵s_____-_____m – avoid people who stress you out and make you feel bad.

When things go wrong, ⁶a_____ t the f_____t that you feel sad, angry or disappointed. It's OK to feel like that. Talk to people you ⁷t_____t, and don't be afraid to ask for help. Focus on your positive qualities and remember that one negative experience doesn't ⁸d_____e you. Recall how you ⁹g_____t t_____h difficult situations in the past. You managed then, and you will again.

Finally, remember that challenging experiences help us develop, grow and be successful!

2 Look at the photos and answer the questions.
  1 What are the people doing?
  2 How are they feeling?
  3 Do you like being in these situations? Why? / Why not?

3 Read the article about different kinds of stress. Do the comments refer to distress (*D*), eustress (*E*) or both (*B*)?
  1 'I've been anxious about my best friend for ages.' ___
  2 'When I'm kitesurfing, I love how I have to concentrate so much that I can't think about anything else.' ___
  3 'I'm starting a new job next week. I'm going to learn so much from it!' ___
  4 'I'm starting a new job next week. Maybe I shouldn't have accepted it. How am I going to get everything else done that I need to do?' ___
  5 'I need a break from this!' ___

4 Complete the blog post with words from the article.

BLOG
New post • 4 hours ago

Make eustress work for you!

While negative stress is bad for our ¹_____, *eustress*, or positive stress, is important for our well-being because it creates feelings of energy and ²_____ in us. We experience eustress when we do things that feel good but a bit uncomfortable at the same time. Take these steps to get more eustress in your life.

* **Develop a positive mindset.** Learn to see difficult situations as exciting ³_____ instead of scary threats.
* **Push yourself.** Try ⁴_____ a new skill, such as a language or a sport.
* **Don't be over-ambitious.** Set goals that will make you work hard but which are also achievable.
* **Be kind to yourself.** Think about what your ⁵_____ are when setting goals, and remember to stop and have some ⁶_____, even when you're doing things you enjoy.

5 Answer the questions.
* Think of a time when you felt negative stress. How did you feel? How did you cope?
* Think of a time when you challenged yourself to do something difficult. How did you feel? What happened?

The power of positive stress

'Agh! I'm really stressed!'

In day-to-day life, we often use the word *stress* to describe negative situations and feelings. However, not all stress is bad.

Of course, negative stress, or *distress*, is a problem. It causes anxiety, is emotionally damaging to our mental health and can lead to burnout, especially when it goes on for a long time. There's also positive stress, though. Also known as *eustress*, from the Greek *eu-* meaning good + *stress*, positive stress is essential for our well-being. Positive stress is what you feel when you push yourself to do something that you want to do but which feels a bit uncomfortable. This could be mastering a new skill, starting a new college, travelling abroad or doing something 'scary-exciting' like watching a horror film or doing an extreme sport. This kind of stress is motivating and doesn't last long. It focuses your energy and attention and makes you perform well. It also gives you feelings of energy and hope.

Another way to think of eustress is that feeling you get when there's a gap between what you have and what you want or need, and the goal is achievable if you put enough effort in. In other words, it's difficult but not impossible. Humans, it seems, thrive on learning, so we feel good when we keep pushing ourselves and making progress. Recognising the difference between stress and eustress can help build resilience. If we see something as a threat which might harm us, then our anxiety levels will rise. However, if we see it as a challenge, then we can enjoy trying to overcome it. We therefore need to remind ourselves to develop a positive mindset, so that we can focus on how we can cope with the unavoidable challenges life brings rather than worrying about what damage they may cause us.

Here are some ways to get more positive stress into your life.
+ Get lots of exercise.
+ Set yourself goals around your interests.
+ Learn something new every day. It doesn't matter if it's big or small.

Even eustress needs to be managed, though, so make sure you leave room in your schedule for downtime too.

Use a variety of phrases to describe and compare photos.

2.8 SPEAKING

STRATEGY Using adjectives

When you are talking about a photo, try to use a range of adjectives to make your description more expressive. You can use both ungradable adjectives (e.g. *amazing*, *brilliant*, *exhausted*, *ridiculous*, *terrible*, *wonderful*) and gradable adjectives (e.g. *bored*, *enjoyable*, *exciting*, *puzzling*, *resentful*, *resilient*).
Ungradable adjectives combine with adverbs like *absolutely*, *completely*, *really*, *totally*.
Gradable adjectives combine with adverbs like *a bit*, *extremely*, *pretty*, *slightly*, *very*.

1 Read the strategy above. Look at the photos and choose the correct alternative.

1 The hiker on the left looks **a bit puzzled / extremely confused**.
2 The other hikers look **totally exhausted / pretty relaxed**.
3 Clearly, it's **quite cold / absolutely freezing**.

4 This photo shows a skateboarder who looks **completely inexperienced / pretty experienced**.
5 He seems **quite happy / a bit frustrated**.
6 The street looks **totally empty / quite busy**.

2 🔊 **2.06** Listen to a student talking about the two photos. Tick (✓) the topics he mentions.
feelings ☐   food ☐   buildings ☐   safety ☐

3 a Complete the sentences with one to three words.
1 _____ photo, you can see three young people in the countryside.
2 I'd say they _____ trying to figure out which way to go next.
3 I can't be _____, but it looks as though they might be in a forest.
4 The man on the right has got a _____ thing for sleeping on or something _____ on his backpack.
5 The second _____ a skateboarder in a city.
6 It _____ any modern city, really.
7 I'd _____ that he's in his mid-twenties.
8 _____ show outdoor activities.
9 For _____, the _____ point is that all these young people are spending time outdoors.
10 I feel _____ that cities should have lots of green spaces where people can exercise.

b 🔊 **2.06** Listen again and check.

4 Match the sentence halves.
1 The man on the left looks a bit confused, ___
2 The skateboarder is on a city street, ___
3 In both photos we can see young people enjoying their free time outdoors, ___
4 The main difference is that the hikers are in the countryside, ___
5 The hikers are in a group, ___
6 Unlike the skateboarder, who is in the middle of an activity, ___

A the hikers have stopped to work out their route.
B whereas the skateboarder is in a city.
C but it looks completely empty.
D but in different situations.
E although the other two people seem quite happy.
F whereas the skateboarder is alone.

PRONUNCIATION Contrastive stress

In English, we normally stress the most important words in a sentence, such as the main nouns, verbs and adjectives. When we emphasise a contrast, we often stress the words that clearly show the two different ideas we want to express.

5 a Read the Pronunciation box. Read sentences 1–6 in Ex 4 out loud. Underline the words in Ex 4 that we would stress to emphasise a contrast between two different ideas.

b 🔊 **2.07** Listen, check and repeat.

6 You are going to write your answer to the speaking task below. Make a note of the main similarities and differences between the two photos.

Compare the photos. Speculate about where the people are, what they are doing and how they are feeling. Then give your opinion about the two different kinds of free-time activities.

7 Plan your work. Use a range of adjectives and phrases for comparing, speculating and stating your opinion. Underline words to show how you would use contrastive stress.

8 Write your script. When you have finished, check that you have …
• described the photos using a range of adjectives and phrases for speculating.
• compared the photos.
• stated your opinion clearly.

Unit 2   25

2.9 WRITING — Plan the content and structure of an opinion essay.

1 Write a few sentences in answer to each of the questions below.
1 Which of the things below do you do as acts of kindness towards yourself?

> connecting with friends   having a long bath
> switching off your mobile phone   taking exercise

2 How do you feel about taking the risks below?
- going on holiday with people you don't know very well
- riding a bike on a busy road without wearing a helmet
- setting up a small business with a family member
- swimming in water where there might be sharks or crocodiles

2 Read the task and the essay. Complete the paragraph plan with topics A–E.

> 'The most effective way to grow, develop and be successful is to take risks.' Write an essay giving your opinion of this statement. Refer to experience, resilience and one more idea of your own.

A the supporting argument that taking risks can lead to a range of new and exciting possibilities

B the supporting argument that, despite the fact that trying difficult or new things can be dangerous, risk-taking often contributes to feelings of well-being

C my overall opinion about risk-taking, repeated more strongly

D the supporting argument that by taking risks, we learn about life and get to know ourselves better, knowing that we might make mistakes sometimes

E some general thoughts on risk-taking, including my opinion and one contrasting argument

Paragraph 1: Introduction: ¹___

Main body: Three paragraphs with supporting arguments with reasons / examples / contrasting arguments
  Paragraph 2: ²___
  Paragraph 3: ³___
  Paragraph 4: ⁴___

Paragraph 5: Conclusion: ⁵___

STRATEGY Planning what to include

When you are planning an opinion essay, think carefully about the topic and your opinion about it. Make a list of ideas or arguments that support your opinion, and some that contrast with it. Evaluate all the ideas and choose the strongest arguments to include.

3 Read the strategy above. Make a list of arguments that support and contrast with the statement in the task below.

> 'Switching off your mobile phone one day a week is one of the kindest things you can do for yourself.' Write an essay giving your opinion of this statement. Refer to well-being, communication and one more idea of your own.

4 Look at the underlined words and phrases in the essay. Decide what function they have, for example, introducing a point or idea, expressing an opinion, sequencing ideas, adding a supporting point and introducing a contrasting point.

> **'The most effective way to grow, develop and be successful is to take risks.' Discuss.**
>
> Risk-taking is often associated with danger. Of course some risks, such as doing extreme sports or visiting dangerous places, can result in harmful consequences. <u>On the whole</u>, however, I personally feel that if we never take risks, it's difficult to grow, develop and be successful as human beings.
>
> Firstly, <u>I firmly believe</u> we need to take risks to gain a variety of life experiences. Of course, we might make mistakes, fail, waste money or simply not enjoy the experience. <u>However</u>, every time we do something risky, we have a new adventure – a new life story to remember and share with others. <u>Moreover</u>, by challenging ourselves we gain knowledge, learn new skills and build resilience. <u>In addition</u> to this, we learn things about ourselves, such as what we enjoy and don't enjoy, and what our strengths and weaknesses are.
>
> Secondly, in terms of well-being, risk-taking can create positive stress, which is good for us. <u>Having said that</u>, we need to be realistic about the degree of risk we take. For example, having a go at surfing is great if you're a strong swimmer and have someone to teach you about technique and safety, but it could lead to negative stress if it's completely beyond your capability.
>
> <u>Finally</u>, taking risks often opens us up to meeting new people, which in turn can lead to new relationships and opportunities. <u>For instance</u>, if you move away from your home town to work or study, you're likely to meet new people who will introduce you to new hobbies and interests, and this of course means you'll be able to try out different things and take new risks.
>
> <u>In summary</u>, as long as we make careful judgements about what physical or emotional damage to ourselves or others a decision might lead to, <u>I personally feel</u> that we should be open to the idea of taking risks for our personal growth and development.

5 Create an essay plan using the five-paragraph structure in Ex 2.

6 Write the essay based on your plan in Ex 5. Write five paragraphs and include at least five phrases from Ex 4.

7 ✓ **CHECK YOUR WORK** Did you …
- follow the plan?
- include grammar and vocabulary related to the topic?
- include phrases for introducing a point or idea, expressing an opinion, sequencing ideas, adding a supporting point, introducing a contrasting point?
- check your spelling, grammar and punctuation?

2.10 REVIEW

Grammar

1 Match the sentence halves.
1 You mustn't ___
2 It can ___
3 You have ___
4 They should ___
5 You'll be ___
6 He isn't supposed ___
7 I don't know. He could ___
8 You don't have ___

A be here soon. It's nearly half past seven.
B be in the garden or he might be in the park.
C eat that! It will make you sick!
D be difficult to make new friends.
E to have your passport or you can't travel.
F to wait for me. You can leave now.
G able to meet Max tomorrow.
H to eat any sugar because of his illness.

2 Choose the correct alternative. Sometimes both answers are possible.

Miguel Thank you for paying for my coffee! You ¹**didn't need to do / needn't have done** that!
Sami Well, I'm in a good mood. It's my birthday.
Miguel Happy birthday! Wait … What's today's date?
Sami The 22nd. Why?
Miguel Oh no! I ²**needed / was supposed** to have handed in an essay yesterday. I completely forgot!
Sami You ³**must / should** have put a reminder on your phone so you wouldn't forget.
Miguel Yeah, you're right. Oh, I can't believe it! I ⁴**could / may** have done that essay on Saturday instead of watching the football at Omar's house.
Sami You were at Omar's? You ⁵**must have / ought to have** met my friend Lucas. He was there.
Miguel Yes, I did. He's really nice.
Sami He'd been quite anxious about going because he only knew Omar, but when he got there, he realised he ⁶**didn't need to be / needn't have been** so worried because everyone was completely focused on the football!
Miguel It was a great match! Right, I've got to go. Thanks again for the coffee. Enjoy your day!

Vocabulary

3 Complete the sentences. Use the definitions in brackets.
1 Were you _____ (upset because you thought I'd said something unkind about you) when I said you were proud of your work?
2 Anna was feeling _____ (really sad) when I spoke to her yesterday.
3 What's that noise? It's really _____ _____ _____ (annoying me).
4 I was _____ (confused) as to why you didn't wait for me today.
5 Holly was _____ (extremely angry) that her sister had borrowed her car without asking.
6 I'm sure you'll feel better when you _____ it _____ (discuss it) with Kaheem.
7 Layla has _____ _____ (had an argument) with Fatima. They aren't speaking to each other.
8 I used to feel _____ (angry about something that seems unfair to you) that my brother was allowed to go to bed later than me.

4 Complete the sentences.
1 Stress can make people ill, but my cousin Maria t_____ on it, which is probably why she loves her job as a firefighter.
2 Jamal wasn't just a bit sad. He was suffering from d_____.
3 If you don't feel good about yourself, learning a new skill can help b_____ s_____-c_____.
4 I've lived a happy life and I don't have any r_____. I'm happy with all the choices I've made.
5 She works six days a week, so she doesn't get much d_____, but she sometimes goes running.
6 I don't know if he has an a_____ to chocolate, but he certainly gets irritated when he hasn't had some for a few hours.
7 When we d_____ a p_____ m_____, we feel more hopeful and optimistic about the future.
8 Thanks to social media, people receive much more i_____ every day than they did 30 years ago.

Cumulative review

5 Complete the blog post with the words and phrases below.

anxiety	calm down	can	chill out	crazy
don't have to	frustrated	had to	mental
must have	should have	well-being

Studies show that spending time in nature can help your ¹_____. Fortunately, you ²_____ go deep into a forest or climb a mountain to experience the benefits of the great outdoors. Just spending time in a park ³_____ be enough. What's your experience?

💬 **Comments**

I get ⁴_____ quite quickly when things aren't going well, but I find that if I go and walk by the river near my house, I ⁵_____ quite quickly. *Kai, 17*

I live in a city, but there's a park nearby where I go and ⁶_____ when things get on top of me. Just sitting there helps reduce my ⁷_____. (I ⁸_____ gone there yesterday when my brother was driving me ⁹_____!) *Lily, 16*

During the 2020 pandemic, I ¹⁰_____ stay at home every day. At least I could spend time in my garden, though, which was really good for my ¹¹_____ health. It ¹²_____ been really difficult for people living in flats. *Toni, 18*

REFLECT Think about the following questions.
1 Which lesson in this unit did you enjoy the most? Why?
2 Which of the grammar points did you find the most difficult? Why?
3 How can you practise understanding new words and phrases in reading texts?
4 What three things can you do to build resilience?

1–2 EXAM SKILLS

Listening

EXAM STRATEGY

When you do a multiple-choice task matching dialogues with photos, look at the pictures carefully before you listen. Identify the topic that links them and think of words to describe each photo. Keep lists of words to describe different topics in your notebook.

1 Read the strategy above. Then read the first question in the exam task in Ex 2 and look at the pictures. What is the linking topic? Think of two or three words that you associate with each picture.

2 ⏵ 2.08 For each question, listen and choose the correct answer: A, B or C.

1 What activity is the boy going to do?
A   B   C

2 Where is Anna going to go to talk to her flatmate?
A   B   C

3 What are they going to do at the weekend?
A   B   C

4 How is Hannah going to travel now?
A   B   C

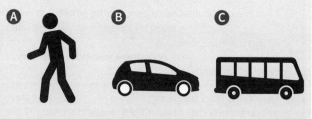

5 What is today's programme about?
A   B   C

Use of English

EXAM STRATEGY

You can practise for a word formation task by choosing words that have prefixes and suffixes and adding as many of these as you can to create different versions of the words.

3 Read the strategy above. Then read the exam task in Ex 4. Look at the first gapped sentence. How many different words can you make with the word given? Which is the correct word?

4 Use the word given in brackets to form a word that fits in each gap (1–10).

Benefits of mindfulness

Do you ever feel that you are not in control of your life? Are you suffering from anxiety or feelings of ¹_____ (DEPRESS)? Life today can be very ²_____ (STRESS), particularly for young people when they are doing exams. During this time, some people become irritated, or ³_____ (RESENT) towards people whose lives seem easier. They may lose friends or find it hard to communicate, which can then lead to feelings of ⁴_____ (HOPE). However, if you are feeling ⁵_____ (HAPPY) in this way, there are things that you can do. One of these is to practise mindfulness. Mindfulness develops our ⁶_____ (ABLE) to connect with the world and with our bodies. It encourages us to notice what is happening in the present moment and to ⁷_____ (POSITIVE) change the way we see life. So how can we become more mindful? There are some simple methods which you can ⁸_____ (EASY) include in your daily life. For example, when you are eating, pay attention to the taste of your food, and when you are moving around, focus on what you see and hear. You can also practise mindfulness by sitting ⁹_____ (QUIET) and focusing on your breathing. These ¹⁰_____ (SUGGEST) can really make a difference.

Reading

EXAM STRATEGY

When you do a multiple-choice task, find evidence in the text to explain both why the option you choose is correct and why the others are wrong.

5 Read the strategy above. Then read the exam task in Ex 6. Focus on the first paragraph and the first question. Which is the correct option? Why? Why are the other options wrong?

1–2 EXAM SKILLS

6 Read the article about a story of survival. For each question, choose the correct answer: A, B, C or D.

Sea adventure

Steven Callahan had been sailing ships since he was young, so when he decided to set sail from Maine on a trip alone to the Canary Islands and then back to the USA in January 1981, he had no sense of anxiety. He was sailing in the *Napoleon Solo*, which was a boat he had built himself. The trip went well, and Callahan made it safely to his destination. It was on his way back, when he left the Canaries, that he ran into trouble.

After about a week, a storm began. It wasn't a huge storm and Callahan didn't feel very worried until suddenly he heard a loud noise. A hole appeared in the boat, and he realised it must have been hit by a whale or a shark. As the boat began to sink, Callahan knew he would never be able to fix the damage. He got into his life raft, but he also needed supplies, which were in the sinking boat. He dived into the ocean and managed to get several items, including food and water.

Incredibly, Callahan was on the raft for a total of 76 days. During that time, he faced terrible danger, but his sailing experience helped him to survive. He was finally rescued when sailors near Guadeloupe spotted him. By that time, he had lost a third of his weight and could barely stand. He was taken to hospital for treatment, but it was many months before he recovered.

After his time at sea, Callahan wrote a book about his experience and continued to design and build boats. He also worked, giving advice, on the film version of the book *Life of Pi* by the Canadian author Yann Martel, which was published in 2001 and won the Man Booker Prize for fiction. In the book, the main character, who is an Indian Tamil boy called Piscine Molitor 'Pi' Patel, is left on a lifeboat in the Pacific Ocean. However, unlike Callahan, he is accompanied by a tiger and is at sea for 227 days.

1 When Steven Callahan set off from America, he …
 A intended not to return.
 B was nervous about travelling alone.
 C was confident about his abilities.
 D had little experience of sailing.
2 Callahan realised he was in danger …
 A after something damaged his boat.
 B as soon as the storm began.
 C the moment he left the Canary Islands.
 D when the bad weather improved.
3 After the boat began to sink, Callahan …
 A ran to get his supplies.
 B spotted a shark.
 C dived into the water.
 D tried to fix the damage.

4 Callahan survived because he …
 A had sufficient supplies.
 B was picked up by a boat.
 C swam to safety.
 D sailed to an island.
5 After his journey, Callahan …
 A made a film about his life.
 B contributed to the filming of *Life of Pi*.
 C wrote a book with Yann Martel.
 D gave up his connections with sailing.

Speaking

EXAM STRATEGY

When you take part in a task that requires you to discuss points and come to an agreement, you can show your initiative by using phrases to keep the conversation moving and bring it to a conclusion.

7 Read the strategy above. Then complete the useful phrases with the words below.

| let's   move   need   shall   think

1 _____ talk about the next point.
2 What do you _____ of this idea?
3 _____ we discuss the other ideas now?
4 I think we should _____ on now.
5 Right. We now _____ to decide on the best ideas.

8 💬 Work in pairs. You are going to discuss what young people should do in order to cope effectively with stress and other mental health problems. Talk to each other about the ideas in the list below and decide which two would be the most useful.
- doing yoga
- practising mindfulness
- having more leisure time
- avoiding social media
- improving diet

Writing

EXAM STRATEGY

When you write a story, vary your use of language by using strong verbs (e.g. *stare* instead of *look*) and reducing your use of adverbs.

9 Read the strategy above. Then replace the words in **bold** with strong verbs.
1 Ben **looked** at the man. Did he know him?
2 Sam **ran fast** down the road.
3 Lucy **closed** the door **loudly**.
4 They **walked around** the caves for hours.

10 You have seen an online advert for a competition asking for rescue stories. Write a story in which you …
- introduce the characters and their situation.
- describe the beginning of their story.
- explain what goes wrong.
- say how they are rescued.

Unit 2   29

3.1 VOCABULARY
Talk about exercise and physical health.

An active life

1 a What can you remember about the vlog? Are the sentences true (*T*) or false (*F*)?
1. *Rajio taiso* is beneficial for people of all ages. T ☐ F ☐
2. Zaki likes *rajio taiso* because it helps him work up a sweat. T ☐ F ☐
3. *Rajio taiso* stretches your muscles at the start of the day. T ☐ F ☐
4. According to Yasmin, one of the main advantages of *rajio taiso* is that it is easy to fit in with your daily routine. T ☐ F ☐
5. *Rajio taiso* and yoga both make you more flexible. T ☐ F ☐
6. Joe started yoga because he finds team sports challenging. T ☐ F ☐
7. According to Daisy, the exercise bike was rather complicated to use at first. T ☐ F ☐
8. The bike has had a positive impact on Daisy's fitness routine. T ☐ F ☐

b ▶ 🔊 3.01 Watch or listen again and check.

2 Choose the correct alternative.
1. Chocolate is so **addictive** / **beneficial** – I just always want more!
2. Nia **worked up** / **took up** a sweat at tennis training.
3. This website has some online classes that are gentle and some that really **increase** / **stretch** your heart rate.
4. Yoga makes you **impact on** / **aware of** your whole body.
5. A short run doesn't **take up** / **fit in** a lot of time.
6. We were **stretched** / **thrilled** to finish the marathon in under four hours.
7. This dance routine is much too **complicated** / **enthusiastic** for me to follow.
8. If you do yoga every day, you'll become more **beneficial** / **flexible**.

3 Complete the advice with words and phrases from the lesson.

4 REAL ENGLISH Complete the dialogue with the phrases below.

| couch potato   job done   keep at it |
| let off steam   that's it |
| too much information |

A Senyo, get off that video game. You are such a ¹_____!
B No, I'm not. I'm learning this new game.
A But you can't ²_____ until you've completed all the levels. That will take days.
B Possibly. It's so exciting, though. The gameplay is amazing, and it really builds on the story from Part 2.
A ³_____, Senyo. Listen, why don't you come to the park with me and ⁴_____? I bet you'll play the video game better after a break.
B ⁵_____? Just half an hour?
A Yes, sure, I promise.
B Let me just finish … this … move. ⁶_____!

5 VOCABULARY BOOSTER Now practise **Keep fit** vocabulary on page 106.

Starting a new exercise routine

So, you've been inspired to start a new exercise routine. Congratulations! Here are some tips that will ¹h_____ a p_____ i_____ on your workout journey.

🎯 First of all, it's vital that you set realistic goals for yourself. Even if you are ²e_____ and motivated, you are likely to struggle unless your new routine ³f_____ i_____ w_____ your existing schedule.

🏃 Next, start small and give yourself time to improve. Of course, it's important to ⁴i_____ y_____ h_____ r_____ and work up a sweat, but do this gradually over a number of weeks – particularly if you are new to sport. Try keeping an exercise diary. This can really ⁵m_____ y_____ a_____ o_____ your progress over time, and help you see when you are ready to move on to more ⁶c_____ workouts.

🤸 Please ensure that you are kind to your body. Remember to ⁷s_____ y_____ m_____ before and after your workout. This will stop you feeling ⁸s_____ and will also prevent injury. It is also crucial to consider your diet. In order to ⁹m_____ y_____ h_____ over time, you must give your body the right fuel for its activities.

❤ Finally, remember what you are training for: your health! It is not ¹⁰b_____ to compare yourself to other people in your gym, or online, or in your school. Be yourself, and enjoy your fitness routine.

30 Unit 3

▶ Grammar animation
GRAMMAR BOOSTER P136

Use comparatives to talk about different exercise routines.

3.2 GRAMMAR

1 Read the sentences. In which sentences is an advanced comparative used …
  A to say that two people or things are equal (or not)? ___ ___
  B to show continuous change? ___ ___
  C to show that two things change together because they are connected? ___ ___

  1 The more people get moving, the better.
  2 The number of people who are overweight is becoming more and more worrying.
  3 During the Covid-19 pandemic, some people couldn't be as active as usual.
  4 Exercising gets easier and easier as you improve your strength and fitness.
  5 The less you practise these exercises, the weaker your muscles will get.
  6 In terms of being active, gardening can be as effective as a trip to the gym.

2 Complete the text with the comparative form of the words below.

  | beneficial   fit   hard (x2)   high
  | popular   short   time-consuming

Ask our fitness expert

Q: Is a ten-minute workout really enough?

A: Ten minutes … That's it? Only joking! The great news is that a ten-minute workout really can be long enough. Short, demanding workout classes have become ¹_____ and _____ in gyms in recent years. It may sound like a temporary trend, but the scientific evidence shows that ten minutes of high-intensity interval training (also known as HIIT) can be ²_____ as 30 minutes of gentle exercise, such as walking.

The idea behind HIIT training is to work ³_____ as you can for a short period of time, followed by a complete stop. The period of activity is known as an 'interval'. As a general rule, the ⁴_____ the interval (usually 1–1.5 minutes), the ⁵_____ the intensity of the effort. This is repeated several times over ten minutes or more. Scientific research proves that HIIT has a significant impact on your body. It's great for burning fat, increasing fitness and even reducing the effects of age on the body. HIIT is good for all abilities because you aim to increase your heart rate to 85%–90% of its maximum. The ⁶_____ you are, the ⁷_____ you have to work – but only during the allowed interval time.

As it's all finished in ten minutes, clearly HIIT is ⁸_____ as going for a jog. Equally, there is more variety: the intervals can involve bikes, weights, jumps, stomach exercises … the list goes on. It's great for working up a sweat!

3 Underline the qualifying word(s) in the sentences. Is the difference small (S), big (B) or equal (E)?
  1 Some people claim Tabata workouts are just as effective as HIIT workouts. ___
  2 The rest periods in Tabata workouts are much shorter than HIIT: just ten seconds. ___
  3 HIIT classes can be a lot louder than some gym classes because the teachers tend to shout positive instructions to help you keep going! ___
  4 If you watch a HIIT class, it can look a bit scarier than a traditional gym class. ___
  5 But if you try one, it's nowhere near as scary as it seems. The shouting really is helpful! ___
  6 Don't forget that rest days are equally as important as exercise days for your body. You need time for recovery. ___

4 Choose the correct alternative using information in the text in Ex 2.
  1 HIIT classes have become **a bit more** / **far more** popular recently.
  2 But HIIT is **much more** / **nothing like** valuable than just a trendy gym class.
  3 Ten minutes of HIIT can be **just as** / **almost as** effective as 30 minutes of walking.
  4 HIIT is **equally** / **not quite** as effective for beginners as for serious athletes.
  5 In HIIT training, your heart rate is expected to be **a bit** / **a lot** higher than its usual level.
  6 Each interval should be **slightly longer than** / **just as long as** the one before, with a rest in between.
  7 Jogging is **nowhere near as** / **just as** varied as a HIIT workout.
  8 Overall, HIIT is **just as** / **nothing like as** scary as you might think it is.

5 Research the intervals below. If you can, try each interval for one minute, working as hard as you can, followed by a one-minute break.
  • mountain climbers
  • burpees
  • spotty dogs

  Make notes using comparative forms of *easy*, *difficult*, *effort* and *fun*.

6 **MEDIATION** Your friend is finding it hard to fit exercise in with their daily routine. Write a short email recommending HIIT and comparing it to running for 30 minutes. Use comparative forms from this lesson, for example …
  • *as beneficial as*
  • *nowhere near as scary as*
  • *far less time-consuming*
  • *just as effective as*

intensity (n) a state of being powerful or extreme

Unit 3   31

3.3 LISTENING
Distinguish facts and speculation in a listening text.

1 What can you remember about the podcast in the Student's Book? Complete the sentences with the words below.

| disputes   originated   recreation
| survival   tribes   warfare

1 In the past, skills that we think of as sporting ability were necessary for _____.
2 The techniques used in many modern sports _____ during ancient times, as ways to hunt for food or stay safe.
3 Some sporting events, such as archery, were used during _____, and would have been practised by soldiers.
4 Lacrosse was played by Indigenous American _____ to prepare young men for battle.
5 Victory at lacrosse may have been used to resolve _____ over land and other resources.
6 Today, in contrast, sport is generally considered as _____ or entertainment.

2 You are going to listen to four texts about sports products. Look at the photos and think about the questions.
- How do these products help people to keep active?
- Who would buy them?
- What features would you expect these items to have?

3 🔊 3.02 Listen to the four texts and choose the correct answer: A, B, C or D. You may listen twice.
1 According to the speaker, where does the 10,000 steps fitness goal come from?
   A academic research from 1965
   B a Japanese fitness tradition
   C research from Harvard Medical School
   D the company that invented the first step counter
2 Why doesn't Aziz want to buy the bike?
   A It isn't the brand he wants.
   B He doesn't trust the seller.
   C He has decided to take up running instead.
   D He thinks he'll find a better deal elsewhere.
3 What camera feature is the customer most interested in?
   A voice control
   B water resistance
   C picture quality
   D internet connectivity
4 What is the central idea explored in the book?
   A the development of modern sports shoes
   B the history of sports clothing around the world
   C that modern shoes are making humans worse at running
   D that humans would be fitter if they followed the example of certain tribes

> **STRATEGY** Distinguishing facts and speculation
>
> When listening to a podcast, lecture or report, etc., it's important to understand whether what the speaker says is a fact or speculation. Facts are often supported by referring to research or other evidence, such as dates or places. Speculation (or the speaker's opinion) is not usually supported by evidence and is often expressed using modal verbs like *could* or *may*, adverbs like *probably* or *likely* and verbs like *think*, *seem* or *believe*.

4 🔊 3.03 Read the strategy above. Listen to the extracts from the texts and decide if they are stating a fact (*F*) or speculation (*S*). Note down any language or information that helped you decide.
1 F / S   5 F / S
2 F / S   6 F / S
3 F / S   7 F / S
4 F / S

5 Rewrite the sentences to emphasise speculation. Use the words in brackets.
1 Shoes are not good for your feet. (likely)
2 These shoes will help you run faster. (seem / people)
3 Karl is running a marathon in July. (might)
4 Modern shoes change the shape of your feet. (thought)

6 Complete the task.
1 Choose one of the products from Ex 2 and research it online.
2 Write three factual sentences using the information you find.
3 Write three speculation sentences to answer this question: 'Do you think the product is suitable for you?'

Talk about how sport can provide the skills for a successful career.

3.4 VOCABULARY

1 Look at the photos. What are the similarities and differences between these roles? Would you expect these people be good at the sports shown? Why? / Why not?

Lifeguard

Referee

First-aider

2 Choose the correct answer: A, B or C.

Amina I've always loved swimming, so it made a lot of sense to train as a lifeguard. You need to ¹_____ strong swimming skills when you qualify, and we renew our qualifications regularly. I'm still at school, but I work here most weekends. People often think lifeguards work alone, but in fact you have to ²_____ work with others all day long. At my pool, there are always two people watching different parts of the water. Also, it takes two or more guards to lift someone from the water if they're injured. I like the amount of variety involved in this job. In particular, you have to ³_____ to changes in the pool users: a family session with lots of young children is very different from a session for confident swimmers. It's a great job, it pays well and I think a full-time career in the leisure industry would suit me.

Jayden I'm a dedicated handball player for my district, and I've also been a handball referee since I was sixteen. When I leave college, I'd like to pursue a career in business, and I believe that being a referee is great preparation for that. You have to get the respect of the players … and sometimes the spectators. They will only ⁴_____ of your decisions if you are fair, calm and consistent. You also have to ⁵_____, because a competitive match can be stressful for everyone involved. I also have to manage my time effectively to get to all the matches and stay on top of my schoolwork.

Mylie I play football for my school football team, but I also volunteer as a sports first-aider at matches in my town. Being a first-aider has helped me find a place in the football community. I used to be quite shy, but now I'm not afraid to speak out if I see risky play on the pitch. Ankle and knee injuries occur very often, and I know that what I do ⁶_____ the player getting the right treatment fast. Even if I'm not needed on the pitch, there's always something to do. Before and after each match, I ⁷_____ checking the contents of the first-aid kit. You have to make sure everything is ready. Of course my first-aid knowledge is beneficial in everyday life too. It shows employers that I care, and that I'm prepared to train and then act decisively.

1	A accept	B demonstrate	C take	
2	A be willing to	B contribute to	C take responsibility for	
3	A cope	B adapt	C accept	
4	A contribute	B take responsibility	C accept the consequences	
5	A cope under pressure	B adapt to changes	C demonstrate your skills	
6	A adapts to	B accepts	C contributes to	
7	A accept the C cope under pressure by	B take responsibility for		

3 Complete the sentences with the words and phrases below.

collaboration	commitment	demands
failure	leadership	organisational skills
self-confidence	teamwork

1 Some players consider leaving the pitch as a sign of _____. I have to help them understand the situation – their health comes first.
2 I need a strong _____ to the sport because my own ability contributes to the success of the role.
3 I need good _____ because I combine this role with my own matches plus my studies.
4 This role has really improved my _____.
5 There's a surprising amount of _____ involved in my role. For example, it takes _____ between two people to complete some of the activities.
6 Injuries are common because the _____ of sport can put the body under a lot of stress.
7 This role demonstrates _____ because I have to manage the teams and also sometimes the spectators during a match.

4 Who said the sentences in Ex 3? Read the texts in Ex 2 again and choose A (Amina), J (Jayden) or M (Mylie).

Sentence 1 A / J / M   Sentence 5 A / J / M
Sentence 2 A / J / M   Sentence 6 A / J / M
Sentence 3 A / J / M   Sentence 7 A / J / M
Sentence 4 A / J / M

5 Replace the underlined words with nouns from Ex 3 and verb phrases from Ex 2 so the sentences do not change in meaning.

1 Throughout your life, your sport routine will have to <u>adjust to differences</u> in your body and lifestyle. You will have to combine any activity with the <u>important things that you have to do</u> of your career.
2 It is fairly obvious that sports like handball and cricket require <u>the actions of a group of people successfully working together</u>, but individual disciplines like running and swimming require <u>the action of working with someone else</u> too.
3 I was a good gymnast, but I didn't have the <u>trust in my own ability</u> to succeed in major competitions. I just didn't <u>deal well with stress and tension</u> very well.
4 If you compete regularly, you'll soon get used to losing. <u>Lack of success</u> actually helps you improve, so show your coach that you <u>are ready and prepared to</u> review your mistakes.

6 Research and choose five Olympic sports you would like to try. Write a list of the skills / abilities you have which you think would suit these sports.

7 **VOCABULARY BOOSTER** Now practise **Transferable skills** vocabulary on page 106.

Unit 3   33

3.5 GRAMMAR
Use articles and quantifiers to talk about street football.

▶ Grammar animation
GRAMMAR BOOSTER P137

1 Read the fact file and choose the correct alternative.

NEW SPORT FACT FILE:
Panna

Rules and history
'Panna' is both a football move and ¹**the / a** competitive game. The move – in which the ball is passed between an opponent's legs – requires ²**– / a** lot of skill. It has several other names, such as 'nutmeg' (UK) or 'petit pont' (France).

Panna originated in Suriname, in ³**the / –** South America, and has spread around the world. ⁴**The / A** rules of the competitive game were only formally agreed in 2007. The pitch is a six-metre circle with a short fence or net around the outside and two goals at opposite ends. Panna is ⁵**a / the** one-on-one sport. Each game lasts for just three minutes, and points are awarded for goals and also for panna moves.

Reasons for success
- Panna is designed for urban life. It uses small spaces and minimal equipment.
- It requires exceptional ball control. The most skilled players demonstrate complicated moves which are more usually seen in freestyle football.

Set up ⁷**– / a** skills club at school.

- Loud street music, live commentary and the close proximity of the spectators all give matches ⁶**the / an** exciting atmosphere.

Prediction
Panna is gaining popularity and the elite now have fans, agents and sponsorship deals. We can expect ⁸**the / –** panna to become more and more professional over the coming years.

2 Complete the rules about the use of articles. Choose the correct alternative and add the highlighted examples from the fact file in Ex 1.

A We use **a/an** / **the** / **–** when there is only one of something, or for a specific example, e.g. _____.

B We use **a/an** / **the** / **–** when we mention something for the first time, and then **a/an** / **the** / **–** for further references to the same thing, e.g. _____ _____.

C We use **a/an** / **the** / **–** when we mean an example of something and we don't need to be more definite, e.g. _____. We use *the* when it is clear what we are talking about.

D We use **a/an** / **the** / **–** with superlatives, e.g. _____.

E We use **a/an** / **the** / **–** with words like *school*, *college*, *work*, etc. when we are talking about their purpose as an institution, e.g. _____.

F We use **a/an** / **the** / **–** for most towns, cities, regions and countries, e.g. _____. We use *the* with a few countries (*the Sudan*, *the United Kingdom*). We also use *the* with geographical features (*the Amazon*, *the Pacific*, *the Arctic*).

G We use **a/an** / **the** / **–** when we talk about something in general, e.g. _____.

H We use **a/an** / **the** / **–** with an adjective to refer to everyone who has that characteristic, e.g. _____.

3 Correct the article mistakes.
1 Road tennis is exciting sport to watch. Spectators can get very close to an action.
2 Martin goes swimming after a work on Tuesdays. He particularly likes an outdoor pool near his office.
3 In ski jumping competitions, you score the points for a longest jump.
4 Panna is extremely popular in Netherlands, which has the large Surinamese population.
5 Snowboarding is not for a shy. You need a self-confidence.
6 Georgia can do football move called 'around the world'. What's best move you can do?
7 Because a pitch is small, panna is great for the players who cannot run long distances.
8 'Can you play a basketball this evening?' 'No, I have to stay in a college until 6.30.'

4 Read the first two paragraphs of the fact file again. Find five examples of quantifiers.

5 Replace the words in **bold** with the words and phrases below so that the meaning does not change.

| a great deal   every one of us   few   much   none of us   some

1 A game of panna doesn't take up **a lot of** time, but mastering the skills takes real commitment. _____
2 **Several** famous football teams use yoga to increase their players' flexibility. _____
3 Gymnastics requires **a lot** of skill. _____
4 **Everyone** wants squash to be an Olympic sport. _____
5 **Not many** people around here have tried the sport of climbing. _____
6 We love watching tennis, but **no one here** has ever played a tennis match. _____

6 Complete the sentences using your own opinions. Include articles and quantifiers.
1 The team sport I like best is _____ because _____.
2 Brand new sports, like panna, are interesting because _____.
3 Sport provision at school is vital because _____.
4 If I could add one new sport to my school curriculum, it would be _____ because _____.

34 Unit 3

3.6 READING

Understand referencing in an article about autism and sport.

1 What can you remember about the review in the Student's Book? Complete the words in the summary.

> The documentary film *Rising Phoenix* explores the world of the Paralympic Games. It partly focuses on Ludwig Guttman, a doctor who ¹s_____ i_____ treatments for injured soldiers. Guttman believed that sport could help many of his patients to ²f_____ t_____ p_____ as they learned to use their wheelchairs. In 1948, he set up a sporting competition for male and female wheelchair users. By 1960, this had become the Paralympic Games. The film also tells the story of several athletes competing in the modern Paralympics. They talk about the ³p_____ b_____ they've had to deal with in order to participate, train and compete. They all have had to ⁴o_____ o_____, some from a very young age.
> *Rising Phoenix* shows that people with physical disabilities can ⁵e_____ a_____ sport. It's an excellent film.

2 🔊 3.04 Read the article about autism and sport. Why does Tom Stoltman describe autism as his 'superpower'?

3 Read the article again. Are the sentences true (*T*) or false (*F*)? Which paragraph (A–E) contains the evidence for your answer?
1 Not all people experience autism in the same way. **T / F** Paragraph: ___
2 Stoltman was proud of his autism when he was at school. **T / F** Paragraph: ___
3 In the past, Stoltman found speaking in public challenging. **T / F** Paragraph: ___
4 Researchers think more girls should be diagnosed with autism. **T / F** Paragraph: ___
5 The sports environment can be very challenging for people with autism. **T / F** Paragraph: ___
6 With assistance, people can recover from autism as they get older. **T / F** Paragraph: ___

STRATEGY Understanding referencing

To understand a text better, it helps to recognise when certain words refer back to an object, a person, an event or an idea which was mentioned earlier in the text. These include …
- subject and object pronouns like *he / she / it / they, him / her / it / them*.
- referents like *this, that, these, those*.
- adverbs referring to place or time like *here, there, then*.
- *so* + adjective, *such* + noun.

4 Read the strategy above. Look at the six reference words in **bold** in the article and identify exactly what each one refers to.

5 Read about Clay Marzo, who is a professional surfer with a mild form of autism. Rewrite the underlined sections using reference words.
1 People with mild autism do not compete in the Paralympics. <u>People with mild autism</u> therefore compete against athletes who might not understand their condition. _____
2 Like many autistic athletes, Marzo is able to focus on the same short task for a long time. <u>Marzo's</u> focus is surfing. _____
3 Many of the problems Marzo has in an urban environment disappear in the ocean. <u>In the ocean</u> he feels calm and at home. _____
4 Marzo won several prizes at a young age. <u>The prizes he won</u> included Open Men's National Champion (USA). _____
5 There is a documentary film about Marzo's career. <u>The documentary film's</u> title is *Just Add Water*. _____

> **autism** (*n*) a disability that can affect social skills and communication skills, and can involve repeating patterns of thought or actions
> **spectrum** (*n*) a range of different positions between two extremes

---

NEWS

Home   World   Business   Tech   Science   **Health**   🔍

Tom Stoltman

You are an athlete at an important competition. Imagine a crowd cheering, bright lights, loud music … For many people, **this** would be a dream come true. Now imagine the same scenario for an athlete with autism. Such sights and sounds can be stressful, even painful. Only a few athletes with autism make it to the top of global sport. One example is Tom Stoltman, who became the World's Strongest Man in 2021.

Ⓑ You probably know someone with autism. It is a lifelong condition which affects communication skills and the way sights, sounds and emotions are processed. **These** issues mean that children with autism often struggle at school. Stoltman, for example, has spoken about his difficulties with maths. For a long time, he kept his autism hidden, even from his friends. But today he describes **it** as his 'superpower': 'Some people with autism are very, very good at maths or very, very good at art – and that's a superpower. That's what makes us "different" and that's what makes us powerful.'

Ⓒ Compared with 20 years ago, doctors today have a better understanding of the condition. As a result, more people are being identified as having autism. However, helping those with autism to achieve their potential is complicated because different people have different symptoms. **That** is why the medical name for autism is 'autism spectrum disorder' or ASD.

Ⓓ Stoltman's physical abilities are very obvious. For example, both of his arms together are over two metres long. But he has faced huge psychological barriers. If he couldn't train when he wanted, or didn't do well at one event, he would struggle to continue. And people kept wanting to talk to him. **Such** complications meant that for years he often asked his brother, Luke – who is also a strength athlete – to talk for him. Today, **he** is much more confident, and he gives talks in schools and even media interviews. With the support of his family and the strongman community, he has found his superpower.

Ⓔ However, life for people with autism varies around the world. More people are identified as having autism in countries that can afford national testing programmes. There's also a significant difference in the experience of women with autism, compared to men with autism. Currently, around four in five children with autism are male. Some researchers believe this may be because females with autism have slightly different symptoms which are not currently well known. The more scientists learn about autism in girls and women, the more confident we can be that help will reach everyone.

3.7 GLOBAL SKILLS

Explore the best ways to handle disagreements.

1 What can you remember about the Student's Book text? Complete the advice about managing reactions with the words below.

| challenge   conflict   emotional   fuss
| hesitate   overreact   personally   propose

If you feel strongly about an issue, it can be easy to ¹_____. However, try to stay calm. If you get ²_____ about it, you are unlikely to get your point across in the best way. Take a moment to assess both the situation and your thoughts – and try not to take it ³_____. Often, it may be best simply to walk away and avoid any ⁴_____ at all. Or you can ⁵_____ talking about it later, particularly if you want to limit the number of people involved.

On the other hand, there are occasions where you shouldn't ⁶_____ to state your opinion and ⁷_____ others to justify their view. Some people feel that speaking up is the same as making a ⁸_____. But perhaps your view hasn't been heard and could make all the difference.

2 Read the post and answer the questions.
1. What does Marek disagree with? Can you tell why?
2. How well has Marek managed his reaction? Explain your thinking.
3. Do you manage your reactions differently online compared to face-to-face situations?
4. Online disagreements have no body language. Do you think this is helpful / unhelpful? Explain your thinking.

3 Read the posts from Marek's friends. Match posts 1–5 to advice A–E.

 @Ted_b23 I know this is important, but the council aren't building a skatepark to upset you! Don't get angry.

 @4real_Martja At the meeting, everyone will be given a chance to speak. Don't forget to wait until it's your turn.

 @NormanH56 The council representatives are just doing their job – the plan is not their fault.

 @hHester_now Why, exactly, do you think the skatepark is a bad idea? You haven't said what the alternative could be. I can think of loads of ideas …

 @Jahal3_1 Remember, the council has the money and the power in this situation. Be polite, even if you don't agree with what they're saying.

A Argue with the idea, not the person. ___
B Show respect, even if you disagree. ___
C Don't interrupt. Listen to other opinions. ___
D Remember to include your points and give reasons for them. ___
E Stay calm and keep a cool head. ___

4 Choose the correct alternative.

@Obe4_home
Marek, it sounds like you're ¹**hesitating** / **taking this personally**. But the council is not building a skatepark to upset you. ²**Getting emotional** / **Proposing** is not helpful. Please try to stay calm and don't ³**overreact** / **challenge**! It's best to ⁴**get emotional** / **avoid conflict** in a discussion meeting.

@therealMaxMart
Marek, I ⁵**propose** / **challenge** you to explain why the skatepark is a bad idea. Also, what alternative idea do you ⁶**propose** / **make a fuss**? I don't think you should ⁷**hesitate** / **make a fuss** unless you have a better suggestion to offer. I've got lots of ideas, so don't ⁸**hesitate** / **overreact** to talk to me about it.

5 Complete one of the tasks below. Use phrases and techniques from this lesson.

- Write a short speech for Marek to read at the meeting. Use these notes and your own ideas.
  - Explain your experiences in the park.
  - Use 'I' phrases.
  - Argue with the idea, not the person.
  - Focus on your suggestion.

- Write an email with advice for Marek to read before he attends the meeting. Use these notes and your own ideas.
  - Listen and wait.
  - Control your body language.
  - Stay calm when disagreeing.
  - Practise what you want to say.

Use a range of phrases to participate in a discussion.

3.8 SPEAKING

1 Look at the photos. What are the health benefits of these park items? Who would use them? What other elements of park design do you think are important?

2 **a** Three students are discussing which of these items would be best to add to their local park. Choose the correct answer: A, B or C.

Abby I feel ¹___ that parks should be for everyone, but my local park is really just for families with young children. There's nothing very useful for our age group, so I think the adult exercise equipment is the best idea.

Pria I understand ²___, but I think you're focusing on equipment. Older people don't need 'stuff' – we can exercise in the open space of the park.

Abby OK, let me clarify ³___. Everyone knows exercise is a great way to maintain your health. Right?

Celia Of course – that's obvious.

Abby But if you go to the park and only see people playing football or with young children, then it feels like you aren't invited.

Pria But surely …

Abby ⁴___, I haven't finished. You aren't invited, there's nothing for you to do, so you give up and go home.

Pria I see. So you think adult exercise equipment is a bit like a 'Welcome' sign for new park users. ⁵___, Celia?

Celia Um … It seems to me that you assume a park is for exercise.

Abby Well, I do think it's the most important function, yes, in terms of what parks are actually used for.

Pria Can I ⁶___ something?

Abby Sure.

Pria Well, I think it's best to focus on the youngest park users. Because the more exercise becomes a habit, the more likely it is that you'll carry on exercising when you're older.

	A	B	C
1	quite strong	quite strongly	a bit of strongly
2	what you're saying	what you say	why you're saying
3	what I tell	what I mean	what I say
4	Hold out	Hold up	Hold on
5	What do you think	What are you thinking	What did you think
6	interrupt	say	finish

b 🔊 **3.05** Listen and check.

3 Read the conversation again. Match completed phrases 1–6 in Ex 2a to categories A–F.
A signalling you want to speak ___
B clarifying a point ___
C disagreeing politely ___
D expressing a preference ___
E including someone in the discussion ___
F managing an interruption ___

STRATEGY Managing the conversation

When taking part in a discussion, everyone has a responsibility to keep the conversation moving forward. It's useful to be able to involve other people, to show that you want to interrupt or say something, and to avoid being interrupted.

4 Read the strategy above. In the script in Ex 2a …
1 Which person takes no responsibility for moving the conversation forward?
2 What impact do you think this has on the outcome of the conversation? Note down your ideas.
3 What advice would you give to this person to help them contribute more in the future? Note down your ideas.

5 **PRONUNCIATION** 🔊 **3.06** Practise reading the sentences using the underlined stresses shown. Listen and check. Then read out loud again.
1 <u>Billy</u>, your <u>brother</u> is <u>twelve</u> or <u>thirteen</u>. Do <u>you</u> have an <u>opinion</u> on <u>this</u>?
2 For <u>me</u>, the most <u>interesting point</u> is that <u>design</u> has a <u>really significant impact</u> on <u>behaviour</u>.
3 <u>Just</u> a minute, I haven't <u>finished</u>. It seems to <u>me</u> that we should be <u>focusing</u> on <u>young teenagers</u>.
4 <u>Sorry</u> if I'm not being <u>clear</u>. The <u>main thing</u> is that <u>all users</u> are <u>considered</u> in <u>park design</u>.
5 I <u>see</u> your point, but I <u>have</u> to <u>disagree</u>. For <u>some people</u>, <u>getting</u> to the park and <u>sitting</u> down to read <u>really</u> is an <u>activity</u>.
6 <u>Personally</u>, I'd prefer to do some <u>yoga</u> under a <u>tree</u> rather than <u>use</u> that <u>equipment</u>.

6 Plan a similar script to Ex 2a.
1 Choose two items of park design to discuss between three students. You can use the park items on this page, or in lesson 3.7, or your own ideas.
2 Think of different opinions about the items. Include polite disagreement within your conversation. Make notes.
3 Decide which phrases for discussing ideas and managing a conversation you will use. Try to use at least one phrase for each function.

7 Write your script. When you have finished, check that you have …
- expressed a range of opinions and politely handled disagreement.
- used a variety of discussion phrases from this lesson.

Unit 3   37

3.9 WRITING — Use impersonal language to write a data-based report.

1 Look at the photo. Answer the questions.

1. How many portions of fruit and vegetables do you eat each day?
2. What do you usually eat at school?
3. How is what you eat at school different from what you eat at home? Which is healthier?

2 Complete the student report with the words below.

| approximately | based | clear | figures |
| nearly | purpose | support | under |

The impact of a healthy-eating initiative on food habits at Leyside School

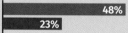

I eat 4 or 5 portions of fruit or vegetables each day
- 48% after the initiative
- 23% before the initiative

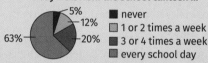

I buy fruit from the school canteen …
- 5% never
- 12% 1 or 2 times a week
- 20% 3 or 4 times a week
- 63% every school day

A Research has shown that healthy eating can be difficult to achieve in secondary schools. This report is ¹_____ on a survey conducted by Year 13 students at Leyside School. Participants were between twelve and eighteen years old. The ²_____ of this report is to announce the results of the survey and consider the impact of a healthy-eating initiative among students at Leyside School.

B Data was collected from 120 out of 800 students. Responses were gathered via a questionnaire in the school playground and also online. Participants were asked twelve multiple-choice questions, so that students answered only A, B, C or D.

C It is encouraging that most participants have improved their eating habits as a result of the initiative. ³_____ half of students report that they are now eating four or five portions of fruit and vegetables each day. Before the initiative, that figure was ⁴_____ 25%. The ⁵_____ also indicate the importance of the school canteen, as ⁶_____ 65% of respondents buy fruit daily when they are in school.

D The results ⁷_____ the conclusion that students didn't find it difficult to change their school eating habits. It is also ⁸_____ that healthy eating habits could be improved further. However, as responses were only collected from 15% of students, we may not have an accurate picture for the whole school.

participant (n) a person who takes part in something, e.g. a survey
response (n) answer, e.g. to a survey

3 Match headings 1–4 to paragraphs A–D.
1. Methods ___
2. Analysis of results ___
3. Evaluation and conclusion ___
4. Introduction and aims ___

> **STRATEGY** Using impersonal language
> When writing a report, try to use more impersonal language so that the reader focuses on the information, not the writer. For example:
> - use passive forms rather than active forms.
> - avoid using personal pronouns such as *I, you* or *we*.
> - use impersonal structures to express opinions or conclusions (e.g. *It is surprising that …* rather than *I was surprised that …*).

4 Read the strategy above. Find examples of passive and impersonal forms in the report.

5 Rewrite the sentences using impersonal language and the words in brackets.
1. We asked students in the school canteen to complete our questionnaire. (were asked)
2. Our participants didn't have to give their names. (were not asked)
3. We also provided an online version of the questionnaire for people to fill in when they liked. (was provided / at a suitable time)
4. We chose four activity categories that we felt best reflected our age group. (were chosen / that best reflected)
5. I was surprised by how much more healthily students ate at school. (surprising)

6 You are going to write a report on the impact of the summer break on activity levels at your school.
1. Plan your Introduction. What is the purpose of your report?
2. Plan the Methods section of your report using passive and impersonal sentences similar to Ex 5.
3. Make notes on this graph for the Results section of your report. Refer to the numbers and data shown.

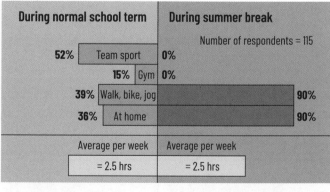

During normal school term		During summer break	
		Number of respondents = 115	
52%	Team sport	0%	
15%	Gym	0%	
39%	Walk, bike, jog	90%	
36%	At home	90%	
Average per week		Average per week	
= 2.5 hrs		= 2.5 hrs	

4. Plan your Evaluation / Conclusion. What does the data suggest / show / indicate? You can include sentence 5 from Ex 5. Were there any problems with the survey?

7 Write your report.

8 ✓ **CHECK YOUR WORK** Did you …
- use the passive and impersonal language?
- give an introduction and conclusion?
- report on methods and analyse results?

3.10 REVIEW

Grammar

1 Complete the second sentence with a comparative so that it means the same as the first sentence. You must include the word in CAPITALS.
1. I enjoy swimming more than I used to. (AND)
   I find swimming _____ enjoyable these days.
2. Aaron ran well in the race, but Miles was slightly faster. BIT
   Aaron ran _____ Miles in the race.
3. Cycling can be dangerous, but I think skiing is a lot worse. MUCH
   I think skiing is _____ than cycling.
4. You are much stronger than me. NOWHERE
   I am _____ as you.
5. Fay and Sami are equally good at skating. JUST
   Fay is _____ Sami at skating.
6. If you try harder, you will improve faster. FASTER
   The harder you try, _____ you will improve.

2 Complete the sentences with one word in each gap.
1. Jen is _____ fittest person I know.
2. He gets upset _____ time his team loses.
3. Some people say that golf is a sport for _____ rich, but I disagree.
4. _____ of us coped very well. As a team, we hate to lose.
5. She was _____ great football player when she was younger.
6. We have _____ hope of winning, but that's better than nothing!
7. That's _____ athlete I was telling you about.
8. At the start of training, there were twelve balls. But we seem to have lost a _____ of them.

Vocabulary

3 Match the sentence halves.
1. It can be hard to fit exercise in ___
2. Lifting weights can be addictive ___
3. It's important to maintain ___
4. He's definitely enthusiastic ___
5. I think looking after the plants in my house has ___
6. Why don't you try jogging home after college? It's a good way to increase ___
7. Don't start a challenging ___
8. I've injured my back. It has really made ___

A your heart rate every day.
B because you want to get stronger and stronger.
C me aware of my whole body. I need to take better care of myself.
D a positive impact on my well-being.
E your health as you get older.
F because he runs almost every day!
G with your daily routine.
H exercise routine straight away if you aren't used to it.

4 Choose the correct alternative.
1. If you **are** / **demonstrate** / **take** willing to work hard, you will improve very quickly.
2. He chose to break the rules and now he has to **deal with** / **accept the** / **cope under** consequences.
3. As team captain, I **deal** / **take** / **cope** responsibility for our failure today.
4. Milo was late for training again. He needs to **be** / **accept** / **demonstrate** better organisational skills.
5. How do you **demonstrate** / **deal with** / **responsibility for** failure? Personally, I like to play basketball and work up a sweat.
6. My team plays in competitions. Over time, I've learned to **cope under** / **be willing** / **demands of** pressure.

Cumulative review

5 Complete the text with the words and phrases below. There are four words you do not need.

| a   adapt   beneficial   contribute   each
| flexible   just   lot   much   muscles
| self-confidence   several   stiff   the (x2)   warmer

Senior Fitness
As we get older, we all need to [1]_____ to our changing bodies. However, many older people don't have enough [2]_____ to go to a gym or a swimming pool. SeniorFitness.com is here to help. Try our range of video workouts that you can do at home.

Strength
Strength exercises don't need to be complicated. Try our series of videos on weight training in [3]_____ chair. [4]_____ chair can also be used for balance exercises (see the 'Stretch' section below). Strong muscles [5]_____ to good health and will help protect you against injuries.

Stretch
As we get older, we all tend to feel more [6]_____. Try our gentle yoga videos and balance exercises. For [7]_____ more adventurous, we also have videos on ballet and tai chi to help you stretch your [8]_____ and improve your balance.

Sweat
It's good to do harder exercise [9]_____ times a week. Try an activity that makes you breathe faster and feel [10]_____. Why not try one of our dance or exercise bike videos? An hour of more intense exercise can be [11]_____ as [12]_____ as two hours of a gentler workout.

> **REFLECT**   Think about the following questions.
> 1. Which lesson in this unit was your favourite? Why?
> 2. Which of the grammar points did you find the most difficult? Why?
> 3. What can you do to practise listening to factual English?
> 4. What three things can you do to handle disagreements more effectively?

Unit 3   39

4.1 VOCABULARY

Use a range of vocabulary to talk about living spaces.

A place like home

1 a What can you remember about the vlog? Are sentences 1–8 about the Taipei apartment (*TA*), shipping container flat (*SC*) or houseboat (*HB*)?
1. The living space was deliberately designed as **open-plan**. ____
2. Yasmin is surprised it has a **well-equipped** kitchen with storage above and below the **work surfaces**. ____
3. This is a **spacious** home that can give its owners the benefits of city **facilities** as well as access to nature. ____
4. Zaki is impressed that this kind of home can be high-tech, with **smart appliances** operated by **remote control**. ____
5. It's a tiny space in a densely populated **urban** area, but it's **affordable**. ____
6. This living space is **energy-efficient** which makes things like **central heating** cheaper. ____
7. This home makes **ingenious** use of its **proportions**. A movable **staircase** gives access to the sleeping area and cupboards that are built high up in the walls. ____
8. Zaki is not sure he could live somewhere with such **restricted** space, even though it uses sustainable materials and has a cool design. ____

b ▶ 4.01 Watch or listen again and check.

2 Choose the correct alternative.
1. I can adjust the solar panels using this ___.
   A central heating B remote control C storage
2. Everyone in the building uses the central ___ and lifts.
   A staircase B proportions C surface
3. I can control the ___ using my phone, so my flat is always the right temperature.
   A central heating B facilities C remote control
4. The ___ at my student hall include a gym.
   A proportions B staircase C facilities
5. My fridge is a ___. It 'knows' what's in it!
   A remote control B smart appliance C work surface
6. There isn't enough ___ in this house. That's why it's such a mess.
   A work surfaces B central heating C storage
7. This room has beautiful ___. It's really spacious.
   A proportions B facilities C surfaces

3 Complete the texts with words in **bold** from Ex 1 that mean the same as the definitions in brackets.

Treehouse
Most treehouses are ¹_____ (having no internal walls) since building space is ²_____ (limited) by the trunk – and therefore a building with no walls works best. However, treehouses can be modern, ³_____ (supplied with everything necessary) homes. Although they can't solve the problems of ⁴_____ (city) overcrowding, treehouses may become increasingly important in rural areas where climate change is leading to increased flooding.

Earthship
Earthships are designed to store heat from the sun, which makes them ⁵_____ (using only small amounts of power). The walls are made from a(n) ⁶_____ (clever) mixture of recycled and natural materials. The entire construction process is ⁷_____ (relatively cheap) because of this. Several Earthships are available to rent as holiday properties, including a ⁸_____ (having plenty of room) six-person home in New Mexico called The Phoenix.

4 **REAL ENGLISH** Complete the dialogue with the phrases below.

| a trade-off   all mod cons   don't get me wrong |
| miss the boat   now you're talking   over the top |

A A bunker home has bedrooms and kitchens and Wi-Fi … ¹_____ … and also enough food for months. Bunker owners think that if you don't prepare now, you might ²_____ and then … well, it's too late.
B Now ³_____, we should all be prepared for global events. But moving into an underground bunker seems ⁴_____.
A I agree. There has to be ⁵_____ between preparation and common sense. How about a treehouse instead?
B ⁶_____!

5 **VOCABULARY BOOSTER** Now practise **Alternative living spaces** vocabulary on page 107.

▶ Grammar animation
GRAMMAR BOOSTER P138

Use future continuous and perfect tenses to talk about plans and make predictions.

4.2 GRAMMAR

1 Look at the photo and read the definition. Then answer the questions.

orientation (n) the action of becoming familiar with a new location or new role. Many universities have an 'orientation week' to help new students.

1 The photo shows an orientation event for new university students. What do you think is happening?
2 What different clubs are there at your school / college?
3 Now imagine a university. What clubs will there be?

2 🔊 **4.02** Listen to the students at a clubs fair like the one in the photo. Complete the future phrases that you hear.

Speaker 1: … by the time I graduate, I'll _____ to sign for two years.
Speaker 2: … by next semester, I'll _____ in a concert!
Speaker 3: Most people will _____ to try lots of new activities.
Speaker 4: … in just a few weeks, you'll _____ lots of new friends.
Speaker 5: I'll _____ table tennis competitively for at least six years.
Speaker 6: Today I'll _____ for film club …

3 🔊 **4.02** Listen again. Match the future phrases from Ex 2 to rules A–C.

A We use the future continuous to talk about an action completed at a specific time in the future, e.g. *I'll be speaking*. ___ ___
B We use the future perfect simple to talk about an action completed by a certain time in the future, e.g. *I'll have spoken*. ___ ___
C We use the future perfect continuous to say how long an action will have been in progress at a certain time in the future. We usually use *for* … to specify the duration, e.g. *I'll have been speaking for* … ___ ___

< Notes

Itinerary – orientation day

10.00 library orientation
11.00 sports centre orientation: check climbing wall isn't too easy find somewhere for some food
14.00 main hall clubs: find animation club, climbing club, orchestra

4 Read Mia's itinerary for the day of the clubs fair. Then choose the correct alternative.

1 At 10.00, she **will be attending** / **will have attended** / **will have been attending** an orientation meeting at the campus library.
2 By 11.00, she **will be leaving** / **will have left** / **will have been leaving** the library and be on her way to the sports centre.
3 You can tell Mia is an experienced climber because she knows she needs to check the facilities. I expect she **will be climbing** / **will have climbed** / **will have been climbing** for years.
4 Between eleven and two, she **will be having** / **will have had** / **will have been having** lunch, although she isn't sure where.
5 By 14.30, she **will be moving** / **will have moved** / **will have been moving** to the main hall to find the clubs she's interested in.
6 By 16.00, she **will be looking** / **will have looked** / **will have been looking** around the hall for six hours.

5 Mia is talking about orientation day with another student from her accommodation. Complete the dialogue with the correct future form of the verbs in brackets.

Leah Do you want to meet at eleven tomorrow for a coffee?
Mia I'm sorry, I can't. At eleven, I ¹_____ (look) round the sports centre. But I can meet you after that. I don't know if there's a café near there, but I ²_____ (walk) past later this afternoon. I'll check.
Leah Actually, there's a great café round the corner from the sports centre.
Mia Oh? Do you know the city already?
Leah Slightly. Because of my flights, I moved in early. By the end of today, I ³_____ (live) here for two weeks already.
Mia I ⁴_____ (ask) you for lots of advice then!
Leah You know, it's quite a long way from the library to the sports centre and back to the main hall. By the end of tomorrow, you ⁵_____ (walk) miles.
Mia Yes, but I ⁶_____ (meet) lots of new people and I ⁷_____ (find out) all the information I need to plan my activity timetable.
Leah Don't forget to actually go to lectures, will you?

6 Imagine it is orientation week at your new university. Using information from the lesson and your own ideas, make sentences using the future continuous, future perfect simple and future perfect continuous.

• I'll be signing up for _____ club because _____.
• Next week, I'll be _____.
• This time next term, I'll be _____.
• By the time I leave university, I'll have been _____.

Unit 4   41

4.3 LISTENING
Recognise discourse markers in order to understand a discussion.

1 What can you remember about the podcast in the Student's Book? Complete the summary.

PODCASTS

GEOCAST – urban teenagers

Laura and Milo express different views on the future of city centres as places to live and work. On the one hand, they see problems, particularly as a result of the pandemic, which caused many companies to ¹g_____ o_____ o_____ b_____. When people had to ²w_____ r_____, this reduced the number of people in the city during the day, which in turn had a significant economic impact on other businesses. Indeed, Milo's mother lost her ³p_____-t_____ j_____. However, Laura points out that there are other reasons for these economic changes, such as online shopping. She thinks all of these factors give an opportunity to reimagine urban spaces and communities. In the future, she hopes that empty ⁴w_____ can be turned into exciting, energy-efficient homes. Milo also paints a positive picture of his current life in a city centre, which is made possible by his father being ⁵s_____-e_____ and working from a ⁶h_____ o_____. Milo enjoys living close to shops and his school, although he wishes there were more things specifically for teenagers.

2 Look at the photo and read the definition. Use a dictionary to complete a second meaning for this adjective.

pop-up (adj)
1 describes a book containing folded pictures which push out to create a raised 3D image as the page is turned
2 describes a _____, restaurant, etc. which deliberately opens in a temporary location for a _____ period of time

3 🔊 4.03 Listen to five people talking about city centres. Match speakers 1–5 to opinions A–H. There are three opinions you do not need.

Which speaker …
A is worried about losing their job? ___
B believes improvements in city life are being led by young people? ___
C is pessimistic about the future of city centres for residents? ___
D would like to see more pop-up restaurants in city centres? ___
E thinks new shops are already having a positive effect? ___
F blames pollution for the decline in city-centre living? ___
G says that customers' shopping habits have changed forever? ___
H is focused on the environmental sustainability of city life? ___

STRATEGY Understanding discourse markers
When you are listening to a talk or discussion, it is useful to be able to understand phrases (called discourse markers) that help you to recognise when the speaker …
A introduces a new point on the same topic (*And similarly, …*)
B gives an example (*One example of this is …*).
C refers back to an earlier point in the discussion (*As we were saying, …*).
D wants to change the subject (*Another thing is …*).
E refers to the wider context (*The bigger picture is …*).

4 🔊 4.03 Read the strategy above. Listen to the speakers from Ex 3 again. Write the discourse markers you hear and match them to rules A–E.
Speaker 1: *And similarly* ___ A
Speaker 2: _____ ___
Speaker 3: _____ ___
Speaker 4: _____ ___
Speaker 5: _____ ___

5 Complete the sentences with the words below.

| broadly   case   example   incidentally
| mentioned   move

1 Let's _____ on to green spaces now. I think we should plant more trees.
2 If you take the _____ of Los Angeles, this city is currently assessing all its current trees and aiming to plant thousands of new ones.
3 One _____ of this innovation is Luxembourg, where all buses, trams and trains are now free.
4 More _____, you can't expect people to stop using their cars unless you offer them a good alternative.
5 _____, did you know that by 2034 all of London's buses will have been updated to electric models?
6 But, like I _____ before, the cost to passengers is also significant.

6 Answer the questions so they are true for you.
1 Are there many empty shops in your nearest town / city? Can you explain why?
2 What kind of pop-up business would you most like to see in an empty store?
3 Are small, independently run stores important? Why? / Why not?

42 Unit 4

Talk about ideas of home and community.

4.4 VOCABULARY

1 Create a spidergram to describe this nomadic home.

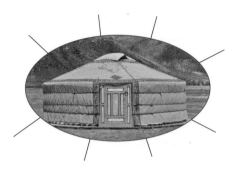

2 Read the film review. Does Aisholpan live in the yurt all year round?

FILM > REVIEWS

The Eagle Huntress

Aisholpan with her eagle. Aisholpan becomes an eagle huntress (a female hunter).

This heart-warming documentary follows thirteen-year-old Aisholpan as she prepares to compete in the famous Eagle Festival in Mongolia.

Aisholpan's nomadic family live in the beautiful Altai Mountains. During the summer months, the tribe lives in **¹lasting for a short time** shelters, called yurts, or gers. Their animals eat the fresh grass, and the people can pack up the yurts and all their possessions in just a few hours. Indeed, this ability to move regularly is the central part of any nomadic **²way of living**. In the winter months, the family moves to a more **³lasting for a long time** building, which offers better protection from the cold in the mountains.

The Altai nomads have trained golden eagles for centuries. These enormous and beautiful birds are used to hunt rabbits and foxes. In the past, the tribe would have been **⁴needing** the food and fur obtained by the eagles' skills. Today, this relationship remains vital to the tribe's cultural identity.

Many people would consider Aisholpan's family to have a low **⁵amount of wealth**. However, the film-makers are careful to show all aspects of their life. For example, during the week, the children attend a boarding school in a nearby **⁶place where people have established a community**. They live in the school for five days each week, before returning to the yurt on their father's motorbike. Aisholpan studies hard and dreams of becoming a doctor.

With the **⁷help and support** of her father, who is an experienced eagle hunter, Aisholpan raises a baby eagle and trains it. This is a physically and mentally demanding challenge requiring skill and strength. When she finally competes in the Eagle Festival, she defeats all the other hunters and wins the trophy.

This film will **⁸attract** many different viewers. On the one hand, it is a sensitive documentary exploring a traditional way of life. On the other hand, it is an exciting story about a competition. The pictures of the Mongolian landscape are stunning, and the film-makers often use a drone to capture an eagle's view of the mountains. Ultimately, the nomads' eagles are the stars of the film.

★★★★½

3 Replace the **bold** phrases 1–8 in the review with the phrases below. There are two phrases you do not need.

| appeal to   assistance   dependent on
| emigrate   existence   permanent   settlement
| standard of living   temporary   wander

1 _____ 5 _____
2 _____ 6 _____
3 _____ 7 _____
4 _____ 8 _____

4 Choose the correct alternative.
1 A yurt is a type of nomadic **settlement / shelter**, similar to a teepee used by the Plains tribes of North America.
2 The family's animals are able to **wander / settle** freely during the summer months.
3 Aisholpan's **extended family / support network**, such as her grandfather, live in the same group of yurts.
4 In some locations, the yurts share a **dependent / communal** water well.
5 Some nomadic tribes around the world are choosing to **emigrate to / settle in** more permanent communities.
6 Some people in Western society are choosing a nomadic existence as a **lifestyle choice / standard of living**.
7 The vast majority of people who **emigrate / wander** to another country for work are in their twenties.
8 If you move to a new country, it's a good idea to seek **assistance / a support network** of people in the same position as you.

5 Complete the additional sections of the film review using words and phrases from Ex 3 and 4.

> I found one part of the film particularly moving. Aisholpan's father is very proud of his daughter, but he is not sure if the other competitors will accept her. He seeks
> ¹_____ from his ²_____.
> First, he travels many miles to visit a friend, another hunter who has competed in the Eagle Festival. Back at home, his
> ³_____ offer their support, including Aisholpan's grandfather. Finally, Aisholpan's mother gives her opinion, saying she is proud of her daughter's
> ⁴_____ and that she wants all her children to be happy. Everyone agrees that Aisholpan should compete, even at her young age.

> At the most exciting point in the story, Aisholpan and her father travel to Ulgii, which is the largest ⁵_____ in their region. As the two of them ride through the busy streets on their horses, the viewer is struck by the contrast between the tribe's nomadic ⁶_____ and the modern world. The different ⁷_____ in town is clearly visible: there are shops and cars. Would Aisholpan be happier in a more ⁸_____ home?

6 **MEDIATION** A relative asks you if *The Eagle Huntress* is worth seeing. Use the film review to write a short email telling them what it is about.

7 **VOCABULARY BOOSTER** Now practise **Nomads** vocabulary on page 107.

Unit 4   43

4.5 GRAMMAR

Use future time clauses and first conditional sentences to refer to future events, arrangements and plans.

▶ Grammar animation
GRAMMAR BOOSTER P139

1 Look at the photo. What kind of scientist lives here?

2 🔊 **4.04** Listen to three weather scientists and check your answer to Ex 1. Complete the phrases you hear and match them to rules A–C.

Speaker 1: … from the moment he _____. ___
Speaker 2: … while I _____ in the weather station … ___
Speaker 3: … after I _____ my first week. ___

A uses the present simple to talk about a future action or state
B uses the present perfect to talk about completed actions at a time in the future
C uses the present continuous to talk about actions in progress in the future

3 Complete the sentences below with suitable time conjunctions. Sometimes more than one answer is possible. There are five time conjunctions you do not need. Then match sentences 1–6 to rules A–C in Ex 2.

| after   as soon as   by the time   immediately
| in case   on condition that   once   the moment
| until   when   while

1 I'll bring my keys _____ you lose yours again. ___
2 I'll clean the kitchen _____ you're tidying the living room. ___
3 _____ you've finished, please go back to your desks. ___
4 It is likely you'll make a terrible noise _____ you're learning to play the violin. But you'll improve! ___
5 You'll feel better _____ you've taken the medicine. ___
6 I *will* help you with this maths _____ you listen in class from now on. ___

4 Write sentences in the first conditional using the words in brackets and an appropriate future form or imperative.
Get some apples while you're there. (you / not / supermarket yet / get / apples / please)
<u>If you haven't been to the supermarket yet, get some apples, please.</u>
1 I hate jogging in the rain. (rain tomorrow / I / workout inside)
_____
2 The flight should land at three. (flight / on time / we / arrive / by three)
_____
3 I definitely recommend the show. (you / not see the show yet / book tickets soon)
_____
4 I'd love to work here. (this company / look for / new employees / I / apply)
_____

5 Oh no! Marcie is going to sing! (Marcie / sing / I / leave the room)
_____
6 I've lived in three different houses. (we move house / I live / four different houses)
_____
7 Have you written your essay? (you / finish your essay / email it / me)
_____
8 I hope you haven't lost my necklace. (you / lose my necklace / I / upset)
_____

5 Complete Rik's blog post with the correct form of the verbs in brackets.

> ≡   HOME   ABOUT   **POSTS**   CONTACT   🔍
>
> 👤 Rik • 🕐 Today
>
> I start work at the weather station next week. Don't worry, I'll write again before I ¹_____ (leave). But what will I be doing once I ²_____ (get) to the top of the mountain?
>
> **Weather data**
> The main job is collecting weather data. We have to collect information every hour, during the day *and* the night. This is very important. If our job isn't done properly, your weather reports ³_____ (not be) accurate. I won't see my colleague Karl very often – even though he's the only other person in the building. While I ⁴_____ (work), he'll be asleep. Then while I ⁵_____ (sleep), he'll be at work.
>
> **Research**
> We also help universities and companies with their research. For example, we test new products to see how they cope in difficult weather. If a product survives at the top of the mountain, it ⁶_____ (survive) anywhere!
>
> **Education**
> I'll be working with schools around the world. As soon as I ⁷_____ (complete) some media training, I'll give virtual talks to children about the weather. There's usually one of those each month.
>
> If you have any questions, ⁸_____ (write) them in the Comments section below.

6 Imagine you are going to live in one of the unusual living spaces mentioned in this unit for six months. What do you expect to enjoy? What difficulties are likely to occur? Complete the sentences using grammar from this lesson and your own ideas.

I'll definitely learn to _____, while I'm _____.
The problems will start as soon as _____.
Once I've _____, I'll _____.
If I work hard, _____.
If I haven't got used to _____ by _____.
If my predictions are correct, _____

44   Unit 4

4.6 READING

Recognise a variety of phrases in order to understand the writer's point of view.

Brain-drain migration

1 What can you remember about the article in the Student's Book? Choose the correct alternative.
   1 Humans have always migrated in their search for the best **habitable** / **uninhabitable** land.
   2 Large migrations create **pressure on resources** / **extreme weather events** such as housing.
   3 Poverty and **flooding** / **food insecurity** led to a large migration to America during the 19th century.
   4 So-called **extreme weather events** / **rising sea levels** are becoming more frequent due to climate change.
   5 Heavy storms can cause **flooding** / **pressure**.
   6 **Rising sea levels** / **Drought** will have a huge impact because many of the world's major cities are near the sea.
   7 Coastal regions may soon become **extreme** / **uninhabitable**.
   8 **Drought** / **Flood** conditions often cause water insecurity.

2 Look at the chart. What do you think it shows?

Stay	Go
friends and family	no support network
OK wages	better wages
known career path	more career opportunities
familiarity	excitement

3 🔊 **4.05** Read the article about a type of migration. Match questions 1–10 to paragraphs A–D.
   Which paragraph …
   1 considers the future of a particular migration trend? ___
   2 suggests brain-drain migration is led by one age group? ___
   3 explains how academic analysis of migration is changing? ___
   4 is sure that migration of young people brings benefits? ___
   5 explores an academic approach to studying migration? ___
   6 describes the negative impact of brain-drain migration on some countries? ___
   7 names places that benefit from brain-drain migration? ___
   8 says that ageing populations have a huge impact on migration in some professions? ___
   9 gives reasons why people choose to leave their country? ___
   10 describes migration without international travel? ___

STRATEGY Recognising the writer's point of view

When reading a text, it is useful to recognise the writer's attitude to the subject they are writing about. In academic texts or articles, writers often use more objective or tentative language to indicate a neutral attitude, or to avoid sounding too certain. This may include …
- verbs like *appears*, *indicates*, *seems*, *suggests*.
- modal verbs like *could*, *may*, *might*.
- adverbs like *arguably*, *possibly*, *understandably*.
- phrases like *It seems likely that …*, *It is by no means certain that …*, *It is generally assumed / believed that …*, *It may be said that …*.

4 Read the strategy above. <u>Underline</u> examples of each feature in the article.

5 Choose one of the following and make a Stay / Go chart.
- Friday evening: do homework or go to cinema?
- University choice: stay near home or go further?

A Everett Lee's influential 'push-pull' idea (1966) explains the main reasons for migration. Push factors might include low standards of living, poor wages, conflict or extreme weather events, while pull factors may include job opportunities or safety. Lee suggests that such reasons are behind most migration decisions. This article looks in detail at so-called 'brain-drain migration,' where students or newly qualified professionals move away from home to make the most of their opportunities. Understandably, this tends to involve those aged 18 to 25.

B Think about student migration. This is generally a form of *internal* migration where young people move within their own country to places of learning. In the UK, smaller cities arguably make the largest gains, with Leeds and Sheffield in the north of England receiving around 30,000 young people each year. Research confirms that these arrivals generate jobs and wealth in the wider community. However, the student brain drain appears to be largely temporary. Most return home, although many will then enter employment markets which have their own brain-drain movements.

C One job sector has a particularly strong brain drain: healthcare. Some countries, for example, in Western Europe, have large numbers of older people compared to their working populations. Over time, this has led to a shortage of doctors and nurses to care for the elderly – and these countries have well-established systems to hire medical professionals from abroad. In contrast to Lee's push-pull idea, recent academic studies of migration focus on the importance of personal networks instead of economic factors. This could explain the success of medical recruitment in countries like the UK and Norway. Successful host countries offer more than wages. They also have communities of other foreign-born nurses. It seems clear that friendships are a vital factor in the decision to stay or go.

D For countries which are 'drained' of their medical professionals, the impact is varied. Of course, money is sent home each month. However, some nations lose too many health workers. In the Philippines, which supplies large numbers of nurses to the United States, the ratio of nurses to patients is 1:60. The US, by contrast, aims for 1:5. It seems unlikely that this trend can continue. Countries with ageing populations must find ways to make their own medical training programmes attractive, leaving younger countries able to support their own health services.

4.7 GLOBAL SKILLS — Understand trends shown in diagrams.

1 What can you remember about the Student's Book lesson? Are the sentences true (T) or false (F)?
  1 International migration has **increased dramatically** over the last 50 years. T ☐ F ☐
  2 There is a correlation between the **rise** in migration and a **downturn** in wages. T ☐ F ☐
  3 The world's rural population has **gone down steadily** since 1950. T ☐ F ☐
  4 There has been a similar **upward trend** in urban populations. T ☐ F ☐
  5 Due to the rise of megacities, urban populations have seen a **slight crash** since 2018. T ☐ F ☐
  6 The percentage of the world's population living in European cities has **decreased** since 1950. T ☐ F ☐
  7 The proportion of the urban population living in Africa and Asia has **gone up** over the same time period. T ☐ F ☐
  8 A particularly **sharp fall** is predicted for the urban population of Africa by 2050. T ☐ F ☐
  9 **Causation** means that a change in one thing produces a change in the other. T ☐ F ☐

2 Read the beginning of a newspaper article and think about the questions.

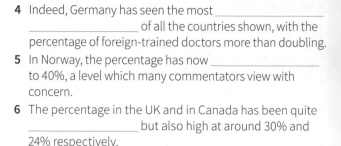

Medical brain drain
Many countries have a shortage of doctors. And the situation is getting worse.

  1 Why might countries hire doctors from abroad?
  2 What issues might arise in the doctors' countries of origin?
  3 What issues might arise in the hiring countries?

3 Look at the bar graph below. Complete the sentences with the correct form of the **bold** words in Ex 1.
  1 The graph shows a clear _____ _____ over time.
  2 Only New Zealand has managed to _____ _____ its use of doctors trained in other countries, although the percentage remains very high.
  3 Although Germany and Slovenia had the lowest levels in 2010, their use of doctors from abroad has seen a _____ _____ to 13% and 16% respectively.
  4 Indeed, Germany has seen the most _____ _____ of all the countries shown, with the percentage of foreign-trained doctors more than doubling.
  5 In Norway, the percentage has now _____ to 40%, a level which many commentators view with concern.
  6 The percentage in the UK and in Canada has been quite _____ but also high at around 30% and 24% respectively.

4 Choose the correct alternative.
  1 The global market in doctors **reflects / shows / presents** several wider trends in society.
  2 For example, we can see a clear correlation **inside / because / between** the number of elderly people in a population and the number of doctors required.
  3 The increase in the global migration of doctors **matches an increase / matches this increase / matches to an increase** in the movement of nurses.
  4 If you compare the data for both professions, you can see that they **match / follow / increase** a similar pattern.
  5 **Corresponding to the graph / As the graph shows / Mirrored by the graph**, there is a clear need for government investment in medical training in these countries.

5 Write about the line graph above.
  • Identify and analyse the trend shown.
  • What is the relationship between this graph and the trend shown in Ex 3?
  • Use phrases and vocabulary from this lesson.

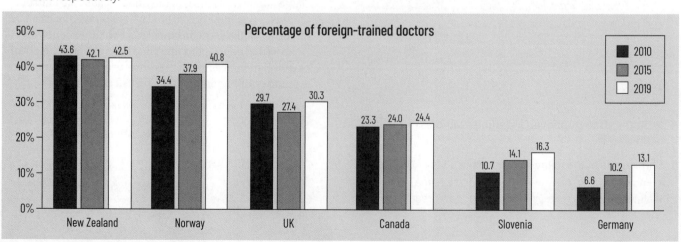

46 Unit 4

Speculate about possible future events or situations.

4.8 SPEAKING

A B C D

1 Look at the photos and the task. Which photo (A–D) would you choose?

> Photos A–D show different types of accommodation. Which of these do you think will be the most common 150 years in the future? Discuss with your group.

2 🔊 **4.06** You are going to explore part of a response to the task in Ex 1. Complete the dialogue with the words below. Then listen and check.

| a situation   a strong possibility   impossible
| myself   quite likely   realistic   the only one

Ava One hundred and fifty years is a long time, but I can't see ¹_____ where most people will be living a nomadic existence, like in photo A. I don't think it's ²_____ to expect that we'll have abandoned our cities. After all, that's where most of the world's population lives.

May It's a good point. I think it's ³_____ that cities will be even more dominant in 150 years. That's why innovative designs like B are so important. I can see ⁴_____ living in one of these floating homes.

Ava I think you're right to be optimistic. It isn't ⁵_____ that society will adapt to meet the challenges of climate change. I can't be ⁶_____ who thinks we'll be OK. Humans are very ingenious!

May Nevertheless, if you think about extreme weather events, not to mention any future pandemics, there's ⁷_____ that migration will increase.

STRATEGY Co-operating and contributing

Co-operation in a discussion is when two or more people work together to reach agreement or make a decision about something. It means listening and responding to what other people say as well as contributing your own ideas.

3 Read the strategy above. What kind of contribution comes after the phrases below? Write *A* for agreement or *D* for disagreement.
1 It's interesting you say that. ___
2 That's what I meant. ___
3 The only problem with that is … ___
4 I hear what you're saying, but … ___
5 It's a good point. ___
6 I think you're right to be … ___
7 That sounds good. ___

4 🔊 **4.07** Listen to the speaker. Make a comment on their opinion using a phrase from Ex 3 and then make your own contribution in agreement. Write two or three sentences.

5 🔊 **4.08** Listen to the speaker. Make a comment on their opinion using a phrase from Ex 3 and then make your own contribution in disagreement. Write two or three sentences.

PRONUNCIATION Chunking

In a discussion or when giving a talk, speakers divide what they say into 'chunks'. These are groups of words or phrases, or sometimes a single word, with short pauses between them. Speakers do this to clearly express a particular idea or to focus on key information. For example:
I think it's likely that [pause] *in future* [pause] *a lot more people* [pause] *will be studying remotely.*
From what I've read, [pause] *there's a good chance that* [pause] *migration* [pause] *will increase in future.*

6 🔊 **4.09** Read the Pronunciation box and listen to this sentence. What error has the speaker made and what is the impact?

It isn't impossible that people will be living in nomadic communities.

7 a Decide how sentences 1–6 could be divided into chunks and predict where the pauses will come.
1 It isn't impossible that people will be living in nomadic communities.
2 Actually, I think it's quite likely that houses in the future will include features from ancient ways of living.
3 Homes that can be packed up and moved have huge benefits in times of drought or flooding.
4 If you think about it, there's a strong possibility that in 150 years homes will have become more mobile.
5 The evidence that we have today points towards photo B, not photo A.
6 It isn't realistic to expect such a dramatic change.

b 🔊 **4.10** Listen and check. Then practise saying the sentences using chunking.

8 Plan a similar script to Ex 2 focusing on photos C and D in Ex 1.
1 Think of different opinions about the photos, but remember to stay focused on the task instructions from Ex 1. Make notes.
2 Decide which phrases to use for speculating about the future and commenting on someone else's opinion. Try to use at least two phrases for each function.

9 Write your script. When you have finished, check that you have …
- included phrases that speculate about the future.
- included phrases that respond to the previous speaker.
- got your ideas across.

Unit 4 47

4.9 WRITING

Write an email to enquire about a work opportunity.

1 Look at the photo and answer the questions.

1 What is street food?
2 Have you ever seen a pop-up restaurant?

STRATEGY Using formal register

In a formal email or letter, it is important to sound polite and professional. You can do this by using …
- formal sentence structures beginning with *It* or *What*: *It is my intention to …*, *What I hope to do is …*.
- indirect questions (especially to make requests): *Could you let me know if that is correct?*
- impersonal phrases: *In all probability, I will …*.
- more formal alternatives to everyday words: *attempt* instead of *try*, *obtain* instead of *get*.

2 Read the strategy above and the email below. In which paragraph does the email …
1 explain future plans? ___
2 ask for more information? ___
3 request action? ___
4 introduce the topic? ___
5 explain interest and experience? ___

Dear Sir / Madam,

A I have heard from a colleague that you are considering opening your empty property on Lyme Street as a pop-up restaurant venue. I ¹**want** to enquire whether this is the case. Could I ask you to consider me as a potential chef?

B I currently run my Sri Lankan street food business from a van near the train station. Please find attached our current menu. I am ²**really** ³**lucky** to have learned Sri Lankan cuisine from the older members of my family, so I offer genuine recipes. Street food is highly suited to a pop-up environment, and I am therefore confident I could offer tasty and high-quality meals. In all probability, I would ⁴**give** three options at each pop-up service: one vegetarian, one meat-based, one fish-based. I only need one other member of staff to ⁵**help** with serving.

C It is my intention to open a permanent restaurant. I am constantly ⁶**looking for** the perfect location in the city centre – but so far without success. Meanwhile, I ⁷**try** to satisfy my customers while also developing my skills as a chef.

D I would appreciate knowing more about the facilities available. I ⁸**think** my minimum requirement is two cooking hobs and a fryer. Access to a freezer would also be ⁹**useful**, though not essential. I should also mention that I would need ¹⁰**about** two hours to prepare food earlier in the day, followed by 30 minutes before the restaurant opens. Could you let me know if that is acceptable?

E I suggest we discuss this in more detail. I would be grateful if you could email or call me.

I look forward to hearing from you.

Mo Chandimal

---

3 Read the email again. Replace **bold** words 1–10 with more formal alternatives.

4 Find in the email …
- one formal sentence beginning with *It* or *What*.
- two indirect questions.
- one impersonal phrase.

5 Choose the correct answer: A, B or C.
1 Could I ask you ___ a sample menu to your email?
  A attach   B to attach   C attaching
2 My current situation ___ I run a small clothing business from my home.
  A is that   B could be   C what
3 What I hope ___ sell my designs to a larger company.
  A would be   B you to   C to do is
4 I wonder if you would mind ___ her contact details to me?
  A send   B to send   C sending
5 It is my intention ___ catering college next year.
  A attend   B to attend   C attending
6 I would appreciate ___ this with you in person.
  A discussing   B discuss   C to discuss

6 Rewrite the requests from an enquiry email as indirect questions.
1 Can you give me a tour of the building?
  Could I _____?
2 How many other chefs will be operating in the pop-up location?
  Would you mind _____?
3 What kitchen and toilet facilities are available?
  Could you _____?
4 Does the owner of the building take a percentage of the income?
  I would like _____.
5 Can you call me tomorrow?
  I would be grateful if _____.
6 Have you received my suggested menu?
  I would appreciate _____.

7 You have heard about a possible pop-up restaurant or pop-up shop location in your local town. You are going to write an email of enquiry.
- Decide what your pop-up business will sell.
- Make notes based on the structure explained in Ex 2.
- Decide which formal and impersonal phrases you will use.

8 Write your email.

9 ✓ CHECK YOUR WORK Did you …
- follow the paragraph structure?
- use impersonal phrases and indirect questions?
- use a variety of formal sentence structures and formal alternatives to everyday words?

48 Unit 4

4.10 REVIEW

Grammar

1 Choose the correct alternative.
1. I'm getting better at Spanish – I'll **be** / **have been** / **have** learning it for six months in May.
2. By the end of next year, I will **have been studying** / **study** / **will be studying** at this school for seven years!
3. He doesn't yet know where he'll **be spending** / **have been spending** / **have spent** the holidays.
4. **Will they be painting** / **Will they have painted** / **Will they have been painting** the living room today or tomorrow?
5. Nobody will be at the party now – they'll all **have gone** / **be going** / **have been going** home.
6. Maria won't **be hearing** / **have been hearing** / **have heard** the news yet. Let's tell her!

2 Complete the sentences using the verbs in brackets. There may be more than one possible answer.
1. If _____ (not finish) your homework by 8 p.m., leave it until tomorrow.
2. By the time _____ (eat) your breakfast, we'll have missed the bus.
3. If _____ (watch) that boring series, I'm going upstairs to read.
4. When _____ (be) in Italy, you'll see some amazing architecture.
5. If you're getting the card, I _____ (buy) the present.
6. It isn't fair – while you're at the cinema, I _____ (write) an essay.

Vocabulary

3 Complete the sentences with the words and phrases below. There are two words or phrases you do not need.

| energy-efficient   ingenious   open-plan |
| proportions   remote control   spacious   staircase |
| urban   well-equipped   work surfaces |

1. As you can see, this _____ house only has one large room – and there's no _____ because it's only on the ground floor!
2. This is a very _____ houseboat, considering its small _____. The kitchen is tiny, but it has everything you need!
3. Don't get me wrong – I like visiting the city. But I don't think _____ life is for me.
4. Please can you pass me the _____ so I can change the channel.
5. Modern homes should be _____ so they are more environmentally friendly.
6. Lianne's flat is small, but it has plenty of _____ storage. It's all very clever.

4 Choose the correct alternative.
1. Eventually, Lucas wants to **settle** / **wander** / **appeal** near the coast and buy his own home.
2. Most of the **shelters** / **lifestyle choices** / **settlements** near here are villages, not towns.
3. Niall studies tigers. The **assistance** / **existence** / **settlements** of these big cats is under threat.
4. Cara is a vegan – it's a **lifestyle choice** / **support network** / **standard of living** for her.
5. I enjoy **wandering** / **settling** / **appealing** around unfamiliar places, especially cities.
6. Around the world, governments are fighting back against poverty, and **support networks** / **standards of living** / **settlements** are gradually improving.
7. The small community is **appealing** / **dependent** / **temporary** on the river for drinking water.
8. A nomadic life doesn't **settle** / **wander** / **appeal** to me.

Cumulative review

5 Complete the text with between one and four words in each gap.

Kwame Gates It's just two weeks before The Big Summer Music Blast. I'm so excited, even though ¹_____ in a tent. Never mind, it's only ²_____ – in four days I'll be back in my own bed! What are you up to this summer? Is anyone staying somewhere more interesting than a tent?

Marie Espinosa I'd love to go to that festival, but it has sold out. If anyone ³_____ a friend with a spare ticket, I'll definitely buy it, **Kwame Gates**.

↩ **Olivia Aydem Marie Espinosa** Me too, but it's so expensive. I wish these events were more ⁴_____.

Jocelyn Mann I can't go anymore! I'll sell you my ticket at a reduced rate on ⁵_____ that you buy me some band T-shirts while you're there.

Thomas Uran I'm going to a tennis camp in Spain for a month. The sports ⁶_____ look amazing – there are great indoor and outdoor courts, a swimming pool and gym! By the end of the summer, hopefully my skills ⁷_____. 😲

Millie Donnerson I'm housesitting for my mum's friend in a beautiful house in the country. She's spending the summer in Australia with her cousins and other ⁸_____ family and deciding whether she wants to ⁹_____ permanently. This will be the first time ¹⁰_____ alone in my entire life!

↩ **Kwame Gates Millie Donnerson** Sounds super exciting. Have a great time!

REFLECT Think about the following questions.
1. Which lesson in this unit was your favourite? Why?
2. Which of the grammar points did you find most difficult? Why?
3. What can you do to practise analysing diagrams?
4. Choose three phrases for commenting on someone's opinion. Try to use them in your next class discussion.

Unit 4   49

3-4 EXAM SKILLS

Listening

EXAM STRATEGY

In a multiple-choice task, read the questions and options carefully before you listen. Look at the key vocabulary and think about its meaning. You might hear some of the words to help define it in the recording.

1 Read the strategy above. Then read the exam task in Ex 2. Look at the first question and the underlined words. Match definitions 1–4 with the words.
  1 people with low-income jobs
  2 people without work
  3 areas such as towns and cities
  4 areas such as parks, fields and gardens

2 🔊 4.11 For each question, listen and choose the correct answer: A, B, C or D.

  1 What is the first topic of today's programme?
    A people without homes in <u>built-up areas</u>
    B <u>poverty</u> in town and countryside
    C plans for more <u>green spaces</u> in the local area
    D the rise in <u>unemployment</u> in cities
  2 Leila says that the charity …
    A is well known amongst homeless people.
    B has a waiting list of volunteers.
    C is given a lot of support from the government.
    D has enough equipment.
  3 Leila thinks that the biggest problem is that …
    A there aren't enough suitable jobs.
    B people need an address to find a job.
    C they don't have any access to computers.
    D employers don't want to employ them.
  4 The system in Finland …
    A gives people a home as soon as they find a job.
    B houses homeless people in green spaces.
    C allows people without jobs to live in apartments.
    D encourages homeless people to move away.
  5 What does Leila say about the scheme's success?
    A It's worked for 20% of homeless people.
    B It's been effective for the majority.
    C It has cost the government more money.
    D It would be better if it gave second chances.

Use of English

EXAM STRATEGY

A multiple-choice cloze task may test collocations. Learn common collocations by writing them in your notebook in the context of an example sentence.

3 Read the strategy above. Then read the first gapped sentence in the exam task in Ex 4. Try to guess the missing word without looking at the options. Check your idea with the options given.

4 Read the text below and choose the correct answer (A, B, C or D) for each gap (1–10).

Copenhagen

Would you like to visit one of the most environmentally friendly urban ¹_____ in the world? We organise 'green' guided tours of Copenhagen, a city which is trying to decrease pressure on ²_____ resources such as water and coal. The city is certainly ³_____ equipped to do this. Already, Copenhagen focuses on alternative energy and encourages people to consider making greener lifestyle ⁴_____. It has a system for recycling rain, has switched to electric buses and has made more road space for bicycles. Here's what you can expect from one of our tours. On arrival, you ⁵_____ to an eco-friendly hotel and have a delicious organic lunch. Your tour will begin as ⁶_____ as you are ready to leave. A guide will take you to the city ⁷_____, where you will see some of the most sustainable buildings in Copenhagen. You will also be given the chance ⁸_____ to some of the most important 'green' architects in the city. By the time you ⁹_____, you will have a new understanding of what a green city can be like. If the idea of this trip appeals to you, please look at our website. There is a special offer which is ending soon, so be quick or you will ¹⁰_____ the boat!

	A	B	C	D
1	ranges	belts	parts	areas
2	physical	environmental	organic	
	D natural			
3	good	well	great	fine
4	choices	picks	elections	options
5	had travelled		will travel	
	C have travelled		are travelling	
6	near	far	soon	close
7	middle	focus	heart	centre
8	to speak	speak	will speak	have spoken
9	to leave	left	leaving	have left
10	drop	lose	miss	fail

Reading

EXAM STRATEGY

Do not worry if you don't understand every word in a reading text. You may be able to work out the meaning through the overall context.

5 Read the strategy above. Then read the first text in Ex 6. Find words to match meanings 1–3.
  1 a shared space
  2 a small version of something else
  3 a small building

3–4 EXAM SKILLS

6 Read the texts below. For each question, choose the correct answer: A, B, C or D.

Last summer, I had my first experience of glamping, the luxury version of camping. Our accommodation was pretty much as I had expected. It consisted of a wooden hut which was one of six on the same site. They were far apart so there was little noise. Inside the hut, there were beds, a mini kitchen with all mod cons, a bathroom and a TV. It was nice not to have communal washing facilities and the views were spectacular, but to be honest, I missed sleeping on the ground and cooking on a fire. Don't get me wrong, I enjoyed it, but if I want luxury, I'll stay in a hotel.

1 What does the writer say about his experience of glamping?
   A He was surprised by the level of comfort.
   B He preferred it to staying in a hotel.
   C He didn't like it as much as camping.
   D He disliked having people nearby.

Are you looking for an unusual place to stay? We set up our business five years ago and have been researching destinations ever since. There are hundreds of suggestions on our website from guitar-shaped luxury hotels in Hollywood to more affordable accommodation such as treehouses in Costa Rica. Each of our properties is checked by employees and each of them is special. We also offer suggestions for activities and recommendations for places to eat. Whichever option you choose, by the end of your stay, you will have enjoyed a unique experience.

2 The advert states that this company …
   A focuses on luxury accommodation.
   B advises on different forms of travel.
   C is based in Europe.
   D only recommends places it has visited.

Hi Joe,
Did I mention I'm thinking of volunteering abroad? Well, I've found a brilliant website that organises voluntary work all over the world. The focus is on making a difference to the planet by helping with conservation and research. You have to pay an amount, but this is relatively small and far less than you would pay for a holiday. You also get accommodation and all your food. They offer loads of projects, so I'm not sure what to choose. Do you fancy having a look? I could do with someone else's opinion. I'll send you the website link in case you get a chance to read it tonight.
See you soon,
Jack

3 What is the purpose of Jack's email?
   A to suggest going on a trip together
   B to ask for advice
   C to describe a holiday he went on
   D to borrow some money

BLOG

Hey. I'm Mu Lan and I live in Singapore. I can't imagine settling in any other location because there are so many things I love about my city. If you don't know, Singapore is very modern and is well known for its innovative architecture and artificial green spaces. It's great for the environment too because the city effectively uses technology to manage things like waste. It's a very busy city and popular with tourists because there is so much to do, but there is a lot of interesting wildlife and beaches too!

4 Mu Lan has written this blog post to …
   A complain about aspects of her city.
   B describe environmental issues.
   C explain what her city offers.
   D recommend specific places to go.

Speaking

EXAM STRATEGY

Prepare for your speaking exam by researching topics you are likely to be asked about in the exam and expanding your knowledge of related vocabulary. Group words together under headings such as *home, family, environment*, etc.

7 💬 Read the strategy above. Then brainstorm words and phrases that relate to the topic of homes and cities. Share your ideas with a partner. Use a dictionary to add more ideas.

8 Answer the questions about homes and cities.
   1 What is your ideal home like?
   2 What are the advantages of living alone or sharing with others?
   3 Would you describe yourself as a creative person when it comes to the interior of your home? Why? / Why not?
   4 What accommodation choices do young people make once they leave home?
   5 How important is it for towns to appeal to young people?
   6 What facilities are there where you live?
   7 How can towns and cities reduce their impact on the environment?
   8 What makes an ideal town or city?

Writing

EXAM STRATEGY

When you complete a piece of writing, make sure you leave enough time to check for errors. You can prepare for this by writing your own checklist of errors so that you automatically focus on these in the exam.

9 Read the strategy above. Then complete the checklist with your own ideas.
   wrong spelling

10 You see this advert on an English-language website.

We are looking for articles about where young people live. Tell us about your nearest town or city. Describe the facilities. Are there enough for young people? What are the good and bad points about this town or city?

Write your article. Check for errors using your checklist. Which ones did you find?

Unit 4   51

5.1 VOCABULARY — Talk about technology.

5 Technology

1 a What can you remember about the vlog? Who said these things? Write Z (Zaki), Y (Yasmin), J (Joe) or D (Daisy).
1 There have been so many **advances in technology** in our lifetimes: social media, smartphones, vlogging. ___
2 What are the **game-changing innovations**? ___
3 I'm a total **geek**. ___
4 I think AI – **artificial intelligence** – is the most interesting development. ___
5 … everything in your phone, including **automatic updates** … uses AI. ___
6 I'm a bit of a **technophobe**. ___
7 What I like is that it's **user-friendly** – the controls are simple and it's easy to read when I'm running. ___
8 This app … let's me **browse** all kinds of music. ___

b ▶ 5.01 Watch or listen again and check.

2 Choose the correct alternative.

TechForum — Home · About · Reviews · Q&A · Sign in

How do you feel about computers and other technology?

Beth I'm not into technology. In fact, I'm a real ¹**technophobe / geek**! I know there have been some ²**user-friendly / significant** developments over the last 20 years, but I'd like to go back in time and live more simply.

Liam I use technology every day, for ³**streaming / browsing** music and ⁴**game-changing / browsing** the internet, but I'm not interested in how it all works.

Kamilli I think we live in interesting times in terms of recent ⁵**advances in technology / updates**. I'm excited about how ⁶**gadgets are / artificial intelligence is** opening up extraordinary new possibilities in business and healthcare.

Rafa To be honest, I'm a bit of a ⁷**technophobe / geek**! I want to own all the latest ⁸**high-tech / significant** devices. I've just bought myself a fitness tracker – my first piece of ⁹**wearable technology / update**.

3 Complete the text with words from Ex 1 and 2.

NEWS › Technology

Mind-reading technology

The brain is an amazingly sophisticated and complex organ – so how can technology ever understand it? Well, now, amazingly, there are ¹_____ that can read your mind!

These computer-based systems use ²_____ in the form of brain signals and translate it to digital commands that are then sent to an output device to carry out a desired action.

With this ³_____ the user can, for example, change the TV channel by focusing their attention on the menu commands on screen. Mind-reading technology could be ⁴_____ in the fields of entertainment, gaming and even medicine. The only disadvantage is that the headsets aren't very ⁵_____, feeling uncomfortable after a short time, but hopefully their design will soon be improved.

4 REAL ENGLISH Complete the dialogue with the phrases below.

| a no-brainer   does that count   get your head around
| not rocket science   piece of kit   take it for granted

Maya What's the most significant advance in technology?
Noah That's ¹_____: the internet. We ²_____, but it's been life-changing.
Maya True, but what about a more recent innovation?
Lucy My electric bike is my favourite ³_____ – you just switch on the motor and go!
Maya But that's ⁴_____. What about the Human Genome Project? Using technology to study DNA. ⁵_____?
Noah Absolutely! I read that overall, humans are 99.9% genetically similar. It's hard to ⁶_____!

5 VOCABULARY BOOSTER Now practise **Technology** vocabulary on page 108.

5.2 GRAMMAR

▶ Grammar animation
GRAMMAR BOOSTER P140

Use second and third conditionals and conjunctions to talk about technology.

1 Choose the correct alternative.

OOPS! I'VE DISCOVERED SOMETHING GREAT!

Many scientific discoveries wouldn't have been made ¹**unless / on condition that** something had happened by chance. Here are three famous accidental innovations.

Millions of children around the world wouldn't have enjoyed using Play-Doh ²**even if / if** it hadn't been for an unsuccessful product for cleaning wallpaper. In 1954, American schoolteacher Kay Zufall was looking for a cheap modelling clay for her young pupils. She'd heard other people were using wallpaper cleaner made by her brother-in-law, Joe McVicker, so she bought some and the children loved it. When Joe saw their creations, he changed the product slightly and rebranded it as a toy, with huge success.

In the early 19th century, you probably ³**wouldn't wear / wouldn't have worn** purple clothes even if you ⁴**had / had had** quite a lot of money, as it was extremely expensive to produce the colour purple naturally. Things changed, however, in 1856 when William Henry Perkin, a young British chemist, accidentally created an artificial purple dye while trying to make a drug to fight malaria.

⁵**Supposing / As long as** you wanted to stick a note to a page in a book for a short time. You ⁶**would want / would have wanted** something sticky, but not too sticky. A Post-it note would be perfect! In the late 1960s, American chemist Dr Spencer Silver was trying to develop a very strong glue. Instead, he created the opposite – a very weak glue. A few years later, a chemical engineer called Art Fry had the idea of using it to create sticky paper bookmarks, and so the Post-it note was invented.

wallpaper (n) thick paper, often with a pattern on it, which is used for covering the walls of a room
modelling clay (n) a soft material you can easily form into different 3D shapes
glue (n) a sticky substance used to join things together

2 Read the text in Ex 1 again and complete the second and third conditional sentences with the verbs in brackets. Sometimes more than one answer is possible.
1 If you _____ (want) to give a young child a simple toy, you could get them some Play-Doh.
2 McVicker _____ (not change) the wallpaper cleaner into a toy if it had been selling well.
3 You _____ (not need) to spend a lot of money if you wanted some purple clothes today.
4 If William Henry Perkin hadn't been trying to make a drug to fight malaria, he _____ (not create) an artificial purple dye.
5 Dr Silver Spencer wouldn't have invented a weak glue if he _____ (not / try) to develop a strong glue.
6 If I needed to mark a page in a book, I _____ (use) a Post-it note or I might just use a piece of paper.

3 Complete the sentences with the conjunctions below. Sometimes more than one answer is possible.

| as long as   even if   on condition that
| providing / provided (that)   supposing (that)   unless

1 I would have an electric car, _____ the battery lasted for more than a few hundred miles.
2 _____ cyber criminals had got hold of your data – what would you do?
3 They could take photos with a drone _____ it wasn't against the law.
4 _____ space travel was cheap and easily available to everyone, I wouldn't want to do it.
5 We couldn't have made these parts _____ we'd had a 3D printer. It's great we've got one.
6 We would be interested in buying the software _____ you were able to train us in how to use it.

4 Complete the second sentence so that it means the same as the first. You must use the word in brackets.
1 I can't imagine posting a picture of a friend online if I wasn't sure they were happy for me to do so. (UNLESS)
I _____ sure they were happy for me to do so.
2 It was lucky we had GPS; otherwise how would we have found this place? (SUPPOSING)
_____ GPS. How would we have found this place?
3 I would travel in a driverless car, but I would need someone else to come with me! (LONG)
I would travel in a driverless car _____ with me!
4 I could live in an underwater city, but I would need to visit the land every few weeks. (CONDITION)
I could live in an underwater city _____ the land every few weeks.
5 We could give him a laptop, but he wouldn't use it. (EVEN)
He wouldn't use a laptop _____ him one.
6 Humans couldn't live on Mars if they didn't have the right life support systems. (PROVIDED)
Humans might _____ the right life support systems.

5 Complete the sentences so they are true for you using appropriate conditionals.
1 I would never _____ even if _____.
2 I wouldn't _____ unless _____.
3 I might _____ if _____.
4 I would _____ on condition that _____.
5 Supposing _____. That would be amazing!
6 I wouldn't have _____ if _____.

Unit 5   53

5.3 LISTENING — Distinguish between supporting and contrasting information.

1 What can you remember about the podcast in the Student's Book? Complete the notes with compound nouns using a word from A and a word from B.

A digital distance on-demand social subscription

B content interaction learning revolution services

Streaming

Pros: ¹ _____ give people unlimited access to a wide range of films and music; they make ² _____ more effective and give more people access to education.

Cons: The availability of so much ³ _____ encourages people to spend too much time on their screens, which can be bad for their well-being; the ⁴ _____ has had a negative influence on musicians' income; online learning takes away the opportunities for ⁵ _____ offered in the 'real' world.

2 Look at the picture and answer the questions.

1 What do robots do that humans aren't capable of?
2 What can humans do that robots aren't capable of?
3 In what fields of everyday life is artificial intelligence currently used?

STRATEGY Distinguishing between supporting and contrasting information

To understand the structure of a spoken text, it's useful to be able to tell when a speaker is adding new information to support a point or introducing contrasting information to argue against it. When supporting or contrasting information is added, linking words are often used. For example:
in addition, needless to say, on top of that, furthermore (supporting information).
having said that, however, on the other hand, although (contrasting information).

3 🔊 **5.02** Read the strategy. Listen to Abe and Maya talk about the pros and cons of artificial intelligence. Tick (✓) the points they mention.

Artificial intelligence

Pros
- It can work without needing to stop and rest. ☐
- It can save organisations money. ☐
- It doesn't make mistakes. ☐
- It's often better at decision-making than humans. ☐
- It doesn't get bored of doing the same thing again and again. ☐
- It supports the work of individuals. ☐

Cons
- It could be very dangerous for humans. ☐
- It doesn't have a sense of what's right and wrong. ☐
- It isn't creative. ☐
- It stops people using their brains so much. ☐
- It's expensive to develop and use. ☐

4 a 🔊 **5.02** Listen again and complete the sentences with one to three words.

1 It's practical, it's rational and not emotional, and _____, it can keep going, without needing a break like us humans.
2 On _____, of course, it doesn't make mistakes.
3 Well, that is pretty impressive, _____ of course in that situation – healthcare – there's a very clear goal that's for the good of people.
4 On _____, I worry about people using AI for negative goals …
5 _____, I like to think that humans are wise as well as intelligent …
6 Well, that's good to know. _____, I do have other concerns.
7 _____, I sometimes wonder if too much AI would make people lazy.

b Now identify the supporting (S) and contrasting (C) ideas in the sentences.

5 Complete the sentences with your own ideas.
1 If services like Netflix didn't make recommendations for what films to watch next, _____.
2 I would be worried about AI if _____.
3 If scientists learned more about the deepest parts of the ocean, maybe _____.
4 If computers felt emotions, _____.
5 If computers replaced doctors completely, _____
_____.

Talk about the effects of technology on the environment.

5.4 VOCABULARY

1 Match the words below to words 1–6 to make collocations.

> energy   footprint   materials
> resources   site   warming

1 landfill _____
2 raw _____
3 alternative _____
4 carbon _____
5 global _____
6 natural _____

2 Match the collocations in Ex 1 to the definitions and examples below.

1 a gradual increase in the overall temperature of the Earth's atmosphere caused by increased levels of carbon dioxide and other polluting chemicals _____
2 the amount of CO_2 released into the atmosphere as a result of what an individual, organisation or community does _____
3 essential things and substances that our planet provides us with, for example, oil, natural gas, wood, fish, air, sunlight, stone, sand, metal, water, land _____
4 things and substances that are used to manufacture other things, for example, oil, natural gas, wood, stone, sand, metal _____
5 an area of land where rubbish is put _____
6 for example, solar power, wind power, hydropower (from water) _____

3 Choose the correct alternative.

- Some ¹**landfill sites / raw materials** are created by digging huge holes in the ground.
- One way to reduce your ²**consumption / carbon footprint** is to switch off your mobile phone overnight.
- Another form of ³**alternative / viable** energy is geothermal energy, which is produced from the heat inside the Earth.
- Over the last 20 years, the ⁴**deforestation / consumption** of wood has increased by 1.1% per year, mainly because of its use in house building.
- What ⁵**raw materials / natural resources** are needed for electric car batteries?
- We should use ⁶**renewable / viable** materials like wood, cotton and bamboo because plants can grow again after they've been cut down.

4 Complete the texts with the correct form of the words and phrases below.

> consumption   deforestation   dispose of
> endanger   environmentally friendly   generated by
> natural resources   renewable   reuse   viable

Our ¹_____ of gadgets, flights and fast fashion ²_____ the planet.

Around 45 million tonnes of computers, televisions, mobile phones and other electronic goods are ³_____ every year. They end up in landfill sites when much of it could be recycled or ⁴_____.

It must be ⁵_____ for industry to become more ⁶_____. For example, it could hugely reduce its carbon footprint by using ⁷_____ energy, such as energy ⁸_____ wind, water and the sun.

Trees are one of the world's most valuable ⁹_____, yet the UN's Food and Agriculture Organization estimates the annual rate of ¹⁰_____ to be 1.3 million km² per decade.

5 Complete the text with vocabulary from the lesson.

ENVIRONMENT NEWS

The future of plant-based foods

Could plant-based foods replace meat and dairy in the future?

The ¹_____ of meat is a problem for the environment, because the methane, CO_2 and nitrous oxide released in its production are all gases which contribute to ²_____.

Farming animals requires significant amounts of energy and water, and clearing land for farmland leads to ³_____. Burning forest creates CO_2 and removes trees which naturally take CO_2 from the atmosphere. Furthermore, the loss of forest ⁴_____ many plant and animal species.

Clearly, plant-based foods are a(n) ⁵_____ alternative to meat. The good news is that technology now exists that makes plant-based meat, cheese and eggs seem more lifelike, which should make them more ⁶_____ as a substitute for meat and dairy.

6 Answer the questions using ideas from the lesson.
1 What natural resources can be found in your country (for example, types of food, stone, oil, plants)?
2 How is energy generated in your country? What alternative energy sources are or could be used?
3 Do you think more people should become vegetarian?

7 **VOCABULARY BOOSTER** Now practise **Effects of technology on the environment** vocabulary on page 108.

Unit 5   55

5.5 GRAMMAR — Use mixed conditionals to talk about plastic.

Grammar animation
GRAMMAR BOOSTER P141

1 Complete the leaflet with the words and phrases below.

> could have been   had never been invented   was   were
> would not be   wouldn't find   wouldn't have taken

The production of plastic needs to STOP!

Many people are trying their best to reduce how much plastic they use, but what really needs to change is the amount of plastic being produced.

Fact: Plastic is produced using oil. In fact, the plastics industry accounts for about 6% of global oil consumption. As a result, the production of plastics generates enormous amounts of air pollution. If plastic ¹_____, global warming ²_____ the problem it is today.

Fact: Most people think that when plastic is put in recycling bins, it is disposed of safely. However, only 9% is recycled globally, and the rest is dumped in the natural environment. Some of it is burned, creating more GHG emissions, and the rest of it ends up on land and in the oceans, endangering wildlife. If all plastic ³_____ recycled or disposed of in a controlled way, the lives of millions of plants and animals ⁴_____ saved over the last 60 years.

Fact: Plastic pollution is contributing to global warming. Until now, the Earth's oceans have absorbed up to 40% of all man-made carbon since we started using machines. Recent research, however, indicates that microplastics prevent this from happening so effectively. Perhaps if people ⁵_____ better educated about our planet, they ⁶_____ it for granted and treated it so badly in recent years, and we ⁷_____ ourselves in the worrying situation we're in today.

We must call on governments now to reduce plastic production!

> **dump** (v) throw away something, especially in a place that is not suitable
> **microplastics** (n) extremely small pieces of waste plastic in the environment

2 **PRONUNCIATION** 🔊 5.03 Listen to and repeat the examples of linking between words in spoken English.
Consonant to vowel
1 **Plastic is** produced **using oil**.
2 The **plastics industry** accounts **for about** 6% of **global oil** consumption.
A /j/ sound linking two vowels
3 **We all** use a lot of plastic.
4 A lot of plastic ends up in **the oceans**.
A /w/ sound linking two vowels
5 Oceans can't absorb carbon **so effectively** because of the amount of plastic in them.
6 Until now, the Earth's oceans have absorbed up **to almost** half of all man-made carbon.

3 Read the text and choose the correct alternative.

In praise of plastic

Plastic often gets bad press, but here are some positives.

Plastic lasts a long time. If water pipes all around the world today weren't made of plastic, billions of litres of water ¹**would be / would have been** wasted over the last 70 years.

Plastic is light. Cars and planes ²**would make / would have made** global warming worse in recent years if they didn't contain so many plastic parts.

Plastic does not conduct electricity. If we ³**couldn't use / couldn't have used** plastic for light switches, for example, what would we have done instead?

Plastic is hygienic. If various uses of plastic in medicine and food production ⁴**hadn't been developed / wasn't developed**, many people ⁵**wouldn't be / wouldn't have been** alive today.

Finally, renewable energy production relies on plastic. If plastic ⁶**wasn't invented / hadn't been invented**, we ⁷**wouldn't be using / wouldn't have been using** today's high-tech solar panels and wind turbines.

4 Complete the mixed conditional sentences using the verbs in brackets, paying attention to the information about what is past (THEN) and present (NOW).
1 (THEN, NOW) If antibiotics _____ (be discovered), I _____ (be) alive today.
2 (NOW, THEN) If you _____ (know) me better, you _____ (say) that.
3 (THEN, NOW) They _____ (offer) you the job if you _____ (not have) such a lot of experience.
4 (THEN, NOW) If they _____ (cut down) so much forest, more species of birds and animals _____ (live) there today.
5 (NOW, THEN) If we _____ (live) closer, we _____ (come) to your concert.
6 (NOW, THEN) There _____ (be) so much rubbish in space if people _____ (think) about space pollution in the early days of space exploration.

5 Answer the questions so they are true for you.
1 How would your everyday life be different if plastic hadn't been invented?
2 How would you be different if you had been born 500 years ago?
3 How would your life be different if you had grown up on the other side of the world?

5.6 READING

Recognise and understand topic sentences in a text.

1 What do you remember about the Student's Book text? Complete the summary with the words below.

| adapt to   maintain their profiles
| obsessed with   peer group   scrolling   targeted

Teens have grown up with the internet and can ¹_____ new social media platforms easily. While some enjoy and, in fact, are ²_____ getting likes, others want to quit social media – they dislike being ³_____ by advertisers and the pressure to ⁴_____. Anastasia quit social media: she prefers to see her friends face to face rather than ⁵_____ through profiles, etc. But others in her ⁶_____ are worried of the consequences of quitting.

2 🔊 **5.04** Read the article and complete the sentences with an appropriate word in each gap.
1. Most teens in the survey felt online learning had had a _____ impact on their future.
2. Lauren _____ concentrate on the screen all day.
3. Noah liked the _____ of online learning.
4. Students with autism _____ online learning because it's less stressful.
5. The author believes online learning _____ have a place in education.

STRATEGY Using topic sentences
Most paragraphs in a text or article have a topic sentence, which is usually, but not always, the first sentence. The topic sentence provides an overview of the main idea in that paragraph. The following sentences contain more information to develop and support that main idea.

3 Read the strategy above. Underline the topic sentence in each paragraph.

4 Read the article again and choose the correct answer: A, B or C.
1. According to the survey, only a small proportion of students felt they ___.
   A would miss the social aspect of school
   B learned better online than in person
   C preferred studying in a classroom to studying online
2. Lauren points out that at school she ___.
   A would do much better if her friends didn't distract her
   B wouldn't have asked her teachers questions if she'd been there during the pandemic
   C would have asked her classmates for help if she'd been there during the pandemic
3. Noah thinks he ___ during the pandemic.
   A would have done better if he'd got up early every day
   B shouldn't have played videos at double speed
   C took a good approach to his studies
4. Students with autism would ___ their lessons were online.
   A be able to maximise their learning if
   B still experience similar anxiety levels even if all
   C get better grades than students without autism if

Classroom learning vs screen learning

Most teens enjoy spending their downtime online, but what about studying online? A recent survey shows most teens prefer in-person school, both for its academic and social aspects. Nearly two thirds found remote learning 'worse' or 'much worse' than in-person learning and felt concerned about doing less well in their studies. Over half of them worry about losing connections with friends too.

Like many teenagers, Lauren had to study remotely during the 2020 pandemic. She explains why she found it tough. 'I hated being on a screen all day because it was hard to focus. I get a bit distracted by my friends in the physical classroom, but it isn't a huge problem. At home, the temptation to take a break and do something different was too much. The worst thing was not being able to ask my teachers or classmates for help and having to wait for a response when I emailed my teacher a question.'

Not everyone found remote learning a problem, however. 'I missed my peers, but home learning was OK,' says Noah, 15. 'I might have felt differently if we'd had "live lessons" with a teacher online, but I could do my lessons whenever I wanted to. Sometimes I got up late, but more often I'd get up early and finish all my lessons by lunchtime. I could take a more flexible approach to the learning itself too. We had to watch a lot of science videos, and the teacher spoke really slowly, so I would play the videos on double speed. I could then spend longer on topics I found more difficult.'

One particular group of students found virtual learning preferable to being in the physical classroom. Students with autism, who face difficulties with communication and social interaction, can experience high levels of anxiety in face-to-face lessons. Furthermore, many of these students do best when they can follow their own interests and work at their own speed. Remote learning benefited them by allowing them to create their ideal study schedule.

Clearly, the concept of traditional learning has changed dramatically in the last few years. Advances in technology offer more students access to cheap and flexible education. So, what's the future of online learning? While 'hybrid learning' – combining in-person and face-to-face study – is likely to become a popular option for universities and colleges, the physical classroom will always be where the most memorable learning takes place.

Unit 5 57

5.7 GLOBAL SKILLS

Explore ideas for creating a positive digital footprint.

1 What can you remember about the podcast in the Student's Book about managing your digital footprint? Complete the sentences.
  1 A passive transfer of information occurs when we browse the internet and visit different websites because our passive digital footprint is made up of the t_____ we leave of our browsing history.
  2 Pay attention to your online security. Check your p_____ s_____ to be sure strangers can't see your posts and photos. Only give away things like your date of birth if you're sure it's r_____ i_____.
  3 Delete accounts you don't use because these i_____ accounts can expose you to h_____, especially if you used a weak password.
  4 Don't communicate online in a way that you wouldn't face to face – be r_____.
  5 Take control of your online image. If someone t_____ you in memes or photos, remember that you can u_____ yourself. You might not want them to be seen when a potential employer is doing a b_____ c_____ on you.

2 Tick (✓) the things that you use the internet for.
  A connecting with friends ☐
  B learning about the world ☐
  C helping other people ☐
  D improving your English ☐
  E expressing your creativity ☐

3 Read the article and match three of the topics A–E in Ex 2 to paragraphs 1–3.
  1 ___   2 ___   3 ___

4 Read the article again and complete the notes with one word in each gap.

WildEarth
- You will need a device with a good internet connection and 1_____.
- Watch some WildEarth videos and 2_____ any questions you have to the WildEarth experts.
- Select a sunrise or 3_____ safari.
- Enjoy your virtual trip!

Be My Eyes
- The app connects 4_____ to 5_____ or partially sighted users. Use the app whenever you need help.
- Sighted users: wait for a 6_____ call. If you're too 7_____, someone else will be able to help.

Eric Whitacre's Virtual Choir
- Register on the website and listen to the latest piece of music.
- 8_____ singing the piece.
- 9_____ yourself singing it.
- 10_____ your recording to the website.
- Enjoy listening to the final performance!

5 **MEDIATION** Your friend has broken their leg and is having to spend a lot of time at home. Write an email suggesting one or two of the websites from the article that you think they might be interested in. Use the information in the text to explain the websites to your friend.

The best of life online

The internet has made our lives richer in so many ways, helping us enjoy the beauty of our planet, connect with others and celebrate the best of humanity's creativity. Here are three opportunities we could never have had without the internet.

1 WildEarth safaris
Do you dream of visiting Africa to see elephants, lions, giraffes and other animals in the wild? It may be difficult to make a physical trip, but WildEarth offers free live-stream safaris from stunning locations in Africa twice a day. Sunrise safaris take place between 6.30 and 9.30 a.m. CAT (Central African Time) and sunset safaris between 2.30 and 6.30 p.m. CAT. All you need is a device to watch the live stream on, including speakers so you can hear the sounds of the animals and the WildEarth expert talking, and a good internet connection. It's worth watching videos of previous WildEarth safaris. You can then email questions for the experts to answer live.

2 Be My Eyes
The internet makes it possible for us to support people anywhere in the world. Be My Eyes is an app that connects volunteers who can see with people who are blind or partially sighted and who need help from time with time with small, everyday tasks like reading the 'use by' date on a carton of milk, for example, or describing the colour of a shirt. Through a live video call, the volunteers guide blind or partially sighted users where to point their camera, what to focus on or when to turn on their torch and then describe what they see. Blind and partially sighted users can use the app to make a video call whenever they need help. Volunteers don't need to take a call if they're busy because fortunately the app already has plenty of volunteers who can help.

3 Eric Whitacre's Virtual Choir
You don't need to be in the same place to sing together! Eric Whitacre's Virtual Choir brings together thousands of singers from around the world to create performances through the use of technology. Once they have logged on, singers in locations all over the world can hear the latest piece that the choir is working on, and practise singing it wherever they are. They then record and upload their videos, which are all combined into a single final performance. The results are beautiful and well worth a listen!

safari (n) a trip to see or hunt wild animals, especially in eastern or southern Africa
live-stream (adj) shown on the internet as they happen
partially sighted (adj) without good eyesight
choir (n) a group of people who sing together

Use signposting phrases in a presentation.

5.8 SPEAKING

1 Look at the photos. What problems do these animals face?

1 coral reef
2 Arabian oryx
3 Amazon wildlife

2 ◆)) 5.05 Listen to a student presentation. Match technology A–E to photos 1–3. There are two technologies you do not need.
 A drones ___
 B GPS tracking ___
 C robots ___
 D solar-powered factories ___
 E the study of DNA ___

3 ◆)) 5.05 Listen again. Are the sentences true (T) or false (F)?
 1 Even if there wasn't any pollution in the oceans, coral would still be dying. T ☐ F ☐
 2 Scientists have invented a high-tech device which looks like another sea creature to monitor the coral. T ☐ F ☐
 3 Scientists will need to develop a new device to help the coral grow again. T ☐ F ☐
 4 The Arabian oryx wouldn't be endangered if it weren't for climate change. T ☐ F ☐
 5 In the United Arab Emirates, oryx were moved to areas where they would have access to freshwater. T ☐ F ☐
 6 Unless BioCarbon Engineering had invented their tree-planting devices, it would be impossible to replant trees in the rainforest. T ☐ F ☐
 7 The tree-planting technology could result in 1 billion trees a year being planted. T ☐ F ☐

STRATEGY Organising a presentation
When giving a presentation, it's important to ensure that you have a clear structure: introduction, main body, conclusion. Use signposting expressions to explain the purpose and structure of your presentation and to join the different parts together. In particular, make it clear when you have finished discussing one point and are starting a new one. This will make it easier for your audience to follow what you are saying.

4 a Read the strategy above. Complete the sentences with the words below.

| areas   begin   concludes   final   look
| move   part   second   subject

 1 The _____ of my presentation today is how technology is being used to protect endangered animals.
 2 I'll be looking at three _____ where people have found innovative solutions.
 3 In the first _____, I'll report on how a high-tech device is helping scientists solve an underwater problem.
 4 _____, I'll talk about a solution to a problem facing animals in desert areas.
 5 In the _____ section, I'll tell you about an innovative solution to deforestation, which gives hope for the animals who live there.
 6 To _____, let's consider what's happening to coral reefs in many parts of the world.
 7 Now, let's _____ on to the desert. Here, climate change is making many areas warmer and drier …
 8 Finally, let's _____ at what's being done to help animals in the Amazon rainforest.
 9 That _____ my talk.

 b ◆)) 5.05 Listen again and check your answers.

5 Match phrases for signposting a presentation A–I to phrases with the same meaning 1–9 in Ex 4.
 A Then, in the second part, … ___
 B Finally, let's consider … ___
 C This presentation will be about … ___
 D Finally, I'll … ___
 E Firstly, … ___
 F To sum up, … ___
 G I'd like to start by talking about … ___
 H Next, I want to turn to … ___
 I My talk will be in three parts. ___

6 Choose one of the topics below and prepare a three-part presentation. Follow the steps.

 • Positive and negative impacts of technology on the environment in your country
 • The advantages and disadvantages of plastic
 • Using the internet in positive ways

 1 Decide what areas of the topic you will talk about, and make notes about the information you will include.
 2 Think about what you will say in the introduction, each part of the main body and the conclusion, and decide what signposting expressions you will use.

7 Write your presentation. When you have finished, check that you have given your presentation a clear structure, and used signposting expressions and vocabulary from this unit.

Unit 5   59

5.9 WRITING
Use a range of phrases to write a balanced review.

1 Write down the names of some apps that you use regularly, for example, search engines, social-media apps and photo-sharing apps.

2 Choose one of the apps and answer the questions.
1 What's its main purpose?
2 What functions does it have?
3 What do you like about?
4 What don't you like about it?
5 Who would you recommend it to?

3 Read the review and number paragraphs A–E in the correct order.

YOUR REVIEWS

A review of an app I like

A ___ On the negative side, I'm not keen on the way a lot of the content looks so perfect. This is not especially helpful if your self-esteem is low, because you can end up thinking that your bedroom / clothes / cooking, etc. will never be good enough. Another drawback is that a lot of people use it to advertise products they're selling, which is slightly annoying when you just want to enjoy the images.

B ___ Moodboard is basically a visual search engine that allows users to find up-to-the-minute ideas for things like home, fashion and food. Users can save and organise images that they like to boards, and share their ideas with other people. It also has a range of features that make it easy to connect with others, such as 'like', 'follow' and 'comment' buttons. It's incredibly user-friendly and also completely free.

C ___ An app I really appreciate is Moodboard, which I use almost every day. I get a lot of design ideas from it, and I also use it to connect with other people. It's extremely attractive and an endless source of style ideas.

D ___ If you are interested in style and design, I would definitely recommend using Moodboard. I would perhaps like to see a bit less advertising and a few more realistic photos, but overall I can't recommend it highly enough.

E ___ What I like most about this app is that people share a lot of DIY (do it yourself) projects, which is great if, like me, you enjoy making things. Another positive is that you can work on boards with other people, which is absolutely brilliant if you're planning something together, like a party. Not only that, but you can also have secret boards which only you and your friends can see, so you can keep your ideas private at the planning stage.

4 Match phrases 1–5 to phrases A–E which have a similar meaning.
1 It appeals to me … ___
2 It's basically a / an … app. ___
3 I'm particularly impressed by … ___
4 Another slight drawback is … ___
5 One way to enhance it would be … ___

A It allows users to …
B I would perhaps like to see …
C What really stands out is …
D It's one of my favourite websites …
E I was a bit disappointed by …

STRATEGY Using modifying adverbs
In a piece of writing, we often use adverbs to strengthen or emphasise a point, or to soften a negative statement.
*I think this is an **absolutely** brilliant feature.*
*The design is **slightly** disappointing.*

5 Read the strategy above. Circle adverbs in the text that strengthen or emphasise a positive point and underline adverbs that soften a negative point.

6 Choose the correct alternative to emphasise the positive points and soften the negative ones.

It's ¹**extremely** / **quite** well designed.
It's ²**somewhat** / **incredibly** popular among teenagers.
It's ³**quite** / **totally** game-changing.
It's ⁴**a bit** / **significantly** more user-friendly than it used to be.
It's ⁵**slightly** / **absolutely** amazing.

It's ⁶**extremely** / **quite** expensive.
It's ⁷**somewhat** / **completely** unnecessary.
It's ⁸**incredibly** / **slightly** disappointing.
It's ⁹**a bit** / **significantly** more complicated than it used to be.
It ¹⁰**isn't especially** / **'s extremely** interesting.

7 Read the advertisement. Use your answers to the questions in Ex 2 to plan your review.

 What's your favourite app?
Write a review of an app you use regularly. Tell us why you find it useful or enjoyable, and let us know what isn't so good about it. Send your review to editor@appreviews.net.uk.

8 Write your review.

9 **CHECK YOUR WORK** Did you …
- use a five-part paragraph structure?
- write an introduction with a brief description of the app?
- describe the purpose and function of the app?
- include both positive and negative views, and recommendations?
- include phrases used in reviews?
- use adverbs to emphasise or soften your comments?

5.10 REVIEW

Grammar

1 Choose the correct answer: A, B or C.
1. I wouldn't go skydiving ___ you paid me $1 million!
   A even if   B supposing   C provided that
2. Provided that you ___ the original box, you could've returned the smartwatch.
   A kept   B would keep   C had kept
3. I would be happy to play music with other people online ___ everyone had a good internet connection.
   A supposing   B unless   C on condition that
4. I wouldn't do the course ___ I could do some of it online.
   A provided that   B as long as   C unless
5. If there ___ a pandemic in 2020, I would never have spent so much time at home.
   A hadn't been   B wouldn't have been   C wasn't
6. They ___ Jack to the concert if they'd known he liked classical music.
   A had invited   B might have invited   C invited

2 Complete the mixed conditional sentences with the phrases below.

| might not be   was   would be   would have used |
| wouldn't have   wouldn't know |

1. We could have watched a film last night if there _____ Wi-Fi here.
2. The company _____ your data if you hadn't completed that quiz online.
3. I _____ the new software more if I found it more user-friendly.
4. Scientists _____ so much about the heart if they hadn't had to develop technology for checking astronauts' hearts.
5. There _____ far fewer trees on Earth if email hadn't become so popular.
6. If you had gone to bed earlier last night, you _____ so sleepy now.

Vocabulary

3 Complete the sentences with the words below.

| browse   geek   high-tech   significant |
| streaming   wearable technology |

1. The first mobile phones were _____ items at the time, but compared to today's phones, they were very big and heavy.
2. _____ has changed the way people watch films and TV because it offers much more choice.
3. Smartwatches and clothes that keep track of their wearer's health conditions are two examples of _____.
4. I love finding out about all the latest technology. I'm a real _____!
5. The internet has been the most _____ development in the recent history of technology.
6. I used to _____ the internet for ages at the weekend, but now I spend a lot more time with my friends instead.

4 Complete the sentences.
1. Don't throw that bag away. I can r_____ it when I go shopping.
2. I'd like to grow all my own food, but it isn't v_____ – I'd still need to buy some items.
3. The oceans wouldn't be so dirty if people had d_____ o_____ plastic more carefully over the last 60 years.
4. It's terrible that so many electronic gadgets end up as waste in a l_____ s_____.
5. Experts are figuring out how to use a_____ i_____ to use data to predict floods in areas that get a lot of rain.
6. Companies that produce goods need r_____ m_____ like oil, wood and iron.
7. Wind is a r_____ energy source.
8. Plastic toothbrushes are convenient, but they aren't e_____ f_____.

Cumulative review

5 Choose the correct alternative.

Looking after our planet, looking after ourselves

We've always had severe weather events from time to time, like heavy rains and strong winds, but ¹**consumption** / **global warming** / **artificial intelligence** is now ²**endangering** / **disposing of** / **generating** the lives of millions of people.

If we ³**would have paid** / **paid** / **had paid** more attention to climate change, we ⁴**didn't** / **couldn't** / **wouldn't** find ourselves in this situation today, but the truth is we are now facing a growing number of natural disasters.

On the positive side, ⁵**gadgets** / **advances** / **geeks** in technology can help experts predict and manage these events. The wildfires that hit California in 2020, for example, ⁶**would have destroyed** / **would destroy** / **might destroy** much larger areas of forest ⁷**unless** / **providing** / **if** firefighters hadn't been able to use ⁸**sophisticated** / **significant** / **viable** drones to map the fires and use fire-stopping technology.

However, we cannot rely on technology to save the planet. ⁹**As long as** / **Even if** / **On condition that** experts had all the time and money in the world, they couldn't fix all the damage we have done. According to recent reports, the ¹⁰**updates** / **consumption** / **deforestation** of energy around the world is likely to increase by between 50% and 100% by 2050. It's therefore essential that we develop innovative technology to use more sources of ¹¹**wearable technology** / **raw materials** / **alternative energy**. We must take all action possible to reduce our ¹²**natural resources** / **carbon footprint** / **landfill sites**.

REFLECT Think about the following questions.
1. Which lesson in this unit was your favourite? Why?
2. Which grammar points did you find most difficult? Why?
3. How could you use the internet in a positive way that you haven't tried before?

6.1 VOCABULARY
Talk about spending and not spending money.

Money matters

1 a What can you remember about the vlog? Answer the questions by writing *Y* (Yasmin) or *Z* (Zaki).
  Who says they …
  1 will get their **s**_____ under control and cut out non-**e**_____? ___
  2 spend money **w**_____ and suggests making a **d**_____ to charity? ___
  3 will keep track of their **f**_____ and **b**_____ up their savings account? ___
  4 don't pay for their gym **m**_____ or guitar **t**_____? ___
  5 enjoy **g**_____ and often **o**_____ friends money? ___
  6 need to cut back on on **e**_____ expenses such as **b**_____ and takeaways? ___
  7 will buy **s**_____ clothes and no **a**_____? ___

b 🔊 **6.01** Watch or listen again and check.

2 Choose the correct alternative.
  1 Making soup is good for **using up / building up** old vegetables.
  2 I try to spend my money **under control / wisely**.
  3 I'd rather **use up / build up** my savings account than waste money on things I don't really need.
  4 It's difficult to reduce **tuition fees / everyday expenses** such as food and travel.
  5 I **keep track of / cut out** my finances by writing down everything I spend.
  6 I owe my **friend / savings account** £20.
  7 If you're **on a limited budget / keeping track of your finances**, you don't have money to spend on extras.
  8 Train **fares / fees** are really expensive these days.
  9 We could try **cutting out / using up** non-essential items to save money.
  10 It's obvious that buying **accessories / second-hand stuff** is better for the environment.
  11 We need to stay calm and get our spending **cut out / under control**.
  12 The school is asking people to **make a donation to / keep track of** the school minibus fund – they hope to raise £3,000.

3 Complete the vlog with the correct form of words and phrases from the lesson.

'Hey guys, welcome back to my channel. My name's Maya Charles, and today I'll be telling you about how I've saved hundreds of dollars as a high-school student here in Australia. So, it all started when I got a job in a shop when I was fifteen, working one day every weekend and several days a week in the holidays. Although I was really excited to be earning my own money, I chose to spend it ¹_____. I spent a bit on ²_____ because that's how I like to relax with my friends, but I tried as far as possible not to buy new things. Instead, I bought ³_____, like a bike and some things for my room. It didn't bother me at all that someone else had owned these things before me. I'm grateful to my parents for encouraging me to save half of what I earned each month, because I've been able to ⁴_____. I have a goal for when I'm in my twenties, which is to buy a car and travel across the USA, and it has really focused my mind. I ⁵_____ so I always know what I've spent and what I've saved, and how close I am to reaching my goal. I've never borrowed money from anyone, and it feels good to know I'm going to be able to make my dream come true without ⁶_____ anyone anything. So that's it, guys. If I've saved all this money, I'm sure you can do the same!'

4 **REAL ENGLISH** Match the phrases below to the definitions.

> break the bank   have my eye on   it all adds up
> save for a rainy day   spend money like water
> strapped for cash

  1 be in need of money
  2 build up money for a time when you really need it
  3 watch somebody or something carefully
  4 cost a lot of money
  5 increase by small amounts until there's a large total
  6 get through money in large quantities

5 **VOCABULARY BOOSTER** Now practise **Spending and not spending money** vocabulary on page 109.

6.2 GRAMMAR

Grammar animation
GRAMMAR BOOSTER P142
Use passive forms to talk about personal finance games.

1 Read the article and choose the correct alternative.

Trending articles
Money and Finance

The gamification of personal finance

'There's a cash crisis, and it's ¹**been created / created** by a cash-strapped super-villain! Everyone's money ²**will lose / will be lost** if nothing is done! Immediate action ³**has been required / is required** to save the day!'

This is the opening sequence of an online game for teenagers called *Cash Crisis*, in which players ⁴**are taken / take part** in a mission to save the day in a graphic-novel-themed adventure. It's more than just a bit of fun, though, as players ⁵**are also taught / are also taught to** financial literacy along the way. This is an example of gamification, where aspects of everyday life, in this case financial skills, ⁶**were being turned into / are turned into** games with goals, challenges, competitions and rewards.

Finding ways to increase young people's financial literacy is important. In 2019, around 7,000 15–18-year-olds in the USA ⁷**were being tested / were tested** on their knowledge of personal finance. The test ⁸**was designed / designed** to find out how much the young people knew about earning, saving and growing wealth. The results revealed the average level of knowledge to be around 65%.

Cash Crisis is just one example of how financial skills ⁹**have been / had been** gamified in the last few years. In other gamified personal finance apps, users ¹⁰**were / are** rewarded for achieving savings goals by seeing their name on a leader board, for example, or getting new features for their digital avatar.

gamification (n) applying elements of game playing such as point scoring, competition with others, rules of play to a product or service in order to encourage people to use it
literacy (n) ability or knowledge in a specified area

2 Complete the sentences with the words and phrases below.

am	are	had already been	has been
is being	was	were being	will be

1 A savings account _____ opened in her name in 2015.
2 A lot of money _____ spent on new roads at the moment.
3 I _____ currently owed about £200.
4 You _____ asked for a £50 deposit tomorrow.
5 When I called the gym about my membership, I found out it _____ paid.
6 Billions of pounds _____ spent on takeaways in the UK every year.
7 When I switched on the TV, celebrities _____ asked to make donations to charity.
8 Our school _____ given £2,000 for new sports equipment.

3 Complete the two passive forms of each active sentence.

1 They will send her a bank card.
  A She _____ a bank card.
  B A bank card _____ her.
2 They have offered Ryan the job.
  A Ryan _____ the job.
  B The job _____ Ryan.
3 Kaheem is teaching everyone the songs.
  A _____ the songs.
  B The songs _____.
4 The official handed me my passport.
  A _____.
  B My passport _____.
5 I gave Lou and Dan access to the bank account.
  A Lou and _____.
  B _____.
6 They still owe us a considerable sum of money.
  A _____.
  B A _____.

4 Choose the correct alternative.

When verbs with two objects are used in passive sentences, it is more common for the **person or people / thing or things** to be the subject of the verb.

5 Write passive sentences using the correct form of the words in brackets.

1 I _____
   (give / a lot of accessories for my birthday). I got a bag, some sunglasses and a watch.
2 You will be shown a training video.
   _____
   (then / you / ask / questions about it).
3 A Thank you for paying for the meal yesterday.
   B That's OK. I was feeling rich. _____
      (I / just / pay)!
4 _____
   (the new app / release / today). I'm looking forward to getting it.
5 _____
   (we / lend / some bicycles). They were a great way to get around the city.
6 _____
   (she / owe / a lot of money). I hope she gets it soon.
7 A What was happening when you arrived?
   B _____
      (the / money / count).
8 _____ (the tuition fee / not / pay / yet). Someone needs to pay them.

6 Complete the sentences with your own ideas.

1 English is taught _____.
2 I have never been given _____.
3 Students are often told _____.
4 A lot of _____ are being made at the moment.
5 I think too much government money is spent on _____.
6 I don't think enough government money is spent on _____.

Unit 6

6.3 LISTENING — Draw conclusions from an interview about anti-consumerism.

1 What can you remember about the podcast in the Student's Book? Complete the sentences with the correct form of the words and phrases below.

consumerism   do without   get rid of
lead a more meaningful life   material possessions
pursue their passion

1 Minimalists believe people generally have too many _____ and blame _____ for this.
2 Joshua Fields Millburn and Ryan Nicodemus both reached a point in their lives when they realised they could _____ all these things in their lives.
3 Millburn gradually _____ his belongings and Nicodemus did it quickly.
4 When owning things was no longer important to them, each of them was able to take the time to _____ instead of remaining in their executive jobs.
5 They both wanted to share their belief that people can _____ if they have less stuff and focus instead on what's important to them.

2 Look at the photos and answer the questions.

1 What's the woman in the first photo doing? Why is she doing this?
2 What does the second photo mean? Do you agree?

3 🔊 6.02 Listen to part of a radio programme about consumerism. Who makes these points, Millie (M) or Omar (O)?

sustainability (n) the ability to avoid using too many natural resources in order to protect the environment

1 A lot of influencers used to make videos about their material possessions. ___
2 When I think about stuff, I think about the production process. ___
3 The feeling of happiness created by material possessions doesn't last long. ___
4 I need my phone. ___
5 I don't buy things I don't need. ___
6 More people will buy 'pre-loved' (second-hand) clothes in the future. ___

STRATEGY Drawing conclusions from what we hear
Listening texts contain information that is not directly stated but can be inferred from the information we are given. We can understand and draw conclusions from the information by thinking about the context and analysing what we have heard.

4 🔊 6.02 Read the strategy above and the statements below. Listen again and choose the correct answer: A, B or C. Which information from the recording allows you to infer this?
1 Millie ___ people know what 'Gen Z' means.
   A thinks   B doesn't think   C isn't sure
2 In about 2017, Millie ___ watching YouTube videos about other people's purchases, or 'hauls'.
   A wanted to stop   B never really liked   C used to enjoy
3 As Millie grew older, she ___.
   A became frustrated that she didn't have as much money as other people
   B developed an interest in environmental issues
   C started making her own 'haul' videos
4 Omar thinks ___.
   A teenagers' attitudes towards brands has remained the same
   B some people need to change their beliefs about what teenagers care about
   C teenagers should be more careful about how they spend their money
5 In relation to consumerism, Omar feels ___ about teenagers' mental health nowadays.
   A depressed   B anxious   C hopeful
6 ___ thinks consumerism is encouraged by mobile phone use.
   A Millie   B Omar   C Neither Omar nor Millie
7 Millie wants her videos to ___ people.
   A inspire   B entertain   C worry
8 Millie ___.
   A prefers second-hand clothes to new ones
   B has enough money to spend on clothes
   C would buy expensive brands if she had more money

5 🔊 6.02 Listen again and complete the sentences with one to three words or numbers in each gap.
1 Millie was born between the late _____ and early _____.
2 She sometimes used to watch children doing reviews of _____ on YouTube.
3 She thinks people turned against consumerist videos because of a growing awareness of _____.
4 Omar points out that teenagers question the _____ they see on their phones.
5 Instead of making 'haul' videos, Millie makes _____ videos.
6 People are also making videos about _____ stuff.

6 Do you think you are a typical 'Gen Z' in relation to shopping and fashion? Why? / Why not? Write a paragraph, giving examples. Think about the points below.

advertising   brands   fashion
second-hand clothes   videos

64 Unit 6

Talk about shopping trends.

6.4 VOCABULARY

1 a Match 1–6 to A–F to make compound nouns.
1 retail ___ A number
2 potential ___ B offer
3 reference ___ C customers
4 confirmation ___ D email
5 shipping ___ E price
6 special ___ F costs

b 🔊 6.03 Listen and check.

2 a **PRONUNCIATION** Complete the table with the compound nouns in Ex 1.

Pronunciation of compound nouns	
When the first part of a compound noun is a noun or a verb, the stress is on the first part.	When the first part of a compound noun is an adjective, the stress is on the second part.
1 _____	5 _____
2 _____	6 _____
3 _____	
4 _____	

b 🔊 6.04 Listen and check.

3 Complete the sentences with the compound nouns in Ex 1 and 2.
1 You'll be sent a _____ with details of your order in the next two hours.
2 I was looking for a new tablet online and I saw a _____. I should have bought it then because a few hours later the price had gone back up.
3 I hadn't checked the _____, so I ended up spending about £10 more than I'd planned.
4 Social media is a great way for companies to inform _____ about their products.
5 I was given a six-digit _____.
6 It certainly seems like a bargain, but have you checked the normal _____ online?

4 Are the sentences true (T) or false (F)?
1 If you want to pick up a bargain, you should look out for special offers. T ☐ F ☐
2 You proceed to the checkout and then you add items to the basket. T ☐ F ☐
3 You get a confirmation email before you purchase a product. T ☐ F ☐
4 Customers should consider the shipping costs when choosing a delivery option. T ☐ F ☐
5 If you've paid above the retail price, then you've definitely picked up a bargain. T ☐ F ☐
6 Generally, it's difficult to track a package if you don't have a reference number for it. T ☐ F ☐

5 Complete the sentences with the correct form of the verbs below.

| add   carry out   choose   pick up |
| proceed   purchase   select   track |

1 Most consumers go through the same basic steps when deciding to _____ a product.
2 I made a mistake when I _____ the item to the basket.
3 If you _____ your package, you would have known when it was going to arrive.
4 I'm hoping to _____ some bargains in the sales.
5 There are three delivery options to _____ from.
6 Now you need to _____ to the checkout.
7 People _____ many more transactions online during the pandemic.
8 Make sure you _____ the right quantity.

6 🔊 6.05 Listen to six people talking and answer the questions. Use vocabulary from the lesson.
1 What has Amina lost? _____
2 Why is Carl pleased? He _____.
3 What is Billy waiting for? _____
4 Why does Katrina mention £40? _____
5 What is Lily trying to do? _____
6 Why does Marc mention $7.99? _____

7 Complete the review with the correct form of words and phrases from the lesson. Sometimes more than one answer is possible.

SHOPPING / YOUR REVIEWS

👤 Supershopper101

MY CASHLESS SHOPPING EXPERIENCE

Shopping in cashless stores means you can ¹_____ without having to queue up and pay. Last week, I had my first experience of this brand-new way of shopping in one of Amazon's cashless stores. You can't ²_____ in a cashless store unless you have the app downloaded on your phone. Once I'd sorted that out, all I had to do was scan a code as I entered the store and then put my phone away. It was absolutely brilliant! Every time I took something from the shelf, the app automatically ³_____. There was no need to ⁴_____ to the checkout because there was no checkout! I simply walked out of the store with my purchases. Later, instead of the kind of ⁵_____ you receive when you order something online, I got an email with information about what I'd bought and how much I'd spent. There were cameras everywhere, and it did feel a bit like stealing when I left the store without paying. Overall, though, it was a quick and easy way to shop, and there must be lots of ⁶_____ out there who would love this convenient way of shopping.

8 **VOCABULARY BOOSTER** Now practise **Shopping trends** vocabulary on page 109.

Unit 6   65

6.5 GRAMMAR

Use advanced passives to talk about community currencies.

▶ Grammar animation
GRAMMAR BOOSTER P143

1 Choose the correct answer: A, B or C.

1 I don't like ___ asked for money in the street.
   A be   B being   C to have been
2 This ticket must ___ used by the end of the month.
   A be   B have been   C being
3 It ___ keeping track of your finances helps you spend your money more wisely.
   A is generally believed that   B is generally believed so   C is generally believed to
4 The confirmation email should ___ sent by now.
   A being   B to be   C have been
5 It feels fantastic ___ paid at last!
   A to have been   B have been   C be
6 I needed ___ taught how to look after my finances.
   A be   B to be   C being
7 The politician was angry about ___ asked about his finances on live TV.
   A be   B to be   C being
8 The first formal banks ___ have been established in Italy in the 14th century.
   A are thought to   B are thought   C are thought that

2 Complete the article with the correct form of the verbs in brackets. Add *that* where necessary.

Community currencies

A community currency is a local currency that can only ¹_____ (use) in a certain area at shops and other businesses that have agreed to accept it as an alternative to the official, national currency. It ²_____ (believe) these currencies strengthen the local economy.

Zoe Waters runs a zero-waste shop in Brixton, an area of London with a local currency, the Brixton pound. 'I always like ³_____ (pay) with the Brixton pound,' says Zoe. 'It's a positive reminder that people are shopping locally rather than going online to spend their money with a big global organisation like Amazon.'

The first local currency ⁴_____ (say / be) the Swiss WIR, which was set up in 1934. Nowadays, community currencies are used in many parts of the world. One area of Mombasa, Kenya's second-largest city, has a local currency called Bangla-Pesa. Businesses in the area are helped by ⁵_____ (give) 400 Bangla-Pesas each month. This is particularly helpful for businesses that are in difficulty, as one restaurant worker explains. 'My boss was struggling to afford the food he needed to stay open. That changed when he started receiving Bangla-Pesas each month. Until then, I could ⁶_____ (tell) any day there was no more work for me, but now my job is secure. And, of course, the food sellers at the market benefit too.'

It seems likely that local currencies will be used in many more areas in the future to build local economic resilience.

3 Complete the second sentence so that it means the same as the first. Use between two and five words including the word in brackets.

1 They might ask you to make a donation. (ASKED)
   You _____ to make a donation.
2 It feels good when someone offers you a job. (BE)
   It feels good _____ a job.
3 I'm sure they've paid you by now. (MUST)
   You _____ by now.
4 It isn't a problem for me when people owe me small amounts of money. (MIND)
   I don't _____ small amounts of money.
5 I want them to tell me clearly what the shipping costs are. (TOLD)
   I want _____ what the shipping costs are.
6 She was afraid that someone would ask her about her finances. (OF)
   She was afraid _____ her finances.
7 We think people first used coins about 2,600 years ago. (THOUGHT)
   It _____ people first used coins about 2,600 years ago.
8 People think his grandfather left him a fortune. (BELIEVED)
   He _____ left a fortune by his grandfather.

4 Complete the sentences with your own ideas. Use passive forms from this lesson. You can use some of the verbs below.

| ask be give owe pay send teach tell |

1 It's nice _____.
2 I hate _____.
3 I'd love to _____.
4 I don't mind _____.
5 I'm looking forward to _____.
6 Money is sometimes said _____.

zero-waste shop (*n*) a shop that sells products that have been made using processes that create as little waste as possible, e.g. by using materials that have been and/or can be recycled

66 Unit 6

Recognise functional language to identify purpose in four texts.

6.6 READING

1 What can you remember about the four texts in the Student's Book? Complete the text with the words below.

| designer label   fashion-conscious   garments
| get dressed up   kit   mix and match
| outfits   stylish

Text 1 explains how fast fashion meets consumer demand for **1**_____ that are both fashionable and cheap.
Text 2 talks about new football **2**_____ such as a **3**_____ 'home' shirt which uses a 3D effect.
Text 3 suggests a clothing rental service for people who want to wear **4**_____ clothing without spending too much money. Customers who want to **5**_____ can rent different **6**_____ or **7**_____ individual items with their existing clothes.
Text 4 describes a superstore in Dundee, Scotland, where **8**_____ residents can buy from a huge range of second-hand clothing.

2 Are the statements generally true of shopping in physical stores (*P*), online stores (*O*) or both (*B*)?
1 You can smell and touch products. ___
2 Technology gives a quick and easy shopping experience. ___
3 There are lots of attractive products to choose from. ___
4 You can have interesting conversations with sales assistants. ___
5 You can use interactive technology. ___
6 You take photos of yourself with the products. ___

> **STRATEGY** Recognising functional language to identify purpose
>
> When you read a text for the first time, look out for fixed expressions that indicate the writer's reason for writing. For example, if the writer's purpose is to advise, the text will probably contain the expression *You should …* . Knowing the reason for writing will help you better understand the text.

3 🔊 **6.06** Read the strategy above. Read the four texts and choose the purpose of each text: A, B, C or D.

A 1 to entertain   2 to argue   3 to instruct   4 to persuade
B 1 to describe   2 to instruct 3 to argue   4 to persuade
C 1 to inform   2 to entertain 3 to persuade   4 to argue
D 1 to entertain   2 to argue   3 to review   4 to instruct

4 Read the texts again. Match questions 1–8 to texts A–D.
Text …
1 ___ focuses on the interaction between a consumer and an employee in a store.
2 ___ gives the pros and cons of one particular store.
3 ___ describes a technology that helps consumers choose products quickly.
4 ___ suggests that our retail experiences will become more interesting.
5 ___ explains how changes to the experience of physical retail are being introduced in one country.
6 ___ mentions a product in store that catches the consumer's attention.
7 ___ gives information about the process of one immersive retail experience from start to finish.
8 ___ invites the reader to try a new piece of technology.

5 Which of the immersive retail experiences described in texts A–D appeals to you most? Why? Write a short paragraph.

A VIRTUAL MIRROR

In our fabulous stores, you can try on ten different make-up looks and find one you LOVE in a matter of seconds – all without applying a single stroke of lipstick!

Our Marvellous Mirror has transformed your shopping experience. The digitally innovative touchscreen allows you to interact with and experience each of our stunning ten looks. Which will suit you best? Have a look in the virtual mirror and see!

The Marvellous Mirror is perfect whether you need to make a quick decision about which product to buy, or want to find a whole new gorgeous look for yourself!

B BOOKS, BOOKS, BOOKS

I was very fortunate to be given the opportunity to visit a Reading Spa at Books by the Sea bookshop.

On my arrival, I was introduced to Becky, an extremely skilled, friendly and knowledgeable sales assistant. We sat and discussed my reading likes and dislikes for about an hour, and I was offered tea and cake. I was then left to browse the shelves while Becky went off and made a selection for me.

When Becky returned with a pile of books, I was thrilled to see so many appealing books I'd never heard of before. The hardest part was choosing which ones to take home with me!

C Experiential retail

While online shopping has gained popularity in recent years, physical stores still have an important place in retail. Of particular interest is immersive retail, which offers consumers the opportunity to experience products through all of their senses, often using technology such as virtual reality, and which is expected to grow rapidly in the coming years.

China is leading the way, with physical stores being adapted to create interesting and unique experiences for customers. Fitting rooms, for example, are equipped with an artificial intelligence system called FashionAI, and smart touchscreen mirrors are used to personalise customers' style choices, offering mix-and-match suggestions and alternative items.

D Amazing shop

One of my favourite shops is Rosa and Stone. It's basically a lifestyle and design store with a wide range of products, including some incredibly cool second-hand stuff. What I like most about the store is how products are presented. Furniture and other products are displayed with men and women's clothing and accessories in a large, bright, white space.

What really stands out is the item right in the middle of the shop – it's always a classic car from the 1960s in perfect condition. These are actually bought by customers from time to time, so it's always worth popping in to see what's there for a 'me-with-another-cool-car' Instagram photo. The store isn't cheap, but I would still definitely recommend a visit.

6.7 GLOBAL SKILLS
Understand and discuss the importance of the small print.

1 What can you remember about the reading and listening in the Student's Book? Complete the sentences.
   1 Most companies present their t_____ and c_____ (legal agreements between a service provider and potential service user), including their r_____ p_____ (what they do when a customer doesn't want to keep a product they've bought from them), on their website.
   2 If you buy something and it's f_____ (not working properly), you should be able to take it back to where you bought it and get a r_____ (money back) as long as you can p_____ (demonstrate with evidence) that you bought it there. You'll need to show your r_____ (document that shows that you have paid; informal) or other p_____ of p_____ (document that shows that you have paid; formal).
   3 When you buy a new electronic gadget, you should keep the w_____ i_____ (written promise given by a manufacturer to the purchaser of one of their objects to repair or replace it if necessary within a certain period of time) in a safe place.
   4 If you see a special promotion online, don't give your details unless you're sure it's g_____ (real).
   5 If you're thinking of getting a s_____-t_____ l_____ (money that is borrowed to provide temporary help), be aware some companies charge very high i_____ r_____ (the amount a lender charges on top of the main amount of money borrowed).

2 Read the article and match headings A–E to paragraphs 1–5.
   A Do your research
   B Keep your receipts
   C Learn how to haggle
   D Consider quality vs quantity
   E Spend your money wisely

3 Read the situations and complete the sentences with ideas from the text.
   1 Sami spent £200 on some new trainers, which the salesperson told him really suited him. Now he's worried that he spent too much on the trainers, because he can't afford to buy anything else.
      A He should have _____ before he went shopping.
      B He shouldn't have _____ the salesperson.
   2 Elena suddenly decided to buy herself a laptop when she was at the shops. When she got it home, she realised it was very slow and didn't have much memory.
      A She should have _____ before she bought it.
      B She could have _____ online or in magazines.
   3 Alisha was pleased with her purchase of some cheap headphones, but they broke after she'd used them a few times.
      She should have remembered that things that are cheap aren't always good _____.
   4 Last Saturday morning, Max paid £30 for some sunglasses at the market. The next day, he found out his friend had paid just £15 for the same sunglasses from the same seller at the end of the day.
      Max should have _____.
      He should have gone to the market _____.
   5 Robbie couldn't get a refund for a tennis racket he'd bought because he lost the receipt.
      He should have _____.

4 **MEDIATION** Your friend Emma has been saving up for two years to buy a motorbike. She is now ready to buy one and has sent you a photo of a cheap one that she has seen that she is interested in buying. Write an email to her with advice based on information in this lesson.

How to be a savvy consumer

However much you might want to reduce the amount of stuff you buy, there are always going to be things you need. There is such a big choice of products and services on offer that it's more important than ever to be a savvy consumer. Here are our top tips.

1 ___
Set your budget before you go shopping. When you're considering buying an item, decide if you really need it, and don't be persuaded by a salesperson into buying something you don't really want or need.

2 ___
This is especially important if you're planning on purchasing an expensive product, when you want quality and reliability for the money you spend. Read online reviews of the products you're considering, although keep in mind that some of the reviews might have been written by the seller!

3 ___
Remember the difference between price and value. Just because something is cheap, it doesn't mean it's a bargain. It's better to buy a few good products that last a long time and bring you pleasure than lots of cheap and badly made items.

4 ___
You might not be able to negotiate the price of your supermarket essentials, but if you're buying something more expensive, like a car, it's worth trying to get the price down. Markets are a great place to negotiate a bargain, but you can try it in shops too. The best time is usually at the end of the day, or any time when it's quiet. Remember, you can also negotiate the price of things like your gym membership.

5 ___
Store them in a safe place as you'll need them as proof of purchase if you have problems at a later date. A clear photo may be accepted as proof of purchase, but we recommend keeping the paper (or emailed) version.

haggle (v) discuss the cost of something with the seller in order to find a price that feels right for both of you
savvy (adj) (informal) having practical knowledge or understanding of something

Use the correct register to assert your rights as a customer.

6.8 SPEAKING

1 Look at the photos. Why might a customer be unhappy with each product?

2 a Complete the dialogues with the words below.

1

| acceptable   be entitled   exchange   manager |
| solution   switch on |

Geeta	Hi. I'd like to ¹_____ these wireless headphones for another pair.
Sales assistant	Could I ask what the problem is?
Geeta	Yes, they won't ²_____.
Sales assistant	Oh. Can I have a look?
Geeta	Sure.
Sales assistant	Hmm. I see what you mean. Is the battery fully charged?
Geeta	Yes.
Sales assistant	Well, if you leave them with us, I'll get one of our in-store technicians to have a look at them in the next couple of days.
Geeta	But I need them today.
Sales assistant	That's all I can offer, I'm afraid. We haven't got any more of these headphones in stock at the moment.
Geeta	Well, it really isn't an acceptable ³_____. I should ⁴_____ to an exchange or a full refund. Can I speak to the ⁵_____, please?
Sales assistant	Wait, do you have your receipt?
Geeta	Yes, it's here.
Sales assistant	Would a refund be ⁶_____?
Geeta	Well, I'd rather have a pair of headphones that work, but yes, that would be fine. Thank you.
Sales assistant	OK, I'll get that processed for you.
Geeta	Thanks.

2

| authorise   customer service   quality   receipt |
| refund   return   right   senior member |

Adam	Hello. I'd like to ⁷_____ this shirt.
Sales assistant	OK, sure. Can I ask why?
Adam	Three of the buttons have come off since I bought it. Look.
Sales assistant	I see. How long ago did you buy it?
Adam	About three weeks ago. I've only worn it twice.
Sales assistant	Could the buttons be sewn back on?
Adam	I don't see why I should have to. Plus, I've lost one of them, anyway.
Sales assistant	OK. Well, we can exchange it for you.
Adam	I'd rather have a ⁸_____.
Sales assistant	Do you have your ⁹_____?
Adam	No, I don't. I didn't keep it because I didn't think I'd need to return the shirt. I basically like it. I think I have the ¹⁰_____ to a refund, though, because I'm really not satisfied with the ¹¹_____ of the product.
Sales assistant	I can't ¹²_____ a refund without a receipt, I'm afraid. I can offer you an exchange, though.
Adam	Well, I must say, I'm disappointed by your ¹³_____. Please can I speak to a more ¹⁴_____ of staff?
Sales assistant	Yes, of course.

b 🔊 6.07 Listen and check.

3 🔊 6.07 Listen to and read the two dialogues again and write *Geeta* or *Adam*.

1 _____ has tried everything to solve the problem.
2 _____ has used the product.
3 _____ has got proof of purchase.
4 _____ isn't happy with the solution offered.

STRATEGY Register

How we say something can be as important as what we say. Choosing the appropriate register for a situation can signal our respect and intention to be polite, even when we are making a complaint. Choosing the wrong register can appear rude. For example:
wrong register: *What did you say?*
right register: *Would you mind saying that again?*
wrong register: *No, I don't want that.*
right register: *I'm afraid that isn't acceptable.*

4 Read the strategy above. Complete the polite phrases for talking about consumer issues.

1 I'd _____ to return these sunglasses.
2 I'm _____ I don't have the proof of purchase.
3 Can I _____ it for another colour?
4 I'd _____ have a refund.
5 _____ to your returns policy, I'm entitled to a refund.
6 I'm afraid I'm not _____ with the service I've been offered.

5 Complete the situation below with your own ideas.

Bako bought _____ in a shop last _____, but when he got home, he realised _____ and he needs to return it / them. He _____ proof of purchase. He is visiting the shop to get a solution. He wants _____. The shop assistant _____. Bako _____ happy with the solution. He expresses his feelings about the process.

6 Use the ideas in Ex 5 to write a dialogue between Bako and the shop assistant. Use language from the lesson and the correct register.

Unit 6   69

6.9 WRITING
Order points into a coherent argument in a for and against essay.

1 Look at the photos. What is happening? How might the two photos be connected?

2 Read the task and essay. Match sentences A–F to gaps 1–6 in the essay.

A What is more, it's possible to make a lot of money by selling used things online.
B Moreover, selling your old clothes is better for the environment than throwing them away as they don't go straight to landfill.
C In conclusion, selling second-hand clothes and accessories online is great for people who have a good eye for style, don't mind the time it takes and like dealing with people.
D Furthermore, buyers can be difficult, for example, agreeing to buy something but then not paying for it.
E The question is whether it's really worth it, given how much effort it takes.
F Having said that, there are disadvantages to selling things online.

> You've been talking in class about the potential benefits of selling second-hand stuff online. Now your teacher has asked you to write an essay exploring the arguments for and against selling second-hand clothes and accessories online.

> There's a big market for second-hand clothes and other accessories online and many people enjoy selling pre-owned, or 'pre-loved', stuff through online shops and auctions. ¹___
>
> It's true that a lot of people like selling their old clothes and accessories because it motivates them to clear out their wardrobe regularly. ²___ Selling online is quicker and easier than selling in person and allows you to reach large numbers of potential customers. ³___ Some people make thousands of pounds each month selling vintage clothes they've bought at charity shops.
>
> ⁴___ It's time-consuming to clean, photograph and write descriptions of what you're selling, and you won't always be paid as much as you hope for. ⁵___ Also, unwanted items could be given to charity shops instead. This would help people who don't have much money for clothes and raise money for the charity.
>
> ⁶___ However, it can take a huge amount of effort, and many of its benefits, such as motivating people to clear out their wardrobe and helping the environment, can be achieved by donating unwanted items to charity shops, an act which is extremely beneficial to others.

> **vintage clothes** (n) good-quality clothes from the past that represent a particular period of fashion

3 Read the whole essay again. Do you agree with the writer's opinion? Why? / Why not?

STRATEGY Ordering points into a coherent argument

After you have chosen the points that you are going to use to support and oppose the topic, you need to put them in order. Ask yourself these questions:
1 Which is the strongest point in each case? (You can use this point to start or finish the paragraph.)
2 Which points logically come after each other?
3 Could any of the points be joined into one sentence?

Ordering your points will make it easier for the reader to follow your argument.

4 Read the strategy above. Follow the instructions.
Find and underline …
1 the sentence in which the author presents their strongest supporting argument.
2 the sentence which contains two separate supporting arguments.
3 the sentence which contains two separate opposing arguments.
4 two opposing arguments which logically follow the argument before it and are in separate sentences.

5 Complete the phrases used in for and against essays.
1 M_____y people … M_____t people …
2 It is often s_____ that … It is t_____ that … It can't be d_____ that …
3 Also, … Besides, … In a_____ … … as w_____ as …
4 Having s_____ that, … In c_____, … On the o_____ hand, …
5 In conclusion, … To c_____, … To s_____ u_____, …

6 Read the task and answer the questions.

> You've been talking in class about the potential benefits of people using electronic payments instead of cash. Now your teacher has asked you to write an essay exploring the pros and cons of a cashless society.

1 Where do you use cash?
2 Where is electronic payment used these days?
3 What's your opinion about the topic? Why?

7 What are the points in favour of / against the topic? Think about the points below and your own ideas and make notes.

> convenience   crime   freedom
> hygiene (cash is touched by lots of different people)
> people who don't have access to bank accounts and banks
> the emotional value of cash   the storing of notes and coins

8 Plan a four-paragraph for and against essay. Order your points into a coherent argument.

9 Write your essay.

10 ✓ **CHECK YOUR WORK** Did you …
- write four paragraphs?
- order your points into a coherent argument?
- include passive structures?
- check spelling, grammar and punctuation?

6.10 REVIEW

Grammar

1 Complete the second sentence using the passive so that it means the same as the first.
1. They released the new app last week.
   The new app _____ yesterday.
2. They are repairing the windows at the bank.
   The windows at the bank _____.
3. He had cancelled the payment.
   The payment _____.
4. They haven't shown us the video yet.
   We _____ the video yet.
5. Someone was counting the money.
   The money _____.
6. They'll offer you free financial advice.
   You _____ free financial advice.
7. Millions of people visit the website every day.
   The website _____ by millions of people every day.
8. She gave Sam the bank card.
   The bank card _____ Sam.

2 Complete the sentences with the correct form of *be*.
1. It's unusual _____ asked how much money you've got.
2. It _____ often thought that online shopping saves people time, but this isn't always true.
3. We should _____ taught more about personal finances when we were at school.
4. I don't like _____ owed money.
5. I hope _____ offered the job.
6. These banknotes are thought _____ made about 600 years ago.
7. I'm fed up with _____ told what to do.
8. The money should _____ transferred to your account today.

Vocabulary

3 Complete the sentences with the words below.

| account budget fares fees membership |
| non-essentials second-hand spending |

1. The tuition _____ are very expensive.
2. How much is your gym _____?
3. I need to get my _____ under control.
4. Sami buys a lot of _____ clothes.
5. I don't have to pay any bus _____ because I cycle everywhere.
6. Amira's working so that she can build up her savings _____.
7. I'd like to buy a ticket, but I'm on a limited _____ this month.
8. I'm trying to save money by cutting out _____, like snacks.

4 Complete the sentences.
1. The r_____ n_____ is 988842106K.
2. You need to c_____ a d_____ o_____ – tomorrow or three to five working days.
3. If you t_____ your p_____, you'll know when it arrives.
4. Did you s_____ the r_____ q_____? We only need three.
5. There are hundreds of s_____ o_____ in store and on sale today!
6. I managed to p_____ a b_____ –this shirt was only £8.
7. You'll receive a c_____ e_____ shortly with all the details of your order.
8. We use advertising on social media to reach p_____ c_____.

Cumulative review

5 Choose the correct answer: A, B or C.

Did you know … ?
- If the first thing you ¹___ when you go shopping is something on your shopping list, you're more likely to buy something that isn't on your list later on.
- Shopping malls ²___ built without windows and clocks so that shoppers don't notice how long they spend there. So next time you're at a mall, watch the time as well as ³___ your finances!
- Old coins and other treasure can ⁴___ found anywhere. In September 2021, divers cleaning up rubbish at the bottom of the sea off the coast of Spain found 53 2,000-year-old coins. Experts believe the coins may ⁵___ hidden there by people who were worried about people stealing them. Keep your eyes open!
- In China, 11 November is Singles' Day, when single people (people not in a relationship) ⁶___ bought and sent gifts – not by other people, but by themselves!
- In early societies ⁷___ was believed that jewellery could protect you from bad luck and illness. These days, many luxury fashion brands make more money from selling ⁸___ such as bags, belts, sunglasses and jewellery than clothes.
- The main reason for shoppers ⁹___ something to their online basket but then not ¹⁰___ to pay is high ¹¹___.
- People must feel most kind and generous at the end of the year, because most ¹²___ are made in December.

1	A purchase	B spend	C use up
2	A had been	B are	C must be
3	A using up	B keeping track of	C building up
4	A be	B have been	C being
5	A to be	B be	C have been
6	A did	B are	C might
7	A it	B what	C this
8	A accessories	B everyday expenses	C special offers
9	A selecting	B picking up	C adding
10	A carrying out	B proceeding	C tracking
11	A shipping costs	B retail price	C potential customers
12	A takeaways	B non-essentials	C charity donations

REFLECT Think about the following questions.
1. Which lesson in this unit did you enjoy the most? Why?
2. Which of the grammar points did you find most difficult?
3. How can you be a wiser consumer?

Unit 6 71

5-6 EXAM SKILLS

Listening

EXAM STRATEGY

When you do a multiple-matching task, read the options carefully and make sure you fully understand their whole meaning. That way you won't be tempted to make a choice simply because you hear a repeated word.

1 Read the strategy above. Then read the exam task in Ex 2. Read explanations 1–3. Which of the options (A–H) do they match?
 1 I want some useful information about money.
 2 I wish I'd behaved differently with my money.
 3 I'm in debt to people I know.

2 ◆ 6.08 You will hear five short extracts in which people are talking about money. Match the speakers (1–5) to the list of statements (A–H). Use the letters only once. There are three statements which you do not need.

Speaker 1: ___
Speaker 2: ___
Speaker 3: ___
Speaker 4: ___
Speaker 5: ___

A I'm saving for something big.
B I'm planning to get some financial advice.
C I never think about how much I spend.
D I regret the things I've done financially.
E I want to be independent in the future.
F I'm worried about changing my circumstances.
G I owe my family and friends a lot of money.
H I make plans if things are going wrong.

Use of English

EXAM STRATEGY

Prepare for key-word transformation tasks by becoming familiar with the type of language points that are often tested, e.g. direct / reported speech, active / passive, past simple / present perfect, etc. Make a list and add to it each time you come across something new.

3 Read the strategy above. Then read the exam task in Ex 4. Read the first pair of sentences. Which language point is being tested?

4 For each question, complete the second sentence so that it has a similar meaning to the first sentence, using the word given. You must use between two and five words, including the word given.

1 Most people know that taking a short-term loan results in high interest.
 WIDELY
 It _____ that taking a short-term loan results in high interest.

2 They are advertising more and more special offers on their website every day.
 ARE
 More and more special offers _____ on their website every day.

3 My savings grew after I stopped buying non-essentials.
 HAVE
 My savings _____ since I stopped buying non-essentials.

4 We will send you details of your new account next week.
 BE
 Details of your new account _____ next week.

5 I advise you to open a savings account.
 TO
 I think you _____ a savings account.

Reading

EXAM STRATEGY

When you do a missing-sentences task, look for connecting words in the sentences. These may give you a clue about what should come before or after the sentences in the text.

5 Read the strategy above. Then read the exam task in Ex 6. Look at the sentences (A–I) and find three connecting words. What is their purpose: contrast, consequence or additional information?

6 Six sentences have been removed from the article. Choose the correct sentence (A–I) to fill the gaps (1–6). There are three extra sentences which you do not need.

Living off grid

Have you ever wanted to give up all your comforts and live a more basic way of life? [1]___ The idea is being adopted by more and more people who have decided that they want to escape their busy lives and live off grid. So, what exactly does this mean? The 'grid' refers to the necessities of modern living that are visible. [2]___ The term also refers to things that you can't see such as the financial system and food supply.

It's generally thought that people who want to escape this kind of modern living do so because they want to protect the planet. They are looking for a more sustainable way of life which doesn't damage the environment.
[3]___ For some, it's because they are fed up with feeling stressed. They want to get away from supermarkets and traffic jams, to feel closer to nature or to find a sense of community which they are unable to find in cities and towns. Or they are driven by money concerns, such as losing their jobs, being in debt or being unable to afford

5–6 EXAM SKILLS

their rent. ⁴___ This is when people feel worried about their lives and decide to find an alternative and cheaper way to live.

Nick Rosen, who is an American campaigner and documentary maker, has written extensively on the topic. He has travelled around and spoken to both individuals and people living in different off-grid communities. ⁵___ His books give advice to those who want to follow a similar lifestyle.

Of course, there are different ways you can go off grid. You might choose to give up all modern comforts provided by society, by generating your own electricity, collecting rainwater and growing your own food. Or you might prefer to maintain some modern comforts and give up others. For example, you can travel around or live in a house or a hut and still be considered living off grid. One community in Somerset, England, called Tinkers Bubble, have made a big commitment. ⁶___ The group has very little contact with any kind of modern life.

Whichever way people choose to live off grid, there's no doubt that the attraction for living close to nature is becoming more and more popular.

A This particular motivation naturally increases in times of financial crisis.
B Nobody enjoys living without any modern comforts.
C They have chosen to be completely independent of modern life and spend their days farming, looking after their homes and cooking.
D These include things like phone wires, TV and internet cables, roads and water systems.
E If you have ever considered this, you are not alone.
F The best thing to do is to give up the idea and move back to a town or a city.
G As a result, he has also become an expert on the subject.
H It is no longer sustainable for people around the world to live in urban areas.
I However, there are other reasons why people make the decision to live a simpler life.

Speaking

EXAM STRATEGY

When you compare two photos, you may be asked to talk about the advantages and disadvantages of an activity or situation. Make sure you give a balanced view with points for either side.

7 Read the strategy above. Then read the exam task in Ex 8 and look at the photos. Write notes expressing two advantages and two disadvantages for both ways of shopping.

8 Work in pairs. Look at the two photos of different ways to shop. Compare the photos and describe the advantages and disadvantages of each.

Writing

EXAM STRATEGY

Prepare for writing formal emails and letters, such as letters of complaint, by learning suitable fixed expressions and phrases that you can use.

9 Read the strategy above. Then complete the sentences with the words below.

| appropriate   circumstances   dissatisfaction
| forward   regret   unfortunately

1 I am writing to express my _____ with …
2 _____, a number of things were wrong.
3 I _____ to say that when I called …
4 Under the _____ I feel it would be _____ if …
5 I look _____ to hearing from you.

10 You bought a smartphone online which arrived with a number of faults. You rang the company two weeks ago to ask them to send you another one, but you have not received it yet. Write a letter to the company using suitable expressions in which you …
- explain why you are writing.
- say what is wrong with the phone.
- describe what happened when you called.
- ask them for action.

Unit 6   73

7.1 VOCABULARY Talk about different art forms.

All about art

1 a What can you remember about the vlog? Complete the summary.

Zaki didn't like the sound of the exhibition ¹o_____ d_____ at their local gallery. He also pointed out that the gallery did not contain any great ²m_____ to look at.

Joe said that ³s_____ a_____ could be found in street art, which often combines ⁴g_____ c_____ with political statements or jokes. Joe recommended a walking tour of Liverpool, which has ⁵s_____ p_____ o_____ w_____ on its streets. In fact, some ⁶a_____ c_____ say Liverpool is the best city in the world for street art.

Daisy suggested an arts festival where they could watch various performances and also ⁷v_____ e_____. She had visited the Manchester International Festival and remembered a dance group who ⁸g_____ a_____ o_____ p_____.

b 7.01 Watch or listen again and check.

2 Complete the adverts with the correct form of the phrases in Ex 1.

Would you like to ¹_____ at Oslo's sculpture gardens? Or see the world-famous paintings ²_____ at the Louvre gallery in Paris? Try one of our virtual guided tours, each presented by a respected ³_____. You will learn more about celebrated ⁴_____ and ⁵_____ from around the world.

Look at the ⁶_____ and skilful technique in this picture! This was created by @gladys_art, who completed our online beginners' art course. Follow our online videos and you too can produce ⁷_____ in just eight weeks.

If you live near Brighton, why not join one of our online singing groups? We meet virtually once a week to sing a wide variety of songs. At the end of each year, our online groups join together to ⁸_____ at Stoller Hall. Why not buy a ticket for this year's event?

3 **REAL ENGLISH** Match the phrases below to the definitions.

| I didn't get it   I was blown away   it does nothing for me
| that's my kind of thing   well worth seeing

1 not improve in any way
2 really impressed
3 not understand
4 enjoyable despite the effort
5 something you like to do

4 Read the online post and comments. Match **bold** phrases 1–8 to art forms A–H.

Alex
6 hours ago

Hi everyone! I tried a ¹**computer headset that creates realistic images and sounds** for the first time today. We used it in art class to take a tour of the Museum of Modern Art in New York. What have you seen in VR?
6 comments

VR is an amazing way to explore ²**paintings, drawings, sculpture, etc**. Have you tried the VR version of Hokusai's masterpiece *The Great Wave Off Kanagawa*?

I went to a VR ³**music performance that you watch as it happens**. It was strange but good!

VR is also being used in ⁴**acting, dance, music, etc**. I watched a piece of ⁵**movement art combining elements of ballet and more modern techniques** called *Dust*. I was blown away!

Have you ever seen the ⁶**show involving songs and dances as part of a story** of *The Lion King*? There's an excellent VR experience of the opening song from the show.

You can use VR to create your own art. The tools are simple, and you can make ⁷**a painting / a sculpture that does not try to show the shape of people or things precisely** easily.

I'm looking forward to the new ⁸**version of a familiar story presented for the theatre** of the Sherlock Holmes books. Parts of the show will involve VR.

A abstract art ___
B live gig ___
C musical production ___
D stage adaptation ___
E VR headset ___
F contemporary dance ___
G the performing arts ___
H the visual arts ___

5 **VOCABULARY BOOSTER** Now practise **Different art forms** vocabulary on page 110.

7.2 GRAMMAR

Grammar animation
GRAMMAR BOOSTER P144

Use reported speech to ask about and report opinions.

1 Look at the photos and answer the questions.
1 What is public art for?
2 Do you think the examples shown here are good art?
3 Do you think the artists were paid for their work?

A Chopin Statue, Warsaw

B Dinky Doors, Cambridge

C Street art, Palermo district of Buenos Aires

2 🔊 **7.02** Listen to the speakers. Match the dialogues to the photos.
1 ___ 2 ___ 3 ___

3 Read Freya's email and find four examples of reported speech.

Hi Aunty,

I'm really enjoying my stay in beautiful Cambridge. Nisha said she'd show me around. I'm also exploring by myself.

Yesterday, I did something I know you'd love. There are two artists who have placed tiny fake doors, called Dinky Doors, all around the city. You can do a walking tour and try to spot them all. Nisha said that this was a great way to get to know Cambridge. So I tried it, and she was right!

The little doors are sculptures. Although they aren't exactly masterpieces, they are cute and funny. You can tell that they were hard work to create. I thought the people of Cambridge would be excited by this public art, but apparently not. I spoke to a lady who was taking a photo of one of the doors. She said that in her opinion the artists weren't well known there. They aren't even paid for their work by the city. They only earn money from things they sell on their website.

Actually, the site is quite interesting too. The two artists always hide their faces, and they make a new video each time they hide a new door. I told Nisha I'd watch all the Dinky Doors videos so we could talk about them. Maybe I'll buy some postcards from their online shop too. I'll send one to you.

Love from,
Freya

4 Rewrite the sentences you found in the email as direct speech.
1 Nisha said, _____
2 Nisha said, _____
3 The lady said, _____
4 I said, _____

5 🔊 **7.02** Listen to the three dialogues again. Then rewrite the sentences as reported speech.
1 Nisha: 'Most people don't know the tiny doors are here.'
2 Freya: 'I'll download the map this evening.'
3 Some critics: 'Graffiti isn't art at all.'
4 Liam: 'We must go on an organised tour.'
5 Tilly: 'My parents visited Warsaw a couple of years ago.'
6 Fred: 'There might be a concert on during my stay.'

6 Tick (✓) the correct reported questions and answers. Correct the wrong ones in your notebook.
1 The tour guide asked us where we were from. ☐
2 She asked if we liked the statue, don't we, and we said we do. ☐
3 You asked did we think it was a good painting. ☐
4 Mum asked I what I want to see first. ☐
5 I asked the tourist can he take a photo of me with the street art. He said he can. ☐
6 I asked Frank if where he favourite street painting was. ☐
7 Emily asked whether I knew the name of any street artists. ☐
8 The guide asked we will recommend the tour online. ☐

7 Read Gloria's opinion of the Dinky Doors project. Rewrite her sentences using reported speech.

'I enjoyed visiting the Dinky Doors. I think they're really clever and fun. You won't find them without the map. Make sure you download it! Where would you place a Dinky Door in your neighbourhood?'

Unit 7 75

7.3 LISTENING
Recognise the new meanings of known words.

1 What can you remember about the podcast in the Student's Book? Choose the correct alternative.

In the early days of cinema, films were ¹**released / noticed / mixed** without a score. Instead, a pianist played music in the cinema. However, as soon as 'talkies' arrived, music was created for each film.

The process of writing a film score takes place after the whole film has been ²**mixed / taken / shot**. First, the composer and the director watch the film. Then the composer does some research so that the music fits well with the film's content. For example, a story that takes place in rural America might use ³**country / natural / classical** music. On the other hand, a collection of songs might be more appropriate. So, a story based in a French city might use ⁴**genres / tracks / shots** by hip-hop ⁵**composers / painters / artists**. The best film scores help the audience to feel the emotions of the actors. For example, Oliver mentions the *Jaws* music which has two repeated ⁶**tracks / notes / genres** to represent the terrifying shark. *Jaws* uses traditional instruments, but these days electronic devices are often used. In all cases, the score is recorded and ⁷**released / mixed / filmed** in a studio.

2 Look at the photos and answer the questions.

1 Where are these concerts taking place?
2 What kind of music is playing?
3 Which concert would you prefer to go to? Why?

3 🔊 **7.03** Listen to six speakers and match them to the texts that they relate to. There is one text you do not need. You may listen twice.

A ___ B ___ C ___ D ___ E ___ F ___ G ___

A I've just heard about an interesting concert. Would you like to come with me? I know classical music is not our usual kind of thing, but we both love video games. Shall we try it?

B You're wrong. I was blown away! I found the performance really exciting. Maybe next time we can watch together? Then you won't be all on your own.

C John said we might get separated during the show. If that happens, everyone meet at the exit afterwards. See you there. XX

D Can't come. Going to a film-score concert.

E Call me back so we can discuss Friday. I think we should go to the cinema. There's a new adaptation I'd like to see.

F Viv said we should view the art exhibits first because it will get busy. I love the designs in these films, so I'm really looking forward to seeing the original drawings. Meet you at the entrance. R xx

G Don't forget to bring a coat and hat. Chidi said we might get pretty cold. Meet you at six. I can't wait. It's my favourite movie of all time!

> **STRATEGY** Recognising the new meaning of a known word
>
> Many words in English have more than one meaning, e.g. *score*. You probably knew the more familiar meaning (the number of points, goals, etc. gained by each player or team in a game), but you may not have known the less familiar one (the music written for a film or play). When you are listening, pay attention to the context to help you identify words with a different meaning. Then use the context to work out the new meaning of the word.

4 a Read the strategy above. What meaning(s) do you know of the words below?

| beat bed flat key pitch skin string

b 🔊 **7.04** Listen to extended versions of Speakers 1–3 from Ex 3. Listen for the words from Ex 4a.

c Match the **bold** words to new meanings A–G used in Ex 4b.

1 I thought the atmosphere was completely **flat**. ___
2 I did buy a new **skin** for my avatar, though. ___
3 You will hear the wonderful **strings** from *Waterfallen*. ___
4 They're also playing the electronic **bed** from *Platforia*. ___
5 I love the African **beats** in that one. ___
6 They're in the same **key**, which is interesting. ___
7 The low **pitch** makes the notes sound even scarier. ___

A the part of an orchestra that contains violins and cellos, among other instruments
B a set of related notes, based on a particular note
C dull and boring
D background music with no singing, for example, on a TV advert or video game
E something you can buy to change the appearance of a character or object on the screen
F units of rhythm
G the quality of sound that allows us to hear 'high' notes or 'low' notes

5 **MEDIATION** Choose one of the events in Ex 3 to recommend to a friend. Write a text message about it and invite them to go with you.

Talk about interpretations of art.

7.4 VOCABULARY

1 Imagine you are at a world-famous art gallery. Answer the questions.
1 Will you try to see all of the artworks?
2 How long will you spend looking at each piece?
3 How long will you spend looking at your favourite painting in the gallery?

2 Read the text. Match underlined phrases 1–8 to the words below.

| colourful   detailed   dramatic   humorous
| realistic   striking   thought-provoking   vivid

SLOW ART

According to a study, most gallery visitors spend around 30 seconds looking at a work of art. But great works of art are ¹causing you to consider the issue more carefully ... and this takes time.

'Slow art' means looking at fewer pictures but looking at them for 5–15 minutes. The difference can be ²very exciting and impressive.

In 30 seconds, you may notice that a painting is ³composed of reds, greens, blues, etc. However, with more time, you might notice a particularly ⁴clear and bright green in one area. In 30 seconds, you may notice that a portrait is ⁵very like real life. But with more time, you might notice an ⁶amusing detail in the background.

Many masterpieces are ⁷very interesting and attract attention, even from several metres away. But if you stand closer, you see that many of them are also very ⁸showing all the tiny parts very clearly. For example, you may see how the paintbrush was used.

3 Complete the sentences with the words in Ex 2.
1 This painting of a battle shows a _____ moment. There's a lot of action and danger.
2 It's a particularly _____ sculpture. Everyone notices it when they come into the room.
3 I don't like _____ portrait paintings. What's the point? You can just take a photo for that.
4 That is a _____ piece of street art. Look at all the different reds and greens.
5 In this painting, the girl's hat is a _____ blue.
6 The artist made several _____ paintings about her country. It helps to know a little bit about her history.
7 I looked at the painting for fifteen minutes. It's very _____, so I had plenty of things to look at.
8 It's good to see a _____ piece. Modern art is sometimes rather serious.

4 Match the sentence halves. There is one sentence ending you do not need.
1 The artist was inspired ___
2 This portrait captures ___
3 I want to draw your attention ___
4 The unusual colours add ___
5 The sculpture portrays ___
6 His work conveys ___
7 The photographer is passionate ___

A to the artist's unusual use of green colours in the sky.
B by her experiences as a child.
C a sculpture of a family.
D one short moment in great detail.
E a sense of the mother's pride in the child.
F a woman and child sitting together.
G a new dimension to the portrait.
H about his city.

5 Complete the article with the correct form of the verb phrases in Ex 4.

My masterpiece

Nada Badran, a tour guide from Dubai, ¹_____ travel and art. In 2020, she was in New Zealand and couldn't get home because of the pandemic. Nada ²_____ the Getty Museum Challenge. This art museum asked members of the public to copy famous paintings using only their own body and objects from their home.

Here is Nada's version of *The Scream* by Edvard Munch. As you can see, her picture is humorous. However, it also ³_____ of great affection for the original painting.

Nada used only a few objects, but the results are impressive. She has ⁴_____ lots of details from the painting. For example, she has ⁵_____ the two men using umbrellas and used spoons as part of the bridge. The different pieces of material on the wooden floor ⁶_____ to the way Munch uses paint. In fact, Nada has ⁷_____ to a picture that is often considered depressing.

Nada's version of *The Scream*

6 Look at this home masterpiece created by Nada. Complete the activity.
1 Find *Self-Portrait with Thorn Necklace and Hummingbird* by Frida Kahlo online.
2 Write a paragraph comparing Nada's picture to the original. Use words and phrases from this lesson.

7 Try making a masterpiece using objects from your home.

8 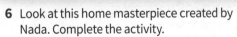 Now practise **Interpretations of art** vocabulary on page 110.

Unit 7   77

7.5 GRAMMAR

Use reporting verbs to discuss what people said.

▶ Grammar animation
GRAMMAR BOOSTER P145

1 Look at the photo and answer the questions.

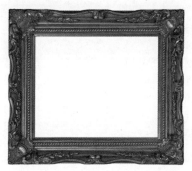

1 Do you think a blank piece of paper can be a work of art? Why? / Why not?
2 How would you describe the 'art' in the photo?

a masterpiece   abstract   artistic   beautiful
complicated   creative   humorous
thought-provoking

2 Read the article and find out how a blank piece of paper became a masterpiece. Do you think this is art?

NEWS
Entertainment & Arts

Erased art

In the 1950s, artist Robert Rauschenberg was thinking about art. What exactly is it? Does art have to make something? Can *removing* marks also be art?

Rauschenberg tried erasing some of his own drawings. He was pleased with the process, but ᵃcomplained that it wasn't very artistic. Instead, he ᵇinsisted on erasing someone else's work – preferably the work of a great artist. He immediately thought of Willem de Kooning, the best-known American artist of that time.

Rauschenberg went to visit de Kooning. During a long conversation, the younger artist ᶜbegged de Kooning to give him a picture for his project. Although de Kooning ᵈadmitted not liking the idea, he understood it straight away … and soon agreed. In fact, de Kooning ᵉrefused to give Rauschenberg a bad picture. 'It has to be something I'd miss,' he said.

Once he had the de Kooning picture, Rauschenberg carefully erased it. This process took many hours and used 40 erasers. A third artist, Jasper Johns, ᶠsuggested that the finished piece should be framed and given a title: *Erased de Kooning Drawing*. Today, the piece is on display at the San Francisco Museum of Modern Art.

Some critics immediately ᵍaccused Rauschenberg of destroying de Kooning's work. However, Rauschenberg ʰinsisted that the erasure was an act of creation. After all, de Kooning had given him permission. What do you think?

erase (v) to rub out or remove marks, usually pencil marks
eraser (n) American English word for a rubber (British English), the classroom object that removes pencil marks
erasure (n) the action of rubbing out or removing marks

3 Match reporting structures 1–7 to underlined examples a–h in the article.
1 verb + *that* + reported statement ___ ___
2 verb + (*not*) *to* + infinitive ___
3 verb + object + (*not*) *to* + infinitive ___
4 verb + (*not*) *-ing* ___
5 verb + preposition + (*not*) *-ing* ___
6 verb + object + preposition + (*not*) *-ing* ___
7 verb + *that* + *should* clause ___

4 Choose the correct answer: A, B or C.
1 They blamed me ___ the tickets.
  A for losing   B to lose   C losing
2 I recommend ___ the Museum of Modern Art while you're here.
  A you to visit   B visiting   C for visiting
3 They ___ not hearing the announcement.
  A complained about   B complained   C complained that
4 I reminded them ___ to the station on time.
  A that they get   B on arriving   C to get
5 She insisted ___ for the broken plate.
  A to pay   B that she pay   C paying
6 He added ___ by the river next time.
  A that we should park   B about parking   C to park
7 We ___ the teacher unless he apologised.
  A warned of telling   B threatened to tell   C advised that tell
8 They proposed ___ again next year.
  A I should apply   B I applied   C that I apply

5 ▶ 7.05 Listen to another unusual art story. Then write reporting sentences in the past tense.
1 The KLF / criticise / music industry / simple ideas
2 In 1992, they / insist / sales / all their records / stop
3 At first / promise / give money / struggling artists
4 Many people / refuse / believe / burn / real money
5 Drummond / admit / regret / burn / money
6 Drummond / recommend / people / should / make up / own mind

6 **PRONUNCIATION** ▶ 7.06 Listen to the reporting verbs and complete the table.

-ed	-ed pronounced as extra syllable
apologised	insisted

7 Write an anecdote about a misunderstanding in an art gallery. Use your own ideas or the situation below. Aim to include six or more different reporting verbs.
• You visited an art gallery with friends and discussed a thought-provoking piece of work.
• You accidentally left your umbrella on the floor. It was there for around 30 minutes before you returned for it.
• People thought the umbrella was part of the exhibit. Some were taking photos.
• You explained the situation.

Use the introduction and conclusion to understand the gist of an article.

7.6 READING

1 What can you remember about the vocabulary in the Student's Book? Match the sentence halves. There are two sentence endings you do not need.
1 Travel is a good way to get ___
2 Some people can visit the four corners ___
3 Planes have made it easier for people to see ___
4 We're going to hit ___
5 You can still find places that are off ___
6 Looking at travel photography really makes me get ___

A into the sea.
B the beaten track.
C itchy feet.
D of the world as part of their job.
E over to another country.
F away from it all and relax.
G the road this summer.
H the world, for example, on holiday.

> **STRATEGY** Using the introduction and conclusion to understand the gist
>
> Articles are clearly organised with an introduction and a conclusion. The introduction gives us an idea of what the article will be about, and the conclusion confirms this, and often leaves us with something to think about. We can get a good idea of the general meaning of a text by reading the first and last paragraphs first.

2 Read the strategy above and the first and last paragraphs of the article. Choose the best summary for the contents page of the magazine.
Our art critic …
A explains the difference between paintings and statues as a way to remember important people.
B discusses the effect of Covid-19 on public art.
C explores the history of statues in public places and their importance in modern cities.

3 Using the introduction, conclusion and photos, write three questions that you expect the rest of the article to answer.

4 🔊 7.07 Read the whole article. Were your ideas in Ex 3 correct?

5 Read the article again. Match sentences A–G to gaps 1–6. There is one sentence you do not need.
A If you wanted a copy of *David* by Michelangelo or *The Thinker* by Rodin, you could have one.
B Surprisingly, they were also very colourful.
C New technology has dramatically changed the way they are produced.
D Public art in general, and statues in particular, have become far more interesting.
E Instead the focus is on making something that lasts longer than the life of a politician, author or composer.
F Wealthy young men on the Grand Tour, for instance, learned that these statues were 'good art' as they visited the major galleries of Europe.
G One of my favourites is Julien Berthier's pigeons.

A plain ancient statue

A modern copy of an ancient statue

Public art

Do you ever look at statues when you walk past them? No, I thought not. When people go to an art gallery, they usually stop and look at the art. Portrait paintings are especially popular gallery attractions. Just think of the *Mona Lisa* and *Girl with a Pearl Earring*. It should be the same for statues. After all, there are no gallery guards to stop us. But public statues share our space … and we're busy. So why exactly are they there?

In Ancient Egypt, Greece and Rome, statues were used to impress the public. They were a display of wealth and power. ¹___ This fact was forgotten when the ancient civilisations disappeared. Of course, when the statues were found in modern times, after many centuries in the ground, the colour had disappeared. Gradually, these plain marble masterpieces came to be seen as beautiful and correct. ²___

Today, our advanced technology allows us to analyse the statues in new ways. We can find tiny clues about the colours used. We now know that statues in Ancient Greece, Rome and Egypt were brightly coloured.

Another lesson we can learn from these ancient pieces is that statues are strong. Perhaps this is why they have often been used to display famous and important people. In these cases, the main aim is *not* to make interesting or high-quality art. ³___ This trend continued into the 19th century, when new industrial techniques changed the art market. Small statues could be manufactured using cheaper metals. ⁴___ In short, sculpture was becoming rather boring.

Fortunately, that trend has now changed. ⁵___ People want statues that they can respond to, that tell interesting stories, that have a visual impact. For example, Bruno Catalano's *Bleu de Chine* considers migration. Statues today can even be humorous. ⁶___ The artist created several perfect bronze bird statues, which he then attached to traditional statues around his home city, Paris. For the people who notice them, they're really funny!

Public art has a positive future. During the recent pandemic, many city residents explored their streets and parks more closely than ever before. They noticed *their* statues, *their* city's art. Some people wondered if the art on display could be better or different. I expect artists around the world will accept that challenge. How exciting!

6 Use a search engine to look at pictures of Julien Berthier's pigeon statues (*Pigeonner*). Write a paragraph answering the questions.
1 Describe the pigeon statues.
2 Where in your neighbourhood / town / city would you place one of the pigeon statues? Why? What effect would you like it to have on members of the public?

Unit 7   79

7.7 GLOBAL SKILLS
Understand issues of copyright and plagiarism.

1 What can you remember about the Student's Book texts? Complete the information with the words below.

> attribution citations copyright direct quotation
> licence logos paraphrase piracy plagiarism
> reference an idea slogans trademark

If the appearance or name of something is special, companies can buy a ¹_____ to protect it. This system also protects company ²_____ and ³_____ such as 'I'm lovin' it' or 'Have a break. Have a Kit-Kat'. However, even though it is illegal, there is a huge trade in fake products.
Artists, authors and musicians have their work protected by ⁴_____ laws. This protection is free to the artists and happens automatically. Anyone who uses the artists' work needs to pay a ⁵_____ fee and include an ⁶_____ which says who the artist is. It is never acceptable to copy someone's work and use it to make money for yourself. This includes the ⁷_____ of videos, films and even software.
⁸_____ means taking someone else's work and using it as though it is yours. Occasionally students do this deliberately by using essay websites. However, many people do it accidentally. To make sure you avoid this problem, it is very important to include ⁹_____ in your work each time you ¹⁰_____. You must do this even if you ¹¹_____ the material in your own words. If you are worried about it, the simplest technique is to use ¹²_____ with clear punctuation marks.

2 Choose the correct alternative.

Popular news stories

Cake wars
Can you get a ¹**licence / paraphrase / trademark** on a cake? Yes, you can. Colin the Caterpillar has one. This cake has been made by the same supermarket company for 30 years and it is a popular choice at children's parties in the UK. However, it is so popular that other supermarkets also make caterpillar cakes with similar names. The original Colin cake has a company ²**logo / copyright / citation** on the packaging but not on the cake. Colin has no ³**attribution / plagiarism / slogan** either. Are the Colin copy cakes an example of ⁴**paraphrases / piracy / direct quotation**? In 2021, Colin's company took one company to court to find out.

caterpillar (n) the adult of this small creature is a butterfly

Whose art is it anyway?
The street artist Banksy has lost a legal fight with a greetings card company. The company makes cards which show graffiti and street art. But no ⁵**attribution / trademark / logo** to Banksy's name was included. Banksy and his legal team argued that these products are illegal and that the card company should agree to pay a ⁶**citation / licence / slogan** fee. However, the court decided that street art cannot be included in ⁷**quotation / plagiarism / copyright** laws because the art is painted without the permission of the building owners.

greetings card (n) paper card, often with colourful pictures, given on birthdays and other special occasions

3 Read the sections from student essays. Which sections show good use of references?

① Banksy is a street artist whose artwork does not convey a sense of timeless beauty as Vermeer's does, but it is still impressive. One example, in my opinion, is *Game Changer*.

② Banksy's artwork, according to Mora Li (2021), 'does not convey a sense of timeless beauty as Vermeer's does' but it is still dramatic and skilful.

③ Mora Li points out some differences between Banksy and Vermeer¹, but there are many similarities between these two artists.
¹Li, M. (2021) *From Galleries to the Streets*, Booksworth, p12.

④ I read a book that explored the similarities and differences between street art and traditional painting.

4 Complete the comments about the student essay sections using words from Ex 1 in the correct form. You can use the same word more than once.

I think Essay 1 is an example of ¹_____. The student has copied a section from the internet. There are no quote marks and no ²_____ to explain which website has been used.
Essay 2 uses a ³_____ with quote marks and a short ⁴_____ to the author they used. I expect there will be a longer 'References' section at the end of the essay.
Essay 3 has a clear ⁵_____ with full information about the source of the ideas. However, this example ⁶_____ the source book instead of using quote marks.
Essay 4 definitely ⁷_____ from a book, but there isn't enough detail. For example, the title of the book is not given.

5 Copyright laws change in some situations. Complete the task. Use vocabulary from this lesson.

DID YOU KNOW?
In many countries, it is legal to copy parts of a song or other artwork if you do it in a funny way. This kind of comedy is called 'parody'.

1 Do you think this is a good part of the copyright law? Why? / Why not?
2 You have posted a parody video of your favourite pop artist for your friends. Write a short comment for the video explaining that this is legal. Use some of the vocabulary from this lesson.

Use a range of vocabulary to select an option.

7.8 SPEAKING

1 Look at the photo and answer the questions.

1 How does this 'thank you' bench make you feel? Would you sit on it?
2 Sometimes public art pieces are about famous people. Sometimes they are about ordinary people. Does this change how you think about them?
3 Where would you place a 'thank you' bench in your neighbourhood? Why did you choose this location?

2 Read the email. Do you have a strong preference for one of these items?

SUBJECT: Mrs Appleby
TO: school mailing list
FROM: school office

As some of you know, Mrs Appleby is retiring at the end of this term. She has been our valued art teacher and colleague for 37 years. We want to create a permanent art project in the school for her. Each class should vote for ONE of the following options:
A a mural on the outside of the art department building
B rename the art department building the 'Jean Appleby building'
C a sculpture outside the art department building
D a formal portrait of Mrs Appleby in the school hall
E a 'thank you' bench in the school playground
Teachers will allow time for discussion of the options in class this week.

mural (n) a large painting or other work of art, drawn onto a wall

---

3 🔊 **7.08** Listen to two students discussing options A and B from the email. Tick (✓) the phrases you hear.
1 The main (dis)advantage is … ☐
2 Good point. And I also believe that … ☐
3 One major benefit / drawback is … ☐
4 Yes, and another thing is, … ☐
5 For me, it's a plus / minus. ☐
6 What are the pros and cons of that? ☐
7 It would have a positive / negative effect on … ☐
8 Absolutely. Not only that, but … ☐

4 Create a list of benefits and drawbacks comparing items A and C in Ex 2.

5 Write a short dialogue using your list from Ex 4 and phrases from Ex 3.

STRATEGY Using a range of vocabulary to avoid repetition
When you are speaking, try to use a range of vocabulary to avoid repeating key words. For example, you could use *get a shot*, *take a picture* or *capture an image* to avoid repeating *take a photo*.

6 a Read the strategy above. Create spidergrams for *remember* and *choose*. Use the words below and add further items using a synonyms dictionary.

| decide   go for   look back   recall

b 🔊 **7.08** Listen again to the students talking. Add any additional words to your diagrams in Ex 6a.

7 Complete the sentences with the correct form of the words below.

| believe   come   go for   go with
| opt   reason   settle   thing

1 The students _____ option D, which was a surprise to the school staff.
2 We need to _____ to a decision. What do you think?
3 For one _____, some of the ideas are much more expensive than others.
4 We all _____ that the abstract painting is the best.
5 Which one are we _____: the museum visit or the theatre trip?
6 The _____ I think that is because I've been to the museum before.
7 I would definitely _____ for a black and white photograph.
8 So that's _____, then. We'll go to the theatre on Saturday the 6th.

8 🔊 **7.09** Listen to two students discussing option C from the email. Then continue the conversation in writing. Follow the instructions using phrases from Ex 3.
1 Agree with the point.
2 Add a further opinion on this topic.
3 Introduce a disadvantage of D.

9 Now consider options D and E from the email. Follow the instructions in writing using phrases from Ex 7.
1 Express a strong preference for D or E.
2 Justify your opinion.

10 🔊 **7.10** Listen to the student who summarises the discussion so far. Then follow the instructions in writing.
1 Disagree and give a strong preference for a different option. Justify your opinion.
2 Conclude the discussion.

Unit 7   81

7.9 WRITING — Use persuasive language to write a formal letter.

1 How do companies and schools use art to present themselves to society? Look at the photos and think of any other ideas.

2 Read the letter and answer the questions.
1 What is the aim of the letter?
2 What arguments does Miles give to support his reaction?
3 What action does Miles propose? How does he support this suggestion?
4 What does he request happens next?

Dear Mr Al-Hamed,

A The proposed design for the sports-hall mural has just been announced on the school website. As one of your final-year art students, I am terribly disappointed. This old-fashioned picture does not represent our school well. In my opinion, this design should be rethought immediately.

B I have spoken to the students in my art class and the majority of us think that a street-art mural would be a better choice. Street art is modern and vibrant, just like your students. However, it is my belief that everyone in the school should be allowed to express their opinion. You always tell us that young people's views matter in this world, but we were not asked our opinion on this design.

C For this reason, I urge you to work with students to produce a new design. Perhaps the final-year art students could select five or six different local artists. Then all the students could be asked to vote for their favourite. Or perhaps you could arrange a competition for students to create a design of their own. This process may take some time, but the artwork itself will last for many years, so this choice must not be treated lightly.

D I propose that you immediately announce the design on the website is not the final choice.

Yours sincerely,

Miles Caley

rethink (v) think again about an idea, an action, etc., especially in order to change it

---

STRATEGY Using persuasive language
We use persuasive language in a formal letter or email to convince the reader to agree with a certain opinion or idea. Persuasive techniques include …
- presenting a personal viewpoint as if it were fact.
- using emotive language to make the reader feel a particular emotion.
- using statistics and figures in a persuasive way.

3 Read the strategy above. Find examples of each technique in Miles's letter.

4 Replace the words in **bold** with a different persuasive phrase so the meaning of the sentences does not change.
1 **I believe** this is the worst possible outcome.
   (I_____ m_____ v_____)
2 It is **essential** that the students are allowed to express themselves. (v_____)
3 We are all **terribly upset** about the decision.
   (s_____ c_____)
4 This is the worst decision **of all time**. (t_____ c_____ h_____ b_____ m_____)
5 I strongly **suggest** that you contact the museum director. (r_____)
6 The dance competition should not be cancelled **on any account**. (n_____ m_____ w_____)

5 Rewrite the sentences to make them more persuasive / formal. There is more than one possible answer.
1 Please don't stop us entering the competition.
2 It is important to have a creative hobby and that's why most of us go to art club.
3 I really don't like the new school logo design.
4 The choir is important to us, so please don't shut it down without thinking hard about it.
5 All my friends think the concert should go ahead.
6 What a brilliant decision.

6 You are going to write a formal letter to the head teacher of your school. Choose an idea and then follow the plan.
- The school logo is being changed without input from students.
- The annual drama performance is being cancelled because there aren't enough teachers available.
- The display of student art is being removed from the office area and replaced with plain colour.

1 For the idea you have chosen, answer the four questions in Ex 2 about you and your letter.
2 Plan one paragraph for each question.
3 Decide which persuasive language techniques you will use. Aim for at least one in each paragraph.

7 Write your letter.

8 ✓ **CHECK YOUR WORK** Did you …
- use persuasive language?
- use a formal register?
- write four paragraphs?
- start and finish your letter correctly?

7.10 REVIEW

Grammar

1 **Complete the reported sentences so they mean the same as the direct sentences. Use the words in brackets.**
   1 'Perhaps I'll come to the art class.' (she)
      Marta said _____.
   2 'Do you want to leave?' 'Yes.' (if / we)
      He asked _____
      _____.
   3 'I went to the cinema last night.' (she / before)
      Funmi said _____
      _____.
   4 'I'm going to try that pasta dish.' (he)
      Kyle said _____.
   5 'Will you tell Kim about the meal?' 'No, I won't.' (whether / I)
      He asked _____
      _____.

2 **Choose the correct answer: A, B or C.**
   1 We insist ___ the results.
     A that should see   B to see   C on seeing
   2 They begged him ___.
     A not giving up   B not to give up   C didn't give up
   3 I propose ___ anything about it.
     A that we do   B doing   C not doing
   4 He ___ often wrong on the subject.
     A added that people were   B added to being   C added that people should
   5 They accused ___ her ideas.
     A the artist of copying   B the artist to copy   C that the artist copy
   6 She refused ___ to his advice.
     A listening   B to listen   C that she listen
   7 Our teacher suggested ___ plenty of rest before the exam.
     A that we get   B we should getting   C to get
   8 He recommended ___ practise our grammar.
     A for us   B to   C that we should

Vocabulary

3 **Match the sentence halves.**
   1 The dance group gave ___
   2 The students went to see a stage ___
   3 At a live gig, ___
   4 Marcus is an excellent singer. He'd like to be ___
   5 We'll need two or three hours to view ___
   6 What a large sculpture! It's really a ___
   7 I prefer the performing arts, ___
   8 There are some gorgeous ___

   A in a musical production, so he's learning to dance.
   B spectacular piece of work.
   C like theatre, dance and music.
   D an outstanding performance last night.
   E the atmosphere is usually very exciting.
   F all the exhibits.
   G adaptation of a famous novel.
   H colours in this street art. It's stunning!

4 **Complete the sentences.**
   1 The novel p_____ life on a small island.
   2 The book contains d_____ descriptions of the island and the people who live there.
   3 There are some h_____ moments, but it isn't a comedy.
   4 This is a s_____ portrait, even though it isn't very realistic.
   5 The film c_____ a sense of sadness.
   6 She wants to d_____ a _____ to the artists who work in her local community.
   7 You can tell that this photographer is p_____ a_____ the sea.
   8 Just look at the v_____ blues and greens in this picture of the ocean.

Cumulative review

5 **Choose the correct alternative.**

Ai-da the art robot

Ai-da is a robot designed to look like a woman. Her name [1]**captures / was inspired by / portrays** the historical computer programmer Ada Lovelace. Ai-da can talk, blink … and paint.

Ai-da's first paintings were mostly [2]**abstract art / visual arts / gorgeous colours**. However, now she is creating self-portraits. Although art critics agree that the works aren't exactly [3]**dramatic / masterpieces / contemporary**, they are certainly [4]**blown away / thought-provoking / realistic**. For example, if robots can create art, then what are humans for? If Ai-da has drawn a self-portrait, does she have a self?

Robots often divide people's opinions, but a robot artist adds a new [5]**dimension / performance / gig** to the debate. Some have refused [6]**seeing / to accept / her of claiming** her work as art. Others have insisted [7]**to call / that should call / that we call** Ai-da 'it', not 'she'. Ai-da was created by a team of experts led by Aidan Meller. In an interview, Meller [8]**encouraged / proposed / accused** everyone to think about the role of humans and technology in their lives. He also said that Ai-da's art [9]**must / can / would** continue to improve. What will she create next?

Some people [10]**said / say / saying** that Ai-da is the future of art. Come and see for yourself. Ai-da's portraits are on [11]**exhibit / stage / display** at the Design Museum until August.

REFLECT Think about the following questions.
1 Which lesson in this unit was your favourite? Why?
2 Do you report speech more often when you speak or when you write? What can you do to practise this skill more frequently?
3 How can you avoid plagiarism in your school essays?
4 How can you make your formal writing more persuasive?

Unit 7 83

8.1 VOCABULARY
Talk about volunteering in the local community.

8 Local and global citizenship

volunteering

1 a What can you remember about the vlog? Complete the summary for each person with the words below.

| charity community contribution elderly homeless
| initiative learning refuges social tuition

Yasmin's grandmother volunteers in a ¹_____ shop because she wants to give something back to her community.
Zaki's mum makes a valuable ²_____ by supporting children with ³_____ disabilities.
Daisy wants to join a local ⁴_____ called On the Street. It offers advice on places to sleep, such as ⁵_____ for people who become ⁶_____.
Joe volunteers for a local ⁷_____ service that helps ⁸_____ people. The service aims to reduce ⁹_____ isolation. Joe is giving George one-to-one ¹⁰_____ in computer skills to help him keep in touch with his family.

b ▶ ◉ **8.01** Watch or listen again and check.

2 Choose the correct alternative.
1. We want to **become / provide / engage with** the issues that cause problems in this community.
2. This charity **provides / suffers / makes** assistance for elderly people.
3. Children can **lack / retain / suffer** hardship if one of their parents is ill for a long time.
4. We are volunteer taxi drivers. We help wheelchair users **retain / engage / provide** their independence.
5. The children are selling cakes to **raise / retain / make** funds for a local charity.
6. Volunteering is a great way for anyone who **engages / lacks / provides** confidence in themselves.

3 Complete the posts using words from Ex 1 and 2.

Kelton Reading Scheme is a ¹l_____ i_____ based in Kelton Primary School. We offer ²o_____ t_____ to all children who ³l_____ c_____ in their reading. Some of the children have recently moved to our country, some are unfamiliar with books, some have ⁴l_____ d_____. If you would like to be a reading volunteer, please contact us to complete our training course.

APPLY

If you have two or more hours of free time each week, your local ⁵c_____ s_____ is looking for volunteers. During the pandemic, many more people have ⁶b_____ h_____. People living on the streets ⁷s_____ h_____ every day. Many are also lonely because they experience ⁸s_____ i_____. All the money from our store goes to the city ⁹r_____ which offers support and a safe place to stay.

APPLY

We are looking for skilled builders and electricians to join our volunteer service. We help ¹⁰e_____ p_____ to ¹¹r_____ their i_____ by making changes to their homes. Join our team and ¹²p_____ a _____ to your local community. Not a builder? You can ¹³m_____ a c_____ to our work by donating money on our website. We ¹⁴r_____ f_____ to pay for the materials and equipment that we use.

APPLY

4 REAL ENGLISH Complete the dialogue with the phrases below. There is one phrase you do not need.

| for a good cause   give something back   keep an eye on
| lend a hand   real eye-opener   safety net

A Aren't you running in the race this year?
B No, I'm a race marshal and ¹_____ runners.
A I know the race is ²_____, but I've forgotten the name of the charity …
B Caring Together. They really helped when my dad was sick a few years ago. It was a ³_____. The charity provides a ⁴_____ for all the children who help care for family members.
A It sounds great – could I volunteer too?
B At the race? Yes, I'm sure you could ⁵_____!

5 VOCABULARY BOOSTER Now practise **Volunteering in the local community** vocabulary on page 111.

8.2 GRAMMAR

Grammar animation
GRAMMAR BOOSTER P146

Use different verb patterns to talk about community service.

1 Look at the photo and answer the questions.

1 Does volunteering take a lot of time?
2 How much time could *you* give to volunteering each week?

2 Choose the correct alternative.

Time banking   About Join Contact

Have you ever wanted ¹**to help / helping** your local community? Are you worried that you don't have enough time? Think again!

Time banking is a way for people to help each other. Everyone can put time into their local online time bank. One hour of your time becomes one time-bank 'credit'. Then you swap your credits with someone in your neighbourhood. For example, Rob offers ²**to wash / washing** James's car every week. In return, James teaches Rob how to fix broken items around his home.

People are often worried that they don't have good skills to offer the time bank. We suggest ³**to think / thinking** of what you do every day. Can you type, cook, garden? Here is Julia's story. 'When I moved here, I knew no one. I heard about the time bank and decided ⁴**to volunteer / volunteering**. At first, I couldn't think what skills to put on my bank profile page. I never considered ⁵**doing / to do** the washing-up and things like that as a skill. But they are! I manage ⁶**to give / giving** four hours each month. It isn't a lot, but it makes a real difference. I enjoy ⁷**talking / to talk** to my neighbours while I wash up or do their ironing. And in return, I have learned how to sew, and I've had a few piano lessons. My advice is: don't avoid ⁸**getting / to get** started. Make a decision and sign up today.'

swap (*v*) give one thing in return for another thing

3 Complete the posts with the correct form of the verbs below. Which verb can use either *-ing* or the infinitive without a change in meaning?

| be   do   look after   swap   use   volunteer

Please can someone teach me how to ride a bike? In return, I hope ¹_____ housework tasks, like washing-up and cleaning. I would prefer ²_____ in the evenings if possible.

I have injured my arm. Can anyone help with my shopping for the next month? I enjoy ³_____ plants and animals, so I could do this for you the next time you are on holiday. Contact me so we can discuss ⁴_____ our time-bank credits.

Do you find maths difficult? I am offering maths lessons in return for computer lessons. I am 76 and avoid ⁵_____ the internet even though I know it could be useful. Online shopping and video calls seem ⁶_____ impossible for me!

4 🔊 **8.02** Listen to the dialogues. Complete the sentences so they keep the same meaning as the dialogues. Use the correct form of the verbs in brackets. Use a dictionary if necessary.
1 Michaela _____ the money to school today. (mean / bring)
2 Tim will never _____ his team win the football World Cup. (forget / watch)
3 Ali should _____ more carefully before she makes a bad decision. (stop / think)
4 Ali _____ the team and she wants to come back. (regret / leave)
5 Jacob _____ his friend's glasses somewhere. (remember / see)
6 Jess _____ the spider, but she couldn't! (try / ignore)

5 Choose the correct sentence: A or B. In some cases, both A and B may be correct.
1 A Do you prefer to watch films at the cinema or at home on TV?
  B Do you prefer watching films at the cinema or at home on TV?
2 A Sorry! I didn't notice you to stand there.
  B Sorry! I didn't notice you standing there.
3 A My school doesn't allow us to bring phones into the classroom.
  B My school doesn't allow us bringing phones into the classroom.
4 A You inspired me to start sewing lessons.
  B You inspired me starting sewing lessons.
5 A He spends too much time to play video games.
  B He spends too much time playing video games.
6 A I found these keys to lie on the floor.
  B I found these keys lying on the floor.
7 A Do you expect us to sit here for hours?
  B Do you expect us sitting here for hours?
8 A They discovered the lost cat to hide in a cupboard.
  B They discovered the lost cat hiding in a cupboard.

6 Complete the sentences with a suitable object, verb and your own ideas.
1 My friend spends too much time on social media. Last year, someone persuaded _____.
2 That's disappointing. I didn't expect _____.
3 It was a surprise because I hadn't seen _____.
4 Don't! If Mum hears _____.
5 Art is wonderful. It inspires _____.
6 Are you enjoying watching the Olympics on TV? I watched _____.

7 You have two hours to put into a volunteering time bank. What skills can you offer?

Unit 8   85

8.3 LISTENING
Recognise features of informal English.

1 What can you remember about the vocabulary in the Student's Book? Match the sentence halves. There are two sentence endings you do not need.
1 Everyone at Skateistan has a real ___
2 I was nervous about coming to these classes, but I said ___
3 You should check ___
4 The garden encourages kids to have ___
5 You may think that going online isn't ___

A out the Skateistan website.
B that hard, but for many people it's a completely new skill.
C laugh together.
D to myself that it would get easier.
E good time on a sailing ship.
F idea about making a difference.
G a go at growing fruit and vegetables.

2 🔊 **8.03** Listen to five people talking about volunteering work. Match each speaker to a photo.

A

B

C

D

E

3 🔊 **8.03** Listen to the speakers again. Choose the correct answer: A, B or C.
1 What does Ashley say is the main role of the volunteers?
 A to give information
 B to listen
 C to call for help
2 Why does Carl think the annual event is a good idea?
 A Because people can't ignore it.
 B Because there are more volunteers.
 C Because tourists can join in.
3 How did the man hear about this group of volunteers?
 A His wife needed to use the group.
 B A work colleague told him about it.
 C His friends were volunteers.
4 During a race, how many volunteer runners support one blind runner?
 A one
 B two
 C three
5 What sort of food does the centre give the animals?
 A food that matches their natural diet
 B food to help them recover
 C food that is deliberately boring

STRATEGY Recognising features of informal English

Recognising common features of connected speech will help you understand informal English spoken at natural speed. Be aware of the following points.
1 When people speak quickly, the sounds at the beginning and end of some words may run together.
 A With two vowels, it may sound as if a consonant has been added: *we often → we yoften*.
 B A consonant at the end of a word can change its sound if the next word starts with a consonant: *I don't know → I dunno*. Some consonants can 'disappear' in common phrases: *I'm going to → I'm gonna*.
 C Unstressed vowels at the beginning and end of words like *of* and *to* often have a schwa sound: /əv/, /tə/.
2 Speakers often use 'filler' words or phrases, for example, *basically, I mean, kind of, like,* or *whatever, really, sort of, to be honest, well, you know*.
3 Speakers often use informal phrases, whereas in more formal situations they might use a neutral phrase or word with a similar meaning.

4 🔊 **8.03** Read the strategy above. Listen again and complete the extract with up to four words. Which feature of informal English (strategies 1–3) does each extract include?
1 When I go home, _____ 'Yes, I've helped someone today'.
2 I _____ people drop litter.
3 The journey was, _____, it was awful, _____.
4 We're a good team and we _____.
5 _____ were kept as pets.

5 **PRONUNCIATION** 🔊 **8.04** Read the sentences out loud. Which extra consonant do you hear between the underlined words? Listen and check.
1 I agree with you.   w / y / r
2 Don't do it like that!   w / y / r
3 I saw Oliver yesterday.   w / y / r
4 I think the media are responsible. w / y / r

6 Choose the correct alternative.
A Why don't you try wheelchair basketball with me?
B I'm not sure. ¹**Sort of / Basically**, I'm worried it might be too difficult. I'm not as fit as you, ²**you know / kind of**.
A I get it. It sounds like it's just for athletes, ³**or whatever / I mean**. But actually it's quite easy. Of course there are new skills to learn, but that's ⁴**sort of / to be honest** the point. Why don't you come and look at my session next week?
B OK. ⁵**Kind of / I mean**, I do want to do more exercise. At the start of this year, I thought, 'You really need to get into shape.'
A Good for you! The coach and the other volunteers are, ⁶**or whatever / like**, friendly and helpful. We have great fun!

7 Match the underlined phrases in Ex 6 to the informal phrases below that have the same meaning.

| a real laugh   check out   have a go at |
| I said to myself   it isn't that hard |

8 **MEDIATION** You and your friend want to become volunteers in the holidays. Choose a volunteer role from the unit so far. Write the script of a voicemail message to your friend summarising the role.

Talk about responding to a humanitarian crisis.

8.4 VOCABULARY

1 Write a short paragraph to describe this picture.

1 What is happening in the picture?
2 What do you think has happened?

2 Choose the correct alternative.

ARTICLES

Transport and tents

When a crisis occurs, international ¹**aid agencies / survivors** arrive as quickly as possible. Everyone wants to help the ²**infrastructure / survivors** and reduce their ³**suffering / refugees**. However, getting to the right location can be difficult.

For example, during a flood, local ⁴**infrastructure / aid agencies** can be impossible to use. If the roads are damaged and there is no electricity, it is very difficult to keep medicines cold. Good transport is therefore a ⁵**priority / relief effort**. Medicines are sometimes delivered using motorbikes, canoes or horses.

During an ⁶**aid agency / armed conflict** or after an earthquake, buildings can become dangerous and large numbers of people become ⁷**refugees / survivors**. In these cases, the ⁸**relief effort / priority** needs large numbers of tents. These temporary shelters become homes, schools and even hospitals.

3 Complete the sentences with the correct form of words and phrases from Ex 2.
1 The _____ caused a huge amount of _____ for ordinary people in this region.
2 Two years later, there are thousands of _____ living in tents because it is not safe to return to the city.
3 I work for an _____, but I don't travel to disaster areas.
4 Sometimes local people are asked to take part in the _____.
5 Although some parts of buildings have been destroyed, the rescue team still hopes to find _____.
6 Our _____ is to fix the bridge because it's a vital part of the town's _____.

4 Read the article and answer the questions.
1 Where do Doctors Without Borders store their tents?
2 How quickly do Doctors Without Borders aim to arrive at a crisis area?
3 What is special about the Doctors Without Borders disaster kits?

Home | About us | News

Doctors without borders

Doctors Without Borders (DWB) is a medical humanitarian organisation. It works around the world to ¹<u>save</u> lives when there is armed conflict, disease or natural disasters. DWB doctors and aid workers are often the first people to arrive at the location of a disaster. How does that happen?

DWB ²<u>removes</u> problems using skill and preparation. Unlike some aid agencies, DWB owns all of its vehicles and equipment. For example, tents are stored in China and Dubai. Medicines, water and vehicles are stored around the world. This makes it easier to ³<u>give out</u> emergency supplies as soon as they are needed. In fact, DWB aims to arrive in a crisis area within 24 hours.

Every day, DWB workers monitor the number of items in the organisation's storage buildings. They use a computer system to ⁴<u>deal with</u> requests for medicine and then ⁵<u>consider</u> if more needs to be ordered. At all times, the medical response is ⁶<u>managed</u> by the medical staff 'on the ground'.

During a humanitarian crisis, all emergency workers expect to ⁷<u>meet</u> a lack of space and equipment. For medical teams in particular, the wrong equipment can ⁸<u>create danger for</u> lives. DWB has created special disaster kits which fold into a small space. These include a whole operating room that is the same size as a table. Using all of these systems, DWB gets the right people, and the right equipment, to the right place.

on the ground (phr) in the place where the practical work takes place

5 Match the underlined words and phrases 1–8 in the article to the verbs with the same meaning below.

assess   co-ordinate   distribute   eliminate
encounter   preserve   process   threaten

6 Complete the sentences with an appropriate form of the verbs in Ex 5.
1 Is the aid agency able _____ resources by helicopter in the mountains?
2 The driver hoped not _____ any problems on the difficult journey ahead.
3 At today's meeting we will discuss _____ the data and how to create a map of the area.
4 The armed conflict last year _____ thousands of lives.
5 They've started _____ the damage caused by flooding.
6 One of the key goals of the World Health Organization is to try and _____ malaria in at least 30 countries by 2030.

7 Go online and visit the DWB website. Answer the questions.
1 When was DWB created?
2 What prize did DWB win in 1999?
3 What is the name of the education course DWB offers for doctors?
4 How does DWB spend money donated by the public?

8 **VOCABULARY BOOSTER** Now practise **Responding to a humanitarian crisis** vocabulary on page 111.

Unit 8   87

8.5 GRAMMAR

Use participle clauses to talk about citizen science.

▶ Grammar animation
GRAMMAR BOOSTER P147

1 Choose the correct alternative.

What is citizen science?

Citizen-science projects use volunteers to collect data. ¹**Involving / Having involved** members of the public allows these projects to gather far more information. For example, ²**helping / helped by** UK gardeners, the Big Garden Bird Watch monitors the number and variety of garden birds. ³**Collected / Having collected** as much data as possible, expert scientists then analyse the information.

2 Read the text and answer the questions.
1 Why is the project called Walrus From Space?
2 How many options are given for each picture?
3 Why are walrus on beaches problematic?

Class 12Y > Winter term. Week 1. Science
Conversations Files Class notes **Assignments**

Walrus are large, sociable mammals

Hello, Class 12Y. This term we will be joining a citizen-science project. ¹<u>Because they live in the Arctic</u>, most of us have never seen a walrus. Now you can with Walrus From Space!
Please follow these steps at home.
1 Create an account at the Walrus From Space website.
2 Complete the training session.
  You will be shown 20 satellite images. For each picture, choose either 'Walrus Present', 'No Walrus Present', 'Other wildlife' or 'Poor image'. The website will give you tips and advice after you have looked at each picture. ²<u>When you practise with the example images</u>, you will become a better walrus detective. Although walrus rest on sea ice when available, they will gather on land during the summer months. This is the best time of year to spot walrus from space, as they tend to come back to the same beaches every summer, so you will notice that most of the 'Walrus Present' pictures show the Arctic coastline, rather than sea ice.
  ³<u>Walrus who are looking for a place to breed and feed</u> tend to rest on the sea ice. They may also choose to rest on beaches. Sometimes ⁴<u>if walrus are prevented from resting on the ice</u>, as a result of a warming world, they gather in large numbers on beaches. Walrus crowds can be dangerous and these huge animals can accidentally hurt each other when they are frightened.
3 Search for walrus.
  ⁵<u>When you have finished the training session</u>, you can begin looking for walrus. ⁶<u>If you record what you see accurately</u>, your data is extremely useful to scientists, who use it to create a detailed report using the 'Walrus Present' images you find.
  *If the layout or detail on the website has changed, follow the on-screen instructions.

3 Rewrite the underlined sentences in the text in Ex 2 using participle clauses.
1 _____, live walrus have never been seen by most of us.
2 _____, you become a better walrus detective.
3 _____ tend to rest on the sea ice.
4 _____, walrus sometimes gather in large numbers on beaches.
5 _____, you can begin looking for walrus.
6 _____, your data is extremely useful to scientists.

4 Match the participle clauses in Ex 3 to rules A–F. You can use the original form of the clauses in Ex 2 to help you decide.
A instead of a relative clause, with a present participle replacing an active tense ___
B instead of a relative clause, with a past participle replacing a passive tense ___
C to show that two things are happening at the same time, using a present participle ___
D to show a sequence of events, using a perfect participle ___
E to express a reason or cause using a present participle ___
F to express a condition, using a past participle ___

5 Choose the correct answer: A, B or C.
1 ___ the rules, it was easy to follow the instructions.
  A After learning
  B Before learning
  C When learned
2 ___ the museum, I noticed a sign about a butterfly project.
  A Since visited
  B While visiting
  C For visiting
3 ___, I have seen several walrus as part of this project.
  A Since joining
  B While joining
  C Before joining
4 I use an identification chart ___ for birds in my garden.
  A on looking
  B by looking
  C when looking
5 ___ the training session, they still found it difficult to see the walrus.
  A Before completing
  B Despite completing
  C When completing
6 ___ the butterfly, Marion felt very excited.
  A On seeing
  B Despite seeing
  C Since seeing

6 Write an instruction text including participle clauses. Choose from one of the following or your own idea.
• Make a simple meal.
• Record a film on your TV.
• Look after a pet or house plant.

7 If possible, explore an online citizen-science project like Walrus From Space.

88 Unit 8

Recognise facts, opinions and speculation in a text.

8.6 READING

1 What can you remember about the Student's Book? Complete the summary with the words below.

| acidity   biodiversity   eradicate
| extinction   parasite   resistant

Around the world, plant ¹_____ is decreasing. In fact, scientists are worried about the ²_____ of many plants in the wild. There are several projects that store seeds to protect them for the future. For example, the Svalbard Global Seed Vault has over 1 million types of seed for food crops.

Malaria is a disease caused by a ³_____ carried by mosquitoes. Until recently, there was no vaccine against malaria. But now there is! Although the new vaccine will not ⁴_____ the disease, it is believed that cases will drop by 40%.

Coral reefs are important ecosystems. Unfortunately, they are dying due to increasing sea temperatures and ⁵_____. One solution is to grow stronger, more ⁶_____ coral in a laboratory. These new corals can then be placed in the ocean to create healthy reefs.

> **STRATEGY** Recognising fact, opinion and speculation
>
> To understand a text fully, it helps to be able to recognise when the writer is presenting a fact, expressing their opinion or speculating.
>
> **Facts** are usually supported by a reference to statistics, numbers or other sources, such as books, articles or reports (*Over 50%, around 5 million, According to the CNN report …*).
>
> To identify the writer's **opinion**, look for adjectives and adverbs that express their opinion (*It's brilliant that …, Unfortunately, we cannot …*) and phrases that connect the reader and writer (*Who doesn't like … ?, We all know …*).
>
> A **speculation** is an idea about what could be true rather than what is objectively true. Look for language such as *could, might, may, … is believed to be, It's likely that …*.

2 🔊 **8.05** Read the strategy above and the article below. Are the three <u>underlined</u> sentences fact (*F*), opinion (*O*) or speculation (*S*)?

3 Read the article again and choose the correct answer: A, B or C.
1 What is the writer's opinion of climate change?
   A that world leaders must act now
   B that it cannot be stopped
   C that the United Nations is correct
2 What will NASA's moon project do?
   A send astronauts back to the moon
   B start construction of a space colony on the moon
   C send humans to Mars from the moon
3 What would be the main benefit of an O'Neill cylinder?
   A It would be closer to Earth than Mars.
   B The technology required is simple.
   C Life inside would be like on Earth.
4 Why doesn't the writer think space exploration can help?
   A We don't have enough time to find 'Planet B'.
   B We can't make our plans based on stories.
   C It is too difficult to move the entire population of the world.

4 Rewrite the opinions as speculations using the words in brackets.
1 People have overcome problems caused by population growth before, so I'm sure we will be OK this time too. (likely)
2 It's brilliant that new technology will save the coral reefs. (may)
3 People say the coral reefs are going to die. (believed / in danger)
4 The politician says that journey times will be reduced by 50 minutes. (possible that / could)

5 Respond to the facts with your own opinion or speculation.
1 According to scientists at the University of Singapore, new coral grows well on Lego.
2 The US government monitors over 27,000 items of space junk. The items are travelling at over 15,000 miles per hour.
3 The Environmental Protection Agency states that 25% of all marine creatures rely on coral reefs at some point during their lives.

FUTURE-PROOFING THE WORLD ... BY LEAVING IT

We are reaching the end of our time on planet Earth. According to a report by the United Nations, global warming will soon lead to a 1.5°C rise in temperature. World leaders have already agreed that this increase will make our current way of life impossible. And I see no signs that countries will work together to reduce climate change. ¹<u>It is therefore likely that the best way to future-proof the world is to leave.</u>

Perhaps we can live on the moon? Jeff Bezos, the boss of Amazon, thinks so. In 2019, he said, 'It's time to go back to the moon. This time to stay.' Bezos is one of several billionaires investing large amounts of money in space colony projects. ²<u>According to *Space Capital* magazine, Bezos has so far invested $7.5 billion in his space company, Blue Origin.</u> NASA also wants to return to the moon although it has a less ambitious aim: landing astronauts on the surface for the first time since the 1970s. Meanwhile Elon Musk, the boss of Tesla, wants to send humans to Mars.

Living on Mars would be extremely difficult, even unpleasant. Perhaps it might be simpler to move our population into enormous spaceships? One idea is the 'O'Neill cylinder', invented by a professor of physics in the 1970s. These huge space colonies would be very similar to living on Earth. ³<u>Who doesn't like the idea of forests and cities on a space station?</u> Unfortunately, we cannot currently build something this size.

Finally, what about space exploration? It's a popular idea, particularly as science-fiction stories often show humans living in other galaxies. Some people believe that humans will move completely onto a new planet: an idea sometimes known as 'Planet B'. However, there is currently no evidence that such a planet exists – it certainly doesn't in our solar system. We only have a few years to solve the Earth's problems. It's time to take action.

> **colony** (*n*) a place (usually foreign, but in this case alien) where a group of people with similar interests / jobs live together
> **cylinder** (*n*) a three-dimensional shape with two circles connected by parallel lines, e.g. a tube or pipe

Unit 8   89

8.7 GLOBAL SKILLS

Discuss issues with people who have a different opinion.

1 What can you remember about the Student's Book text? Complete the summary with the words below.

| acknowledge   avoid   challenge   find |
| goes   make   set   show   speak |

It's important not to ¹_____ judgements about people if they say something that ²_____ against your values. Try to ³_____ confrontation. Instead, listen carefully and ⁴_____ respect. The best way to ⁵_____ prejudice and discrimination is with better arguments, not insults. Do some research so you can ⁶_____ from an informed position on matters that are important to you.

For smaller disagreements, particularly with people you need to work with, the best approach is to try to ⁷_____ aside your differences. You can ⁸_____ your different perspectives and leave it there, or you can work to ⁹_____ a compromise.

2 🔊 **8.06** Listen to two people discussing a quiz. Choose the correct alternative.

Speaker 1 chose ¹**As / Bs** in the quiz. She believes that often the best approach is to ²**hold your tongue / stand your ground**. You can't expect everyone to agree all the time. However, in a situation with friends, she thinks she would ³**hold her tongue / stand her ground**.

Speaker 2 chose mostly ⁴**As / Bs** in the quiz. He thinks people need to ⁵**stand their ground / look for common ground** and the best way to do that is to speak up. He believes that everyone should read the news so they can ⁶**get their heads around / hold their tongue** the important issues of the day. Otherwise, the loudest person wins instead of the best argument.

3 Read the quiz. Complete the gaps with an appropriate form of phrases from Ex 1 and 2. Then answer the quiz questions.

4 Choose the correct answer: A, B or C.
1 It's important to ___ prejudice. If you don't, nothing will change.
   A speak   B challenge   C set
2 People will listen to you if you ___.
   A go against your values   B make judgements
   C speak from an informed position
3 It's sad that you've argued. I wish you two would ___ and be friends again.
   A show respect   B set aside your differences
   C get your heads around
4 If there's a disagreement, I tend to ___ to show that there's always something we can agree on.
   A look for common ground   B go against my values
   C make judgements
5 You should say something and ___.
   A stand your ground   B hold your tongue
   C avoid confrontation
6 You don't have to choose between his idea or your idea – you can ___.
   A find a compromise   B make a judgement
   C set them aside

5 Choose one situation and write about how you would respond. Use phrases from this lesson.
A Several people in your class are posting things online that you find offensive.
B You want to get a part-time job, but your parents worry this will affect your school grades.
C There's a new student in your class: James. You've heard some people being mean about him in the school cafeteria. Now your best friend wants to tell James what you heard.

Quiz

1 The strangers

You are in a shop with your young brother or sister. Two people next to you are having a conversation that strongly ¹g_____ a_____ y_____ v_____.

Do you ...

A walk away? The situation is not important, so it is best to ²a_____ c_____. You can't possibly change their opinion in a shop.

B speak up? You believe that you should ³c_____ p_____ o_____ d_____ when you meet them. You need to show your sibling that this is important.

2 The teammates

After losing a match, your teammates begin angrily discussing what went wrong.

Do you ...

A join the discussion? You are a team, so you need to ⁴a_____ y_____ d_____ p_____. By ⁵s_____ a_____ y_____ d_____, it becomes possible to ⁶f_____ a c_____ and work successfully together.

B listen from a distance? You don't want to express your opinion in case people ⁷m_____ j_____ about you. After all, that's what you're doing.

3 The debate

In an English class, you and another student have to prepare a presentation on animal welfare. You are a vegetarian and this is a subject you are passionate about.

Do you ...

A prepare an informative but neutral presentation? This is the best way to express yourself. You can ⁸s_____ f_____ a_____ i_____ p_____ and ⁹s_____ r_____ for your classmates.

B prepare an informative but argumentative presentation? This is the best way to express yourself. You will only use facts, but you can make people reconsider their eating habits by shocking them.

Use a range of phrases to engage with others' ideas in a debate.

8.8 SPEAKING

1 Read the debate topic and the student's ideas. Which ones are for and which are against the issue?

> Space tourism should be banned.

		For	Against
1	Space tourism is dangerous. A pilot has died.	☐	☐
2	It may produce new technology that will benefit us all.	☐	☐
3	I know I would love to travel into space.	☐	☐
4	It is very expensive, and the money could be spent on better things.	☐	☐
5	Rockets are not environmentally friendly.	☐	☐
6	Tourism is important for the world's economy. Space tourism will be important too.	☐	☐

STRATEGY Listening actively

In a debate or formal discussion, it is important to show the other speakers that you are listening, and that you have understood and respect their ideas. You can do this by listening 'actively'.
- **A** Use body language to show you are paying attention: keep an upright posture, maintain eye contact and nod your head occasionally.
- **B** Show that you are listening by expressing interest and engagement, for example, *Really?*, *That's interesting*, *OK*, *right*, *I see*, *Wow!*, *No way!*
- **C** Ask follow-up questions, for example, *Why is that? What makes you say that?*

2 Read the strategy above and look at the photo below. Answer the questions.

1 Describe the body language you see.
2 How can the person on the left improve her body language?
3 Think about your own body language and how you express interest / engagement as you listen.

3 🔊 **8.07** Listen to Dianne talking about space tourism. Answer the questions.
1 Which ideas from Ex 1 does Dianne mention?
2 What follow-up question would you ask Dianne?

4 Read the debate topic. Make a list of points for and against the issue.

> We should do more to reduce light pollution.

5 Read the dialogue and choose the correct alternative.
A ¹I think we **look at / share** the view that light pollution is bad. However, I believe there are far more important environmental issues, like plastic waste and global warming …
B ²I hear **what you're saying / that you agree with me**, but surely all of these issues are connected. We need to have more respect for our environment. And that includes the light from our cities. ³This is something I feel **strongly / afraid** about. I believe we should switch off most street lights, say between midnight and 4 a.m.
A ⁴I respect your **point of view / saying**, but that simply isn't practical. Street lights are important for safety. They can't be switched off. ⁵There's **no question about that / an interesting perspective** for me.
B ⁶Let's accept that we don't **agree / feel strongly** about street lights. ⁷What if we look at it from **another angle / different eyes**? How about lights inside businesses and homes?
A ⁸I hadn't **accepted / considered** that aspect, but I don't think it can make a big enough impact.
B ⁹**I'm afraid / I respect** I'm really passionate about this. The behaviour of individual citizens can make a huge difference.

6 Match the underlined phrases in Ex 5 to headings A–C.
A Acknowledging a different perspective ___ ___ ___
B Finding common ground ___ ___ ___
C Emphasising your position ___ ___ ___

7 Read the opinions. Write a response to each one following the instructions.
1 'International air travel causes huge environmental damage.'
Ask a follow-up question: _____

2 'Pollution in our city is terrible. I think families should only be allowed one car.'
Use a phrase to find common ground: _____

3 'Volunteers should be given extra holidays because of all the good work they do.'
Acknowledge a different perspective and make a point of your own: _____

4 'It is too easy to buy unhealthy food. The government should ban fast food.'
State your own position and then emphasise it: _____

5 'A lot of photos on social media have been changed using computer software. They're fake.'
Acknowledge a different perspective. Make a point of your own, then ask a follow-up question based on the speaker's point: _____

Unit 8 91

8.9 WRITING

Write a well-structured discursive essay using nominalisation.

1 Read the essay task. Answer the questions to help you decide your own position on this topic.

'Fishing is bad for the planet.' Discuss.

1 Do you eat fish? If yes, do you know where it comes from and how it is caught?
2 Do you think dolphins should be protected? How about sharks and turtles?
3 How many people do you predict work in the fishing industry?
4 Who owns the ocean? Who should take responsibility for it?

2 Read a response to the essay task in Ex 1. Complete the planning chart to show the structure of the essay.

Introduction	State position:
	Key fact:
Paragraph 1	Point 1:
	Evidence / example:
Paragraph 2	Point 2:
	Evidence / example:
Conclusion	Restate your position:

A Every day, fishing boats accidentally catch dolphins, sharks and other protected species. This is called 'bycatch' and it is a huge problem, particularly for the largest, most intelligent animals in our oceans. According to scientific evidence, one fishing region accidentally killed between 6,000 and 10,000 dolphins in one year. Another major problem is 'overfishing', which means that too many fish are caught. If overfishing occurs for several years in a row, fish life can be completely eliminated.

B The fishing industry is extremely important for people around the world. Over 59 million people work to catch or farm fish. Fishing problems can therefore have a huge impact on people as well as on the environment. For example, in 1992, a large fishing industry in Canada went out of business because too many fish had been caught. When there were no more fish, there was no more work. Approximately 35,000 people lost their jobs. However, this damaging event ¹led people to create the Marine Stewardship Council.

C Although individual countries have responsibility for the sea near their coastlines, two thirds of the ocean is known as 'the high seas' and belongs to everyone. Therefore ²we need to emphasise working together to protect our ocean. According to the Convention for Biological Diversity, the international community wants to protect 30% of the ocean by 2030. This will include more places where no fishing is allowed. ³Using different fishing equipment can also help. For example, fishing boats can use different nets to stop bycatch.

D Overall, I believe the fishing industry is currently bad for the planet. However, this is largely due to a lack of understanding and low levels of international assistance. The situation can and must improve. ⁴Developing new fishing techniques and improving public awareness will make a huge difference.

Marine Stewardship Council (MSC) is an international organisation that works to protect the ocean and its fishing industries. It allows fishing companies to use MSC labels on fish products if they meet good standards for reducing bycatch and overfishing.

STRATEGY Using nominalisation

Nominalisation is the use of nouns and noun phrases instead of verbs and verb phrases. It is a common feature of certain kinds of writing, especially essays. Using nominalisation will make your writing sound more formal and objective.
For example, instead of …
Developing the technology took two years.
This information enables us **to understand** the problem better.
we can write …
The development of the technology took two years.
This information enables **a better understanding of** the problem.

3 Read the strategy above. Rewrite underlined phrases 1–4 in the student essay using nominalisation. Use a dictionary if necessary to find the noun forms of *create, emphasise, using* and *developing*.

4 Rewrite the sentences using nominalisation. Change the words in **bold**.

1 **Analysing** the data showed that overfishing was happening.
_____ the data showed that overfishing was happening.
2 We **define** 'bycatch' as 'species that are caught accidentally during fishing'.
_____ 'bycatch' is 'species that are caught accidentally during fishing'.
3 Everyone is responsible for **protecting** the ocean.
_____ the ocean is everyone's responsibility.
4 They **investigated** for twelve months.
_____ took twelve months.

5 You are going to write an essay. Complete the tasks.

'I can't help the oceans.' Discuss.

1 Read the task.
2 Decide on your position.
3 Copy the planning chart from Ex 2 into your notebook and complete it for this essay.

6 Write your essay.

7 ✓ **CHECK YOUR WORK** Did you …
• follow your plan?
• use nominalisation to make your writing sound more formal?
• include grammar and vocabulary related to the topic?
• check your spelling, grammar and punctuation?

8.10 REVIEW

Grammar

1 Complete the mini-dialogues with the correct form of the words in brackets.
1 'Have you heard their new song?' 'I think I _____ on the radio yesterday.' (hear / it / play)
2 'Isn't it a great song?' 'Do you think so? I don't _____ it that much.' (remember / like)
3 'Why are all the lights on?' 'Dad must have _____ them off when he left.' (forget / switch)
4 'What are you wearing to the party?' 'I've _____ me her red jacket.' (persuade / my sister / lend)
5 'You cannot borrow my jacket! I _____ it!' 'But you promised I could wear it!' (refuse / allow)
6 'Why isn't he worried?' 'He's only a child. You can't _____ the situation.' (expect / him / understand)
7 'Why didn't you tell me?' 'I'm sorry. I completely _____ it.' (forget / mention)
8 'I want to help, but I don't know how.' 'I _____ a donation to the refuge.' (recommend / give)

2 Choose the correct alternative.
1 **Since moving / Moved** to the city, Nell is a lot more confident.
2 **Having seen / Seen** as part of a bigger situation, her decision makes sense.
3 **While worrying / Worried by** the situation, we decided to discuss it with our teacher.
4 **Before speaking / Having spoken** to Mike, I understand now.
5 **When walking / Walking** in the mountains, always tell someone where you plan to go.
6 **Having known / Despite knowing** her for years, her response wasn't a surprise to me.
7 **On studying / Despite studying** the piano for three years, he was still a beginner.
8 **Considered / Considering** another way, he was making good progress at the piano.

Vocabulary

3 The verbs in **bold** are in the wrong sentences. Change them to make correct sentences.
1 I like formal debates in class. It allows us to **make** with the issues of the day.
2 This refuge is a safety net for families who **raise** homeless.
3 Would you like to **retain** a contribution to our charity shop?
4 We hope to **engage** funds for a new roof for the community library.
5 It can be challenging for elderly people to **provide** their independence.
6 I work for an educational charity. We **become** assistance for older teenagers with learning disabilities.

4 Match the sentence halves.
1 After a natural disaster, aid ___
2 Rescue workers helped hundreds of survivors ___
3 The storm has finished, but the relief ___
4 This government wants to eliminate ___
5 Medical staff need good equipment ___
6 The charity used helicopters to distribute ___

A the suffering caused by water insecurity.
B to leave the flooded area.
C agencies are often the first organisations to arrive.
D to help them preserve lives.
E effort will last for many months.
F food and water because the local infrastructure was damaged.

Cumulative review

5 Complete the text with the words and phrases below. There are three words or phrases you do not need.

| assess   faced   facing   hardship   lack   learned
| learning   leaving   one-to-one   process   refugees
| teaching   to learn   to work   working

> **How do you use technology to help others? We'd particularly like to hear from volunteers and charity workers.**
>
> **KumalJ** I'm an engineering student in Nepal. My part of the country experienced a terrible earthquake not long ago. ¹_____ with dangerous buildings, technology has been an important part of the response. On ²_____ about a crisis-mapping project based in my university, I signed up as a volunteer. We've used drones to take videos and ³_____ the damage. Then we ⁴_____ the video information to create maps for the local community. The project has allowed me ⁵_____ many new skills, and I've particularly enjoyed ⁶_____ with the drones. I hope ⁷_____ for a crisis-mapping organisation when I graduate.
>
> **IonaL** Hi! I volunteer with a language charity called Buddy. We give small online classes and ⁸_____ tuition to people who have arrived in my country but do not speak the language. Several of my students are ⁹_____ who have left their home country to escape a humanitarian crisis. While ¹⁰_____, they suffered real ¹¹_____. At the start of the course, people often ¹²_____ confidence, and it's very rewarding to see that change over time. It's a great way to give something back, and I've made several good friends.

> **REFLECT** Think about the following questions.
> 1 Which lesson in this unit was your favourite? Why?
> 2 Which of the grammar points did you find most difficult? Why?
> 3 What can you do to practise listening to informal English?
> 4 What three things can you do to improve your active listening skills?

7–8 EXAM SKILLS

Listening

EXAM STRATEGY

When you do a multiple-choice task, you may hear words which are the same as the words in the options. Read the options carefully and think about the context and meaning. Decide whether the words you hear are making the same points.

1 Read the strategy above. Then read the first question and set of options in the exam task in Ex 2.

Which statement (A–D) …
1 describes a work proposal?
2 describes a problem?
3 makes a comparison?
4 talks about numbers?

2 🔊 8.08 For each question, listen and choose the correct answer: A, B, C or D.

1 You hear two people talking about volunteering. What does the young man say about his experience?
   A The morning was the most enjoyable part.
   B The majority of the staff were volunteers.
   C The customers were sometimes difficult.
   D The manager offered him a paid position.

2 You hear someone addressing a group of people. What is the speaker's purpose?
   A to invite people to support the elderly
   B to report on different successes for the group
   C to encourage people to pick up litter
   D to ask for volunteers to run the weekly meetings

3 You hear a young woman talking about raising money. What does she say about the experience?
   A She was disappointed in the response.
   B She encountered difficulties setting up a website.
   C She found different ways to sell donations.
   D She lacked confidence in her ability to make sales.

4 You hear two friends talking about doing some voluntary work. What do they decide to try to do?
   A help homeless people
   B volunteer in two different places
   C listen to young children read
   D help out in a charity shop

5 You hear a man talking about the voluntary organisation he represents. What is the speaker's purpose?
   A to ask for donations to his organisation
   B to provide information about voluntary work abroad
   C to describe his role as a team leader
   D to persuade students to do paid charity work

Use of English

EXAM STRATEGY

The missing words in an open cloze task may test vocabulary or grammar. First identify what the gap is testing. For grammar items, consider whether the missing word is an auxiliary verb, a linking verb, etc. For vocabulary items, consider whether the word is part of a set phrase or a phrasal verb.

3 Read the strategy above. Then read the exam task in Ex 4. Read the first sentence. Is the gap testing vocabulary or grammar? What is the missing word?

4 Read the text below and think of the word which best fits each gap (1–10). Use only one word in each gap.

Protecting bees

Bees are an important part of the natural world, but sadly they ¹_____ being threatened by disease, climate change and the use of chemicals. Considering these problems, it's hard ²_____ feel optimistic about the future. However, many organisations have ³_____ campaigning to help bees and people are starting to listen. For example, on investigating the problem, the European Commission decided to ban certain chemicals. This is good news, but more needs to be done. One of the ways in which ordinary people can ⁴_____ a contribution is by encouraging bees into their gardens. Before you go ⁵_____ to plant your flowers, however, it's a good idea to find out which flowers attract bees. Different bees are active at different times, so you'll need to plant a variety of flowers ⁶_____ order to encourage them throughout the year. After you have successfully attracted the bees, you can ⁷_____ an eye on their numbers. Many nature organisations collect this information so they are ⁸_____ to assess the situation. Of course, there are other ways you can ⁹_____ a hand to the cause. Why not donate to charities which have been set ¹⁰_____ to help bees?

Reading

EXAM STRATEGY

In 'True, False or Doesn't Say' tasks, the statements follow the order of the text. Find the part of the text that matches each statement. If the information you need is not in the right place, or only part of the meaning is there, the answer is not given.

5 Read the strategy above. Then read the first paragraph of the text in the exam task in Ex 6. Read the first statement and find any reference to the topic in the paragraph. Is the answer *T* (true), *F* (false) or *DS* (doesn't say)? Why?

94 Unit 8

7–8 EXAM SKILLS

6 Read the article about space. For each statement (1–8), write *T* (true), *F* (false) or *DS* (doesn't say).

Space technology by Eleanor Poole

Critics see space exploration as a waste of money which would be better spent on fighting poverty on Earth. There is criticism too of wealthy people who insist on travelling into space. However, there is another side to this argument. Some scientists, including myself, believe that one of the best ways of solving Earth's problems is through space technology itself.

Satellites are an example of how space technology provides data about how our planet is changing. When the damage to the Earth's atmosphere was identified by satellites, governments around the world signed an agreement to make research into climate change a priority. Satellites also monitor parts of the Earth which are difficult to reach. They can locate oil spills and provide data on wildlife and habitats.

Space technology helps us understand more about the human body. Scientists have discovered that some of the changes that take place in astronauts during space travel are similar to problems associated with ageing. Other research has produced findings that help people suffering from diseases such as heart problems.

Such technology can also be adapted for everyday purposes, for example, GPS navigation systems and the cameras in our phones, which were originally developed for spaceships. Space allows us to connect through satellite TV, phones and internet access.

As well as giving us technology, space inspires young people who are often fascinated by the stars and who see astronauts as role models. They are encouraged to become scientists and engineers, which are necessary jobs for the development of our world.

There is also an argument which suggests it is good for wealthy people to travel into space. After seeing how small Earth is from space, many astronauts talk about having a new understanding of the environment. If wealthy people who go there come back with the same attitude, they may invest in saving our planet.

1 The writer has never travelled into space. ___
2 Information from satellites helped world leaders decide to fight climate change. ___
3 Satellites are unable to gather information from remote places. ___
4 Scientists say that similar health problems can affect both astronauts and the elderly. ___
5 Space technology was used in the first heart operation. ___
6 Phone cameras were inspired by space technology. ___
7 The writer became a scientist after being inspired by an astronaut. ___
8 The writer thinks only trained astronauts should travel into space. ___

Speaking

EXAM STRATEGY

In a role-play, when you discuss and make decisions about different options, make sure you have several ideas that you can talk about. When you have fully explored an option, move onto the next using phrases such as *Let's talk about the next point*.

7 Read the strategy above. Then read the exam task in Ex 8. Think of two reasons why taking part in a marathon would be a good idea for students and two reasons why it would not be. Do the same for the other points.

8 💬 Work in pairs. Imagine the following situation. Your teacher has asked you to make suggestions for ways the students in your class can raise funds for a local charity. Talk to your partner about how practical and effective each of the ideas below is. Try to agree on one of them. Use appropriate phrases to move on to each new point.

- taking part in a marathon
- collecting items for a sale
- holding a cake sale at school

Writing

EXAM STRATEGY

Prepare for writing informal emails and letters by learning suitable fixed expressions and phrases that you can use.

9 Read the strategy above. Which of the expressions below would you expect to read in an informal email?

1 It's great to hear from you.
2 Thank you for getting in touch.
3 I am writing to inform you …
4 I was wondering what you're doing later.
5 I look forward to hearing from you.
6 See you soon!

10 Read the email from your English-speaking friend, Max. Write an email reply to Max, answering his questions. Use your own experience of volunteering or imagine some voluntary work you have done. Use appropriate expressions and phrases.

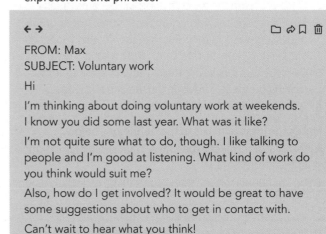

FROM: Max
SUBJECT: Voluntary work

Hi

I'm thinking about doing voluntary work at weekends. I know you did some last year. What was it like?

I'm not quite sure what to do, though. I like talking to people and I'm good at listening. What kind of work do you think would suit me?

Also, how do I get involved? It would be great to have some suggestions about who to get in contact with.

Can't wait to hear what you think!

Max

Unit 8 95

1 HOW TO LEARN VOCABULARY

Idioms

1 a Look at the phrases in **bold** below. What do we call phrases like these? What do they have in common?
  1 Oh, dear! I think I **put my foot in it** when I asked Andy if Sue was coming to the party. He looked quite upset. I don't think they're friends anymore.
  2 I **didn't know what hit me** when I started my new job. It was very tough and it took me ages to get used to it.
  3 I had to **learn** the poem **by heart** because we weren't allowed to read on stage.

b Look at Ex 1a again. Are the sentences true (*T*) or false (*F*)?
  A Speaker 1 has physically stepped in something. ___
  B Speaker 2 was not physically hurt by an object. ___
  C Speaker 3 used their heart to learn the poem. ___

2 Match the phrases in **bold** in Ex 1 to the definitions below.
  A memorise ___
  B say or do something that upsets, offends or embarrasses somebody ___
  C be so surprised by something unpleasant or shocking that you do not know how to react ___

WORD SKILLS Idioms

An idiom is a group of words whose meaning is different from the literal meanings of the individual words. The literal meaning of a word or phrase is its basic meaning. For example, the literal meaning of *Break a leg!* is 'damage your leg by breaking a bone, usually accidentally', whereas the idiom *Break a leg!* means 'Good luck!' It isn't always easy to recognise an idiom, but if a phrase looks strange or unusual, it's a good idea to look it up in a dictionary. When looking up an idiom, choose the most important word in the phrase and look for the idiom under its definition. Sometimes you might have to look it up under a couple of words before you find it.

3 Read the information above. Underline the idioms in the sentences below.
  1 Peter ignores everything we say and won't listen to advice. He's going to have to learn the hard way.
  2 I've been here all my life, so I know this town backwards.
  3 Once you learn the ropes, the job will become much easier.
  4 Marina refused to take her jumper to school this morning because it was so sunny. But then the weather changed and she felt really cold all day. That certainly taught her a lesson!
  5 Our teachers make sure their students are learning and making progress. They don't just teach to the test.
  6 Pablo is such an irritating person. He knows all the answers!

4 Match the idioms in Ex 3 to the definitions below.
  A learn, as a result of experience, what should not be done in the future ___
  B be confident that you know something, especially when you actually do not ___
  C know somebody / something extremely well ___
  D teach students only what is necessary in order to pass exams, rather than help them develop a range of skills ___
  E find out about something by learning from your mistakes or from unpleasant experiences, rather than from being told ___
  F learn how a particular job should be done ___

5 Rewrite the sentences with the correct form of the idioms below. Look them up in the dictionary first if necessary.

  an old head on young shoulders   one of the old school
  pass with flying colours   put your thinking cap on
  too cool for school

  1 I'm going to give this problem my full attention and try to solve it now.
  _____
  2 I got 100% in the exam.
  _____
  3 Soraya behaves in a sensible and grown-up way even though she's only ten.
  _____
  4 Martin wears such fashionable clothes – he looks amazing!
  _____
  5 My grandfather never goes out without putting on a jacket and tie. He's so old-fashioned.
  _____

LEARNING STRATEGY Making idioms memorable

When you come across an idiom, you can use different strategies to make it memorable.

Context
Write a funny sentence or short story using the idiom, for example:

Freddy said he **knew** *our neighbourhood* **like the back of his hand**, *but when his father asked him to take his uncle to the bus station, he got completely lost and his uncle missed the bus.*

Drawing
Draw a little picture next to the idiom, for example:

learn by heart

Personalise
Use the idiom in a sentence about your own experience, for example:

I **didn't know what hit me** *when I started football training. It was really hard!*

6 Read the strategy. Look at the underlined idioms in the sentences below. Choose one of the methods above to make the idioms memorable.
  1 I didn't need to continue with my studies. The university of life was enough for me.
  2 Gina dropped out of university and went travelling.
  3 There is more than one school of thought on the subject of how to bring children up.
  4 Their research into sustainable energy has broken new ground.

7 Find two idioms in the dictionary by looking up one of the verbs below. Write them in your vocabulary notebook with an example sentence or a drawing.

  give   read   sing   write

96 How to learn vocabulary

2 HOW TO LEARN VOCABULARY

Collocations

1 Choose the correct alternative.
1 Going through hard times helps people **accomplish / build / produce** resilience.
2 It's impossible to go through life without **examining / facing / seeing** challenges.
3 You need to **accept / agree / believe** the fact that you can't always solve a problem.
4 Although I have a very challenging job, it isn't a problem because I **succeed at / thrive on / win at** stress.
5 My teachers have helped me **build / construct / create** self-confidence.

WORD SKILLS Collocations

A collocation is two or more words which are often used together. It is useful to learn them because they expand your vocabulary and make your English sound natural. You can make collocations with different parts of speech:

verb + noun (V+N)	make a commitment
verb + adverb (V+A)	return safely
adjective + noun (A+N)	strange coincidence
adverb + verb (A+V)	quite agree
adverb + adjective (A+A)	completely satisfied

2 Read the information above. Complete the sentences.
1 Words that go together like those in Ex 1 are called _____.
2 They are important because they make your language sound _____.

3 <u>Underline</u> the collocations in the sentences.
1 I am eternally grateful for all your help. _____
2 You should listen carefully to what she says. _____
3 You need to accept responsibility for your actions. _____
4 We were absolutely delighted to have been invited. _____
5 I strongly recommend that you watch this. _____
6 Please make an effort to co-operate. _____
7 We were late because of the heavy traffic. _____
8 It was a huge mistake not to go. _____
9 Work hard and you'll succeed. _____
10 Mindfulness is widely believed to be helpful. _____

4 What parts of speech are the collocations in Ex 3? Write V+N, V+A, A+N, A+V or A+A next to each sentence.

5 Complete the <u>underlined</u> collocations in A with the same verb and in B with the same noun.

A
1 If you can't _____ <u>competition</u>, you shouldn't take part in the race.
2 You'll have to _____ <u>the consequences</u> of your actions.
3 You need to be able to _____ <u>problems</u> rather than run away from them.
4 After making so many mistakes, she could _____ <u>the threat</u> of losing her job.

B
5 Work-related _____ is a problem for many people doing this job.
6 Once I learned to <u>deal with</u> _____ in my new job, I began to enjoy it.
7 Poverty and lack of education <u>cause more</u> _____ than people think.
8 Yoga and meditation can be very helpful for people who <u>suffer from</u> _____.

LEARNING STRATEGY Recording and remembering collocations using mind maps

When you come across a new collocation, it's a good idea to record it, adding the parts of speech of each word. Once you know more than three collocations using the same word, make a mind map to help you remember them. For example:

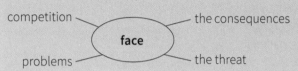

6 Read the strategy. Complete the mind maps with the words below.

| anticipation   a reputation   a working relationship |
| an invitation   an offer   responsibility   returns   trust |

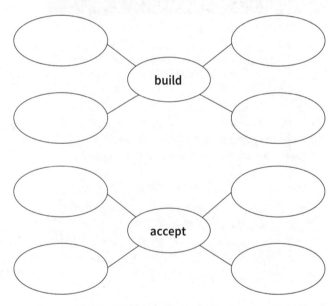

7 Look at the pairs of collocations below and choose two. Find two more collocations using the same word from each pair. Make a mind map to remind you of them. You can use a dictionary to help you.

take a risk / take time (V+N)
live well / live dangerously (V+A)
gradual progress / quick progress (A+N)
strongly dislike / strongly agree (A+V)
absolutely sure / absolutely right (A+A)

3 HOW TO LEARN VOCABULARY

Word building

1 Look at the words below. What do they all have in common?

dangerous
addictive
failure
completely
challenging
dutiful
responsibility
celebration

2 Now look at these words. What do they all have in common?

midnight
overcharge
prehistory
international
unusual
impatient
contrast
translation

WORD SKILLS Recognising prefixes and suffixes and identifying the base word

You can increase your vocabulary by using prefixes and suffixes. A prefix often changes the meaning of a base word, for example, *dis-* changes *agree* into the opposite: *disagree*. A suffix often changes the word into a different part of speech, for example, *-ure* added to the verb *fail* changes it into a noun: *failure*. In some cases, the spelling might change slightly, for example, the verb *please* + *-ure* becomes *pleasure* without an *e* before *-ure*. Once you have identified the base word (*agree*, *fail*, *please*), you can build more words using prefixes and suffixes.

Common prefixes include: *anti-, co-, dis-, ex-, extra-, im-, un-, mid-, non-, pre-, re-, over-,* etc.

Common suffixes include: *-al, -able, -ed, -ence, -ible, -ic, -ion, -ity, -ful, -ial, -ing, -ly, -ment, -ous, -ship, -ure,* etc.

3 Read the information above. Identify the base words in Ex 1 and Ex 2 and write them down next to each word.

4 Complete the sentences using a prefix or a suffix and the base word in brackets. Think about what part of speech it should be.
1 If you have _____ skills, it means you can use something you've learned in one context in a different one. (transfer)
2 I'm much more _____ now that I've been doing yoga. (flex)
3 Rita has developed very good _____ skills since becoming captain of the team. (organise)
4 We're looking for someone with good _____ skills to fill this role. (lead)
5 Talent and hard work are _____ important if you want to succeed in sport. (equal)
6 Although he isn't very good, Tim is an _____ tennis player. (enthuse)
7 You need to practise _____ if you want to be good at any sport. (regular)
8 'With great power comes great _____' is a very famous quote. (responsible)
9 Successful _____ between colleagues has hugely increased the company's profits. (collaborate)

LEARNING STRATEGY Making a word-building table

One way to increase your vocabulary and remember new words with prefixes and suffixes is to make a table like the one below. You can add to it every time you come across a new example.

Not all words can be made into all parts of speech. For example, you can have *confidence* (noun) and you can be *confident* (adjective), but you can't make a verb from *confidence*. You have to say something like *to become confident* or *to build confidence*. Note that the verb *confide* has a completely different meaning (*to tell someone your secrets*). If in doubt, check in your dictionary.

Verb	Noun	Adjective	Adverb	Opposite
–	confidence	confident	confidently	–
succeed	success	successful	successfully	unsuccessful / unsuccessfully

5 Read the strategy. Complete the table below. Check the spelling in your dictionary.

Verb	Noun	Adjective	Adverb	Opposite
benefit				
		transferable		
	stress			
				irresponsible
	duty			
complicate				
				inequality
commit				

6 Find more words with prefixes and suffixes in Units 1–3 and add them to your table.

4 HOW TO LEARN VOCABULARY

Noun phrases

1 Underline the subjects in the sentences. What do you notice about them?
1. One-storey houses without any stairs are called bungalows.
2. Modern open-plan flats with big windows are very popular at the moment.
3. Automatic window blinds are very convenient.
4. Commuting by bus is slower than going by train.
5. The development of green spaces is a priority for the government.

WORD SKILLS Noun phrases

A noun phrase is a group of words that behaves in the same way as a noun. It can be the subject or object of a sentence and is used to give detail, to clarify and make something more specific. It also makes your writing less repetitive. Compare A and B below:

A There is a flat above mine. It is huge and modern. It is being sold.
B The huge, modern flat above mine is being sold.

The noun phrase in sentence B is the subject of the sentence and tells you what you need to know in a more concise and interesting way.

All noun phrases have a **head noun**, which is the main noun or compound noun in the phrase. We use **premodifiers** before the head noun. These can be determiners (*a*, *the*, *these*), quantifiers (*lots of*, *some*), numbers (*two*, *three*), adjectives (*lovely*, *modern*) or compound adjectives (*open-plan*, *old-fashioned*). The words that come after the head noun are **postmodifiers** (words that give more information about the head noun). For example:

The house they bought last week is very modern.
head noun: *house*
postmodifier: *they bought last week*
The fact that house prices are going up is terrible.
head noun: *fact*

2 Read the information above. Look at the noun phrases and underline the head noun.
1. modern university-owned halls of residence
2. comfortable study bedrooms with their own bathroom
3. other people in a similar situation
4. an affordable flat to rent near the city centre
5. a convenient place to live
6. a growing community of modern nomads
7. an unwillingness to put down roots
8. a home with all mod cons

3 Complete the noun phrases with the words below.

| housing   light bulbs   settlement   societies
| solar panels   staircase   use   work surfaces

1. affordable, energy-efficient _____ for the city's street lights
2. six _____ on the roof
3. a temporary _____ in the desert
4. beautiful stone _____ in the kitchen
5. ingenious _____ of space
6. a beautiful wooden _____ leading up to the studio
7. enough affordable _____ in our town
8. many traditional _____ around the world

LEARNING STRATEGY Using noun phrases to add detail and make your writing more interesting

Using noun phrases in your writing will make it sound more interesting, especially if you are writing a descriptive text or a story. It will also help you avoid repetition.

When you are writing, try to add detail to nouns, using pre- and postmodifiers. It is especially useful to do this when you are writing a second draft or revising your work.

4 Read the strategy. Write one sentence with the information given. Underline the noun phrases.

We live in a house. The house is new and made of wood. It's by the river. It's an eco-house.
We live in a new, wooden eco-house by the river.

1. There are lots of buildings. The buildings are affordable. They are empty. They are in the city centre.
   There are _____.
2. They studied many societies. The societies were all around the world. They were traditional. They were nomadic.
   They studied _____.
3. There is a community of modern nomads. The community is growing. They are in the US.
   There is _____.
4. The Student Housing Company provides accommodation. The accommodation is high quality. It is private. It is for foreign university students.
   The Student Housing Company _____
   _____.

5 Make noun phrases using the nouns below or use nouns of your choice. For example:

house	*a big modern house by the sea*
bedroom	_____
kitchen	_____
living room	_____
garden	_____
van	_____
boat	_____
container	_____

How to learn vocabulary 99

5 HOW TO LEARN VOCABULARY

Compound adjectives and nouns

1 a Look at the sentences below and underline seven compound words.
  1 You should be aware that your personal data could be used without your consent.
  2 The company needs to update its website because it isn't well designed.
  3 We are worried about the children's well-being.
  4 After university, she got a highly paid job in the financial sector.
  5 My eighteen-year-old brother has just left school.

  b Which are compound nouns? Which are compound adjectives? Which one is a compound verb? How do you know?

WORD SKILLS Compound adjectives and nouns

Compound nouns are made up of two or more words which can be noun + noun (*distance learning*), adjective + noun (*personal data*), noun + verb (*landfill*) or adverb + noun (*well-being*). They can be two or more separate words, one word or hyphenated.

Compound adjectives are also made up of two or more words which can be nouns, adjectives, adverbs and present or past participles. They are usually hyphenated when they come before a noun (*face-to-face meeting, high-quality materials, nine-year-old computer*), but not hyphenated after a noun (*the materials are high quality, the computer is nine years old*).

Note: compound adjectives are not hyphenated before a noun when the first word is an -*ly* adverb (*poorly designed tools, highly intelligent student*).

2 Read the information above. Complete the table with the compound adjectives and nouns below.

| digital revolution   distance learning   film-making |
| five-part   game changing   high quality |
| user experience   user-friendly |

Compound nouns	Compound adjectives

3 Complete the sentences with compound nouns and adjectives from Ex 2. Hyphenate (-) the compound adjectives if necessary.
  1 They used to be quite complicated, but most computer programs are very _____ these days.
  2 The _____ started in the 1980s and brought with it the internet, mobile phones and social media.
  3 We've watched two episodes of a _____ series on the environmental impact of plastic pollution.
  4 _____ technology such as robotics has changed the way surgeons perform operations.
  5 _____ became common during the pandemic when people couldn't leave home to go to school.
  6 We need to improve the _____ if we want more people to use our website.
  7 I studied _____ at university and now have a job as a TV programme director.
  8 _____ online courses, as good as face-to-face ones, are now available worldwide.

LEARNING STRATEGY Looking up compound words in a dictionary

It is worth looking up a compound word in the dictionary, but you won't always find the definition from looking up the first word. In other words, they don't have their own entry. However, you can usually find the meaning by checking each word. For example, you probably won't find the compound adjective *high-energy* in the dictionary, so you will have to work out the meaning from looking up both words and guessing the meaning from context, for example, 'high-energy batteries'. For compound adjectives, look up the second word first as it usually gives you a better clue. In this case, *energy* means 'a source of power' and *high* means 'greater than normal'.

Once you've worked out the meaning of a new compound adjective or noun, record it with its definition and an example sentence to help you remember it.

4 Read the strategy. Look at the compound words in **bold** in the sentences below. Then follow the instructions A–C below.
  1 I think it's better for **social interaction** to be in person rather than online. _____
  2 I would like to buy a **lightweight** tablet to replace my heavy laptop. _____
  3 Famous people almost always have a massive **digital footprint**. _____
  4 The most famous **video-sharing** website in the world is YouTube. _____
  5 I use a monthly **subscription service** to stream videos and music. _____
  6 Greenland is the least **densely populated** country in the world. _____

  A Write *CN* for compound noun and *CA* for compound adjective next to each sentence.
  B Put a tick (✓) next to the compound words that have their own dictionary entry.
  C Find out what the others mean from looking up the first or second word, or both if necessary.

5 Look at the words below. Choose the ones that you do not know and look them up in a dictionary. Record them with an example sentence. Add *CA* (compound adjective) or *CN* (compound noun) to each example.

badly finished   _____
global warming   _____
highly valued   _____
landfill   _____
pop-up   _____
raw materials   _____
second rate   _____
well maintained _____

6 HOW TO LEARN VOCABULARY

Connotation

1 Look at sentences 1–3. What is similar about them? Then answer questions A–C.
1 She's interested in other people.
2 She's curious about other people.
3 She's nosey about other people.

A Which sentence is neutral?
B Which is negative or critical?
C Which is positive and more approving?

WORD SKILLS Connotations

Connotation means an idea suggested by a word in addition to its main meaning. For example, the word *strict* makes you think of authority, perhaps a severe teacher, while the word *intellectual* might make you think of someone intelligent and well educated, perhaps a university professor.

Another example is the word *dazzling*, which means *so bright that you can't see for a while*, for example, *Those headlights were so dazzling I was almost blinded*. In this case it has no specific connotations, but it can also be used to describe a person or a thing that is very impressive or beautiful, for example, *She looked dazzling in her gorgeous dress*. In this case, *dazzling* means 'beautiful' or 'very attractive'. It has positive connotations.

Some words have positive connotations, some are neutral and others have negative connotations. For example:
*Anna is **thrifty**. She manages to live well on very little money.*
*Bob is **prudent** with money. He doesn't want to get into debt.*
*Sue is **stingy**. She hates spending money.*
All three words mean 'careful with money', but *thrifty* has positive connotations, *prudent* is neutral and *stingy* has negative connotations.

2 Read the information above. Look at the sentences below. Decide if the words in **bold** in each section (A–D) have positive (P), neutral (N) or negative (NEG) connotations. Use your dictionary to look up the words you don't know.

A
1 The volcano has been **inactive** for decades. _____
2 George is terribly **lazy** and never gets anything done. _____
3 Soraya is **laid-back** and relaxed about most things. _____

B
4 His behaviour is very **childish**. He needs to grow up. _____
5 She's a **young** woman of 23. _____
6 Although she's over 40, she's still very **youthful**. _____

C
7 Our **elderly** neighbours are very charming. _____
8 He was **old** when he died. _____
9 My 90-year-old aunt is too **decrepit** to leave the house. _____

D
10 George has some really **weird** ideas. _____
11 She likes to wear clothes which are **different**. _____
12 That was a **unique** and unforgettable experience. _____

LEARNING STRATEGY Recognising connotations

You can often guess connotation from context, but sometimes it isn't clear and it is therefore helpful to look the word up in a dictionary. For example, if you look up *childish*, you will get two definitions. The first one gives you the basic, neutral definition: *connected with or typical of a child*. The second definition gives you a clue about connotation: *(disapproving) (of an adult) behaving in a stupid or silly way*. You know, therefore, that in this context *childish* has negative connotations.

3 Read the strategy. Complete the table with the words below. Use your dictionary to look up the words you do not know.

| assertive | confident | extravagant |
| stink | stubborn | workaholic |

Positive connotation	Negative connotation
industrious	
	arrogant
resolute	
generous	
	domineering
aroma	

4 Complete the sentences with words from Ex 3.
1 Tina says her job is too busy for her to spend time with her family, but in reality, she's a _____.
2 Some people think Daniel is domineering, but I think that's an unfair criticism. He's just quite _____.
3 What a horrible _____! It's like rotten meat.
4 It's OK to be generous, but you really shouldn't be so _____. You can't afford it and you'll get into debt.
5 Anya is much more _____ than before. She is more sure of herself and her abilities and she's doing a great job.
6 Stop being so _____! Just admit you were wrong and change your mind.
7 Every morning, we woke up to the _____ of freshly baked bread. It was wonderful.
8 We felt safe with Paul as the leader of our expedition. He was always _____, calm and determined that we would all reach our destination.

5 Look at the pairs of words below. Decide which word has a more negative connotation. Use your dictionary to look up the words you do not know. Then write example sentences to help you remember how to use them.

a liar	a storyteller
private	stand-offish
haggard	tired
plain	nondescript

How to learn vocabulary **101**

7 HOW TO LEARN VOCABULARY

Position and order of adjectives

1 Look at the pairs of sentences. One is correct and the other is wrong. Tick (✓) the correct one. Can you work out what is wrong with the other sentence?

1. **A** We saw an interesting new Spanish film last night. ☐
   B We saw a Spanish new interesting film last night. ☐
2. **A** The story ends with a woman standing alone on a beach. ☐
   B The story ends with an alone woman standing on a beach. ☐

WORD SKILLS Position and order of adjectives

Generally, adjectives come before a noun (*That's a **famous** painting.*) or after a verb (*That painting is **famous**.*).

However, there are some adjectives that don't usually go before a noun, for example, *well* and *ill* and adjectives that start with the prefix *a-* (*alive, awake, annoyed, alone, asleep,* etc.).

She is ill. NOT ~~She is an ill woman.~~

The children are awake. NOT ~~They are awake children.~~

You can use more than one adjective before a noun, but it is unusual to use more than three or four.

When you have more than one adjective before a noun, we put them in the following order:

opinion → size → shape → age → colour → nationality / origin → material

For example:

a striking, huge, new building

some stunning, large, black pearl earrings

a thought-provoking, new, international production

Notice that when adjectives are of the same category, e.g. colour or materials, we separate them with *and*. For example:

*a black **and** white photo*

*a gold **and** silver necklace*

*some fascinating **and** unusual ideas*

2 Read the information above. Put the phrases in the correct order. Underline the nouns first.

1. a / French / remarkable / gold / mirror / round
2. a/an / 1950s / American / humorous / cartoon
3. a / painting of a / vivid / gorgeous / sunset
4. a / silver / stunning / sculpture / small
5. some / glass / colourful / vases / Italian
6. a / Danish / marvellous / TV series / new
7. a/an / table / oval / wooden / valuable / antique
8. a/an / young / world-famous / musician / Mexican

3 Rewrite the sentences with the words in brackets in the correct place. Make any necessary changes.

1. We saw a play. (Norwegian / modern / unusual)

   _____

2. It's a photo. (black / white / fascinating / 1940s)

   _____

3. It's a building. (metal / glass / pyramid-shaped)

   _____

4. I visited a museum in Spain. (modern / world-famous / huge)

   _____

5. He painted a portrait of a man sitting on a sofa. (young / interesting / red-haired)

   _____

LEARNING STRATEGY Making adjectives memorable

One way to make new adjectives more memorable is to use them in a sentence which is true for you, for example:

outstanding

I thought Florence Pugh's performance in the film Little Women *was outstanding.*

remarkable

I think The Hobbit *is the most remarkable book I've ever read.*

You can also think of works of art, films or plays that you know and that you really like and write short descriptions of them, using as many adjectives as you can. For example:

Christina of Denmark

Hans Holbein painted this **striking** portrait of the **beautiful sixteen-year-old** Danish princess in 1538. He was asked to paint it by King Henry VIII, who was looking for a fourth wife. It is one of Holbein's **best-known** paintings and one of the most **famous** in the National Gallery in London. Although it is not a **colourful** painting, the **dramatic** contrast between her **black** clothes and **pale young** face and **white** hands is **stunning**. It is also **thought-provoking**. Why was someone so young wearing black? Henry VIII loved the painting and kept it for the rest of his life, but he didn't marry Christina because her uncle, Emperor Charles V, wouldn't allow it.

4 Read the strategy. Complete the sentences below so they are true for you.

1. I think _____ is the most striking masterpiece I've ever seen.
2. _____ is a modern painting with vivid colours.
3. _____ is a detailed and realistic portrait.

5 Choose a painting, a play, a film or a piece of music that you particularly like. Write a short description of it using as many adjectives as you can in the correct order.

8 HOW TO LEARN VOCABULARY

Three-word phrasal verbs

1 a Underline the phrasal verbs in the pairs of sentences. What do you notice about them?
  1 A If you look up, you'll see lots of stars in the sky.
    B Ruth and Charlie look up to their older sister, Helen.
  2 A You'll have to go through the document carefully before you sign it.
    B I'm sorry, but I've changed my mind and I can't go through with the sale of my house.
  3 A The sun comes up at six every morning.
    B Have you come up with a solution yet?

b Match definitions A–F to the phrasal verbs in Ex 1a.
  A examine _____
  B rises _____
  C raise your eyes _____
  D do what is necessary to complete _____
  E found, discovered _____
  F admire and respect _____

WORD SKILLS Three-word phrasal verbs

Two-word phrasal verbs have two parts: a verb + a particle.

Three-word phrasal verbs have three parts: a verb + a particle + a preposition. For this reason, they are often called phrasal-prepositional verbs.

Guessing the meaning of three-word phrasal verbs is often harder than for two-word phrasal verbs, so it's a good idea to look them up in the dictionary if you can't guess the meaning from context.

Three-word phrasal verbs are always transitive, and almost always inseparable. In other words, they have an object and you can't separate the verb and the particle and preposition, for example:

look forward to + object

I **look forward to** the weekend.

NOT ~~I look the weekend forward to~~. or ~~I look forward the weekend to~~.

The only exception is when a three-part phrasal verb has two objects, for example:

put down to: put something down to something else

I **put** his bad mood **down to** tiredness. (= His bad mood is caused by his tiredness.)

Note: these are not very common, so as a rule, don't separate three-word phrasal verbs.

2 Read the information above. Look at the phrasal verbs below and tick (✓) the ones you know or have come across before. Check the others in your dictionary.

| get back to   go down with   grow out of   keep up with
| look down on   own up to   run out of   stand up for

3 Replace the underlined words in the sentences with the correct form of the phrasal verbs in Ex 2.
  1 It's important to defend the rights of refugees.
  2 The victims of the earthquake are hoping to return to their old life soon.
  3 After the floods, they soon finished their supply of food and fuel.
  4 You should admit your mistakes straight away.
  5 Children generally stop habits like biting their nails as they get older.
  6 You shouldn't think you are better than people just because they have less than you do.
  7 They continued to be in contact with old friends after the crisis even though they were all living in different countries.
  8 They were worried that people would become ill with water-related diseases like cholera after the floods.

LEARNING STRATEGY Checking the meaning of phrasal verbs

If you don't know the meaning of a phrasal verb and you can't work it out from its context, you should look it up in a dictionary. There will often be more than one definition, so you will have to read through all the possibilities before you decide which the correct one is. For example:

grow out of *phrasal verb*

grow out of something [no passive]
1 (of a child) to become too big to fit into a piece of clothing
  *He's already **grown out of** his school uniform.*
2 to stop doing something as you become older
  *Many children have to sleep with the light on, but they **grow out of** it.*
3 to develop from something
  *The idea for the book **grew out of** a visit to India.*

Using phrasal verbs makes your language sound more natural and less formal, so it's worth learning them and using them as much as possible.

To help you remember new phrasal verbs, write them in your vocabulary notebook with their definition and one or two example sentences. If possible, make these sentences true for you so they are easier to remember.

4 Read the strategy. Look at the sentences below. Underline the three-word phrasal verbs. Look them up in a dictionary and record them with their definition and another example sentence which is true for you.
  1 Their parents made up for their absence during the week by spending all their time with their children at the weekend.
  2 I can't put up with all this noise!
  3 Although they parked illegally, they got away with it. They didn't even get a ticket.
  4 I'm going to hold on to my signed copies of his book in case they go up in value.
  5 I'm not going to accept this offer. I'm going to hold out for a better one.
  6 They managed to pass off as students and get cheaper tickets for the exhibition.

5 Choose three phrasal verbs from the list below and write them in your vocabulary notebook with examples. Add them to the ones you recorded in Ex 4.

| break up with   come across as   cut down on
| face up to   fall out with   lead up to   live up to
| look out for   make off with   watch out for

How to learn vocabulary 103

1 VOCABULARY BOOSTER

Skills and natural talents and The ages we do things best

1 **PRACTISE** Complete the sentences with correct form of the words below.

| attempt   be motivated   focus your attention
| gain experience   hopeless   inspire   master

1 Hannah is brilliant at running long distance, but she's _____ at short distances because she's too slow.
2 I _____ to learn the rules of cricket, but gave up because they're so complicated.
3 If you get a job with our sales team, it won't be long before you _____ the art of selling.
4 I'm going to work at the theatre company voluntarily in order to _____.
5 Watching his cousin play tennis _____ Simran to take up the sport.
6 Instead of worrying about failing, you should _____ on revising for your exam.
7 Lisa _____ to practise the violin every day when she was chosen to join the school orchestra.

2 Match the sentence halves.
1 It's much easier to **recall** ___
2 It's useful to be good at **mental** ___
3 Although Amira **has an extensive** ___
4 It's difficult to **absorb** ___
5 I couldn't concentrate because you were ___
6 Although it's never too late to **acquire** ___
7 My grandma is 85 and **is** ___

A **vocabulary**, her grammar is quite poor.
B **names** if you repeat them often.
C **distracting** me with all your chatting.
D **arithmetic** when you're out shopping and being given change.
E a **second language**, it's easier when you're a child.
F **wise** and knowledgeable.
G **information** when you're looking at your phone at the same time.

3 **EXTEND** Complete the interview with the correct form of the words and phrases below.

| be a natural   build rapport   capitalise on
| fulfil our potential   have strict self-control
| push our boundaries   show leadership
| think outside the box

Interviewer Today I'm talking to George, captain of the under-18s football team. Hello, George. How does it feel to have won all your matches this year?
George It's a fantastic feeling. I'm so proud of our team. I always thought we were going to do well and now I can say that we've ¹_____.
Interviewer So what's the secret of your success?
George We worked really hard and we were prepared to ²_____ and go beyond what we thought we could achieve.
Interviewer Yes, you certainly proved that. And it must help to have Sam in your team.
George Of course. Sam is our star player. He ³_____ striker. He knows what to do instinctively and he's always there when the other players need him.
Interviewer Just in time to score another goal!
George Exactly. And as we kept on winning matches, we ⁴_____ our success. Every time we won, we agreed we would try even harder to win the next time.
Interviewer And what about you? Everybody says that as captain, you have ⁵_____. The team really respect you and do what you say.
George It's been easy, to be honest. We managed to ⁶_____ very early. All the players get on well and there's nothing they wouldn't do for each other.
Interviewer So what advice would you give another team?
George Two things, really. First, you need to play as a team and you have to ⁷_____. You can't be ruled by your feelings. Our players behave really well on the pitch and don't lose their tempers.
Interviewer Yes, everybody noticed that. And what's the second thing?
George Well, you want to be a little bit different, unpredictable. So when you're discussing strategies, you need to ⁸_____. You don't want the opposing team to be able to predict what you're going to do next.
Interviewer Well, it's really worked for you and the team. Congratulations!

4 Decide if you agree (A) or disagree (D) with the sentences. Rewrite the ones you do not agree with.
1 You can easily succeed at school without strict self-control.
2 In team games it's better not to think outside the box, but to do what has always worked in the past.
3 It's easy to build rapport with someone if you have a lot in common.
4 Everybody should push their boundaries when they are young.
5 If you aren't a natural at a sport, you shouldn't play it.
6 It's difficult to capitalise on success unless you are prepared to work hard.
7 If you're the captain of a team, it's more important for people to like you than to show leadership.
8 You can fulfil your potential by always doing your best.

5 Do a survey to find out the average age that friends, family and classmates learned particular skills. Choose five from the list below or make your own list.

| cooking   cycling   driving   ironing   knitting
| playing a musical instrument   sewing on a button
| skateboarding   swimming   typing

Ask questions to find out if it was the best age to learn the skill or if it would have been better at an earlier or later age. Write a short report with your findings. Add your own conclusion.

2 VOCABULARY BOOSTER

Feelings and other people's behaviour and Ways to improve your well-being

1 **PRACTISE** Complete the sentences with the correct form of the words in brackets. In each case, there is one word you do not need.
1. I know Rita is _____ **you crazy**, but it's no good getting angry. You need to _____ **down** and tell her how you feel. (calm, drive, fall)
2. Before _____ **a commitment** to a new exercise plan, you need to _____ **account** of factors like time, expense and how effective you think it will be. (evaluate, make, take)
3. Louise and Belinda _____ **over** their recent disagreement and have now _____ **up** with each other. (make, fall, talk)
4. I don't want to _____ **out** with Aziz, but he's really _____ **on my nerves** at the moment. (face, fall, get)
5. Make sure that you've _____ **all the options** available before you decide to _____ **a commitment** to such a stressful job. (drive, evaluate, make)
6. To _____ **a challenge** like running a marathon, you need to be able to _____ **your focus**. (face, drive, maintain)

2 Complete the text with the missing words. The first letter of each word is given.

When it comes to ¹m_____ h_____ problems, most of us have heard about people who worry a lot and suffer from ²a_____, or people who are often very sad and suffer from ³d_____. We might know about people with screen addiction, but do you know anyone who has an ⁴a_____ to work? Believe it or not, this is a serious condition and people who suffer from it are often very ill. For Ted, it started as soon as he went to school. He spent all his spare time doing homework and could never go out and play or take some ⁵d_____. His parents worried that he was so exhausted he would end up suffering from ⁶b_____ before he even got to university. But this didn't happen. He finished university and got a job straight away and worked fourteen-hour days – until one day he realised that at the age of 40 he had few friends, no family or children and that he had focused on work his entire life. He had many ⁷r_____ and felt sad that his life was so empty. But this was the beginning of his recovery because he had finally recognised that he had a problem and that he needed to do something about it. He had therapy and focused on improving his ⁸w_____-_____, doing more activities outside of work and having fun. He used to always follow work meetings and check emails in his free time, but he doesn't anymore. It wasn't easy to switch off his phone and stop giving his opinion or providing ⁹i_____ from home, but he has made a lot of progress. So much so, that next month he is going on holiday with a new group of friends. He also enjoys his job more and he believes he's better at it!

3 **EXTEND** Look at the words below. Which can be changed to mean the opposite by using the suffix -*less* or the prefix *in*-?

| competent   considerate   proactive   resilient
| self-critical   tactful   vulnerable   worthless

4 Match the phrases below to their opposites from Ex 3.
1. weak and unable to recover quickly _____
2. confident and conceited _____
3. very valuable _____

5 Complete the sentences with words from Ex 3 or their opposites.
1. Bill is incredibly _____. He's always upsetting people by saying the first thing that comes into his head. I wish he'd be a bit more _____.
2. Miranda seems conceited, but in fact I know she doubts herself all the time and is quite _____.
3. As a young man, Ade felt completely _____, but now that he's old, he is often scared and feels quite _____.
4. I know you thought they were very _____, but I'm afraid these objects are _____. You won't make any money if you sell them.
5. Although Chris seems very _____ and good at his job, he's actually hopeless at it. He's totally _____.
6. Don't be so selfish and _____. You should think about other people's feelings.
7. Although Leyla may seem weak, she is in fact very strong and _____.
8. You need to be more _____ if you want to get things done quickly and efficiently. It's no good being so passive and _____.

6 Write a multiple-choice questionnaire to find out about your family members' and friends' feelings. Find out …
- what makes them anxious.
- what they do to increase their well-being.
- what makes them want to throw in the towel.
- what they regret.
- what drives them crazy.
- what makes them feel vulnerable, etc.

Ask at least five people to complete your questionnaire. Then write a short report and prepare to give a presentation to the class.

1. Which of these makes you feel the most anxious?
   A being late for school or work
   B losing your keys or glasses
   C not finishing your homework
2. What do you do to increase your well-being?
   A make sure you've done all your work on time
   B see friends and family
   C watch a funny film

Vocabulary Booster   105

3 VOCABULARY BOOSTER

Keep fit and Transferable skills

1 **PRACTISE** Complete the text with the words below.

| addictive beneficial challenging complicated |
| enthusiastic flexible injury inspired |
| stiff thrilled |

Although exercise is almost always ¹_____, when you can't stop doing it and it becomes ²_____, it can do more harm than good. Sylvia's case is an example of what can go wrong. She was ³_____ to take up running during the Olympic Games. She found it very ⁴_____ at first because she was unfit, but soon she was running every day, usually with a running club. She was very keen and became one of their most ⁵_____ runners, and having gained a lot of strength and fitness, she was also one of their best. She was always very careful to do lots of stretching before and after running and as a result, she was very ⁶_____ and never got ⁷_____ or sore even after doing a marathon. But then things became ⁸_____. She found that one run a day wasn't enough, so she started running two or three times a day. She stopped seeing friends because she no longer had time for them. Luckily for Sylvia, a knee ⁹_____ meant she had to stop running and that gave her time to recognise that she had a problem. After a few months, she was able to get back to it, but now she only runs three times a week and she is ¹⁰_____ to have overcome her addiction.

2 Match the sentence halves.
1 It's easier to **take responsibility** ___
2 It's important to be able to **adapt** ___
3 Athletes need to **be willing** ___
4 Consistently excellent training can **contribute** ___
5 If you've made a mistake during a game, you need to **accept** ___
6 You have to learn to **cope under** ___
7 You need to be able to **deal** ___
8 It is important for athletes **to demonstrate** ___

A **enormously to** the success of a team.
B **an ability** to accept criticism as well as praise.
C **pressure** if you want to be a professional athlete.
D **for** the successes of the team rather than its failures.
E **to** accept that they can't win every time.
F **with failure** as well as success if you want to succeed as a professional player in your sport.
G **to** playing in countries with different weather conditions from your own.
H **the consequences of** your actions and apologise.

3 **EXTEND** Choose the correct answer: A, B or C.
1 How important is it for parents and children to ___ for each other?
  A stay ahead   B devote time   C have mutual respect
2 What might happen if you ___ and do something really adventurous?
  A leave your comfort zone
  B do yourself proud
  C keep something in perspective
3 Why should you ___ your dreams?
  A try out   B pursue   C stay ahead of
4 How would you react if you'd succeeded in something and ___?
  A had mutual respect   B kept something in perspective   C done yourself proud
5 How much time should people in their early twenties ___ to sport or exercise if they want to be really fit?
  A try out   B devote   C pursue
6 Why is it important not to get upset and to ___ if you've failed to achieve one of your goals?
  A devote time to something   B leave your comfort zone   C keep things in perspective
7 What routes or walks do you ___ because you've done them so many times?
  A devote time to   B know like the back of your hand   C do yourself proud
8 How can you ___ your homework?
  A stay ahead of   B keep in perspective   C pursue

4 Match the questions in Ex 3 to the answers below. Are there any you do not agree with or that do not apply to you?
A There is always another chance to succeed. Never give up!
B I'd be very happy with my performance, but I'd try not to boast about it or appear too conceited.
C I could do the walk to school with my eyes closed.
D It's essential that they listen to each other and respect each other's opinions.
E Do it immediately. Don't leave it to the last minute.
F They need to spend at least an hour a day being active.
G You only have one life so you should try to achieve the things you hope for.
H You'll probably learn a lot about yourself from having new and unusual experiences.

5 Create an exercise plan for one of the following:
• someone who is enthusiastic about team sports but works full time and so has little free time
• someone who has just recovered from a shoulder injury and is scared of damaging it
• someone who doesn't cope well under pressure but needs to get fit
• an older person who needs to become more flexible
• a young person who isn't good at dealing with failure but wants to play in a team
• someone who loves sports but has just moved to a new city and doesn't know anyone

Explain what they should and should not do. Make sure you give reasons. Present your plan to the class and ask them to guess who it is for.

106   Vocabulary Booster

4 VOCABULARY BOOSTER

Alternative living spaces and Nomads

1 **PRACTISE** Complete the texts with the correct form of the words below. For each text, there are two words you do not need.

| appeal to   dependent   emigrate
| ingenious   proportions   restricted

We are looking for a flat to rent and we've seen one that really **1**_____ us. The living room has generous **2**_____ which means it can fit a table and chairs as well as a big sofa. It has been designed in such a(n) **3**_____ way that you can divide the room easily with sliding doors and have two separate spaces if you want. The only disadvantage is that parking is **4**_____ in that part of town, so we'd have to park our car in a garage a few blocks away.

| assistance   dependent   existence
| ingenious   settle   wander

My 90-year-old grandfather has moved into sheltered housing because he needs **5**_____ with day-to-day living, especially shopping and cooking. He **6**_____ in very well and feels safer now that he isn't **7**_____ on his children and neighbours, but has someone in the same building who can help at any time of the day or night. He's much happier too because after my grandmother died, he'd lived a very lonely **8**_____, but now he can enjoy the company of other residents and has made lots of new friends.

| appeal to   emigrate   existence
| proportions   settle   wander

My sister and her husband decided to spend a few years travelling before they **9**_____ down. After **10**_____ around Europe and Asia, they've finally decided to **11**_____ to Thailand. They're planning to open a restaurant near the beach. That kind of lifestyle really doesn't **12**_____ me, but I know they'll love it!

2 Match the words below to the photos.

| remote control   shelter   smart appliances
| staircase   urban area   work surfaces

3 Complete the sentences with words from Ex 2.
1 There isn't a _____ in the house because it's a bungalow, so everything is on one floor.
2 Do you have any _____ in your house that you can control from your phone?
3 It's very difficult to cook in this kitchen because there aren't enough _____.
4 Most people live in _____ because there are more jobs available.
5 When we went on a weekend expedition to the countryside, we had to build a _____ to sleep in.
6 I can't turn on my TV without a _____.

4 **EXTEND** Match 1–6 to A–F.
1 be ___   A necessities
2 be uprooted ___   B an assumption
3 make ___   C disadvantaged
4 live ___   D your own destiny
5 have basic ___   E from your home
6 control ___   F in social housing

5 Complete the questions with words from Ex 4.
1 What basic _____ do you think all people should have access to?
2 Why do you think people in rural areas are often more _____ than people living in urban areas?
3 Why do children often suffer the most _____ in difficult times?
4 What are the advantages and disadvantages of living in _____?
5 Do you know anyone who has been _____ from their home?
6 Have you ever _____ that was wrong? What was it?

6 Answer the questions in Ex 5. Then ask four people you know the same or similar questions. Compare answers. Write a short report and prepare to give a presentation to the class.

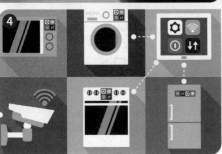

5 VOCABULARY BOOSTER

Technology and Effects of technology on the environment

1 **PRACTISE** Choose the correct alternative.
   1 Installing solar panels has been **game-changing / environmentally friendly** for us as our electricity bills have gone down dramatically.
   2 Solar power is a **sophisticated / viable** alternative to coal and gas.
   3 Our office is really **high-tech / renewable** with all the latest innovations, including smart desks and lights that you can control from your phone.
   4 We need to use **environmentally friendly / user-friendly** packaging that is either biodegradable or recyclable.
   5 There have been **renewable / significant** advances in automotive technology in the last 20 years.
   6 Criminals use increasingly **game-changing / sophisticated** methods to trick people into believing they are communicating with their bank.
   7 If we can't manufacture **innovative / significant** products, we will no longer be up to date and relevant in the market.
   8 Wind, wave, geothermal and solar power are good for the environment because they provide **game-changing / renewable** energy.
   9 The heating system in our flat is so complicated that I've decided to change it to a more **high-tech / user-friendly** one.

2 Complete the questions with the missing words. The first letter of each word is given.
   1 What's the best way to d_____ of unwanted computers and phones?
   2 Why is it important for businesses to post u_____ on social media?
   3 What can we use instead of fossil fuels to g_____ power?
   4 Which metal used in smartphone batteries should always be r_____ instead of being thrown away?
   5 What happens when you b_____ the internet?
   6 How did people listen to music and watch films at home before s_____ was invented?
   7 In what way does new technology e_____ our planet?

3 **EXTEND** Match the questions in Ex 2 to the answers below.
   A A lot of energy is used in the manufacture and use of new gadgets and this encourages us to regularly dispose of our old ones.
   B Wind and solar power are alternatives.
   C They should always be recycled by experts.
   D They usually purchased CDs and either bought or rented DVDs.
   E If they don't, their customers won't be aware of their latest products or developments.
   F You use a lot of energy.
   G Lithium.

4 Complete the sentences and short texts with the words below.

| biodiversity   carbon capture   carbon storage
| climate change denial   conservationists   eco-anxiety
| ecology   monoculture   zero-emission

   1 Sir David Attenborough is one of the most famous _____ in the world.
   2 If you're interested in the relation of plants and living creatures to each other and to their environment, you should study _____ at university.
   3 Zero Avia is a British American company developing planes that can fly using hydrogen instead of kerosene, which is a fossil fuel. Unlike kerosene, hydrogen does not produce carbon dioxide emissions. The aim of the company is to make _____ air travel available for everyone.
   4 Costa Rica is a tiny country in Central America which contains 5% of the world's _____, including more varieties of butterfly than all of Africa.
   5 Organic farmers know that the practice of _____, when you grow crops on their own, is more likely to encourage pests and diseases that can only be treated with chemicals.
   6 _____ isn't a recognised mental illness, but it is increasing as people worry more about climate change.
   7 The biggest machine in the world designed for _____ and _____ is in Iceland. It has been built to take 4,000 tonnes (4 million kilograms) of carbon dioxide out of the air every year and turn it into stone.
   8 _____ can be a big problem for scientists wanting governments to act now to reduce global warming.

5 What do you think an individual can do to help protect the environment? What needs to be done by governments? Ask friends and family. Prepare to give a presentation to the class and give reasons for your choices.

Individual action	Government action
make sure you dispose of your waste correctly	build more recycling centres
buy goods that aren't wrapped in plastic	ban plastic bags and packaging in shops

108 Vocabulary Booster

6 VOCABULARY BOOSTER

Spending and not spending money and Shopping trends

1 **PRACTISE** Complete the sentences with the words below.

| build up | cut out | keep track | limited budget |
| owe | spend your money | under control | use up |

1 If you're careful and _____ wisely, you are unlikely to get into financial difficulties.
2 Why don't you download an app that helps you _____ of your finances so you never spend more than you have?
3 It's a good idea to be on a very _____ if you're saving up to buy something special.
4 If you're worried about debt, make sure you don't _____ anyone any money.
5 You should _____ your savings account so you have a bit more to spend when you go to university.
6 To avoid waste, everyone should make sure they _____ all the things they already have in their kitchens, like tinned and frozen food, before doing any more food shopping.
7 It's best to _____ non-essentials like takeaways and coffees out with friends if you want to save up for something expensive.
8 One of the best ways to get your spending _____ is to make a budget every month and keep to it.

2 What do you think of the advice given in Ex 1? Order the sentences from the most helpful (1) to the least helpful (8) for you.

3 Choose the correct answer: A, B or C.
1 I'm not going to buy this because the ___ is higher than the price of the item.
  A delivery option B shipping cost C reference number
2 The ___ of these shoes is high because they only manufacture a few pairs every year.
  A retail price B reference number C purchase
3 I don't think the transaction has gone through because I haven't received a ___.
  A check out B special offer C confirmation email
4 You need to make sure you save the ___ when you make an online purchase in case you need to return the item.
  A package B reference number C retail price
5 How many ___ do we need for this particular product to make a profit?
  A potential customers B shipping costs C delivery options
6 You really shouldn't buy an item just because it's on ___. Only buy it if you really need it or you absolutely love it.
  A special offer B bargain C retail price

4 **EXTEND** Match the sentence halves.
1 When you are **overdrawn**, ___
2 You need a credit card or debit card ___
3 When you get **free shipping**, ___
4 We'll have paid off our loan ___
5 I'm completely broke so I can't ___
6 This shirt was an **impulse buy** as ___
7 Our bills have gone up again. We've got ___
8 The company had to do some **cost-cutting** ___

A to **tighten our belts** or we'll end up in debt.
B **pay my way** if we go out tonight.
C when we make our final **repayment** next month.
D you owe money to your bank.
E because of poor sales last year. This means nobody will get a salary raise this year.
F you don't have to pay for your purchase to be sent to you.
G to make a **contactless payment**.
H I really didn't mean to buy any new clothes – I just couldn't resist!

5 Complete the sentences with your own ideas.
1 If free shipping is offered …
2 I think impulse buying is …
3 If I can't pay my way …
4 Cost-cutting often happens in companies when …
5 Some people don't like making contactless payments because …
6 The best way to avoid being overdrawn is …
7 If you can't make a repayment when you've borrowed money, you should …
8 Sometimes you have to tighten your belt because …

6 Imagine you need to save money to pay for something that you really want to do, for example, get driving lessons or go on holiday with a group of friends. Which of the following would you do? Which would you not do? Give reasons for your choices.
• Keep track of your finances by writing down everything that you spend.
• Have a weekly budget and never go over it.
• Never impulse-buy.
• Buy second-hand clothes when you can.
• Get a Saturday job.
• Ask friends and neighbours if they need any jobs done, like babysitting or helping in the garden.
• Only buy things online if you can get free shipping.

Make a list of ten rules you would follow in order to achieve your aim.

My money-saving rules

1 Every time you buy something, write it down in a notebook or on your phone.
2 …

7 VOCABULARY BOOSTER

Different art forms and Interpretations of art

1 PRACTISE Complete the sentences with the words below.

abstract art	contemporary dance	live gig
musical production	performing arts
stage adaptation	visual arts	VR headset

1 We now know that people have been interested in the _____ since prehistoric times, with the discovery of animal drawings on cave walls made over 30,000 years ago.
2 It's much more entertaining and memorable to go to a _____ than listen to music on your phone.
3 We went to the theatre and saw a wonderful _____ of Michael Morpurgo's *War Horse*. I think it was just as good as the books.
4 _____ doesn't represent people, places or objects, but it often makes you think more as a result.
5 DNA VR is the first virtual-reality place in London where you can play lots of games and have amazing experiences. All you need to do is put on a _____ and enter another world.
6 Although I like ballet, I prefer _____ because it's more modern and experimental.
7 What I really like about _____ is the fact that it's done for an audience, so in some ways each performance is a unique experience.
8 The _____ of *Les Misérables* is probably more famous today than the book, written by the French author Victor Hugo in the 19th century.

2 Choose the correct alternative.

3 EXTEND Complete the sentences with the correct form of the words below.

| canvas | landscape | line drawing | performance art |
| spray paint | surrealism | watercolour |

1 Before painting his portrait, the artist made many quick _____ of his face in his sketchbook.
2 Dalí's famous *Lobster Telephone* is an example of _____. It is an old-fashioned black telephone with a lobster on top, which you would pick up to answer the phone.
3 We went to the theatre to see some _____ where the artist painted a huge canvas on stage while an orchestra played a symphony.
4 Before the 16th century, most paintings were made on wood rather than on _____.
5 Most _____ are painted on paper made of cotton or wood.
6 Students from the art college have been allowed to use _____ to make a work of art along a wall in the centre of town.
7 My favourite painting is of a _____ with mountains, a river and a gorgeous sunset.

4 Look at the words in Ex 3. Which two describe a tool or something you may need in order to create a work of art? Which one describes an art movement?

5 Do a short project about the top five works of art in your country.

> **Top Five Works of Art**
> - Research in books or online and make a list of the top five most important artworks and where they can be seen.
> - Ask friends and family if they have seen them and what they think of them.

Write a short report and prepare to give a presentation to the class. If possible, bring in photos to show the class.

The Sculpture Park

If you're looking for a great day out near London, why not visit the Sculpture Park in Surrey? You can enjoy it all year round and see sculptures surrounded by trees and flowers in summer or in a more ¹**colourful / dramatic** landscape in winter, when they can be seen against a white background of snow. There are all sorts of sculptures in the park, from ²**realistic / vivid** ones that look like animals wandering through the landscape to ³**detailed / humorous** ones that make you laugh. A favourite with children is the ⁴**colourful / thought-provoking** sculpture of flamingos in bright blue, pink and yellow. And not only can you spend the day there, you can even buy a sculpture and take it home with you.

The National Gallery

You shouldn't miss an opportunity to see the stunning artworks at the National Gallery in London. One of the most popular is Vincent van Gogh's famous *Sunflowers*, described by the artist himself as 'a picture all in yellow', and in fact the ⁵**realistic / vivid** yellows are almost as bright today as they were when he painted it. Other artworks of the same period include Henri Rousseau's painting *Surprised!* This is a dramatic painting of a tiger in the jungle showing his huge teeth, eyes wide open, probably about to catch another animal for his dinner. It is an unusual and very ⁶**humorous / striking** image which must have been shocking when it was first shown in 1891 before people had got used to seeing photos and films of wildlife. There are also much older works, including one of the most famous paintings in the world, *The Arnolfini Portrait*, painted by Jan van Eyck in 1434. It is an extraordinarily ⁷**detailed / dramatic** painting of a young couple. It shows them in their home and we can see every small part of the room they are standing in, the furniture and what they are wearing, including the fur around their clothes. It looks incredibly real. People have been fascinated by this ⁸**thought-provoking / vivid** portrait for centuries, wondering who the couple were and what happened to them. Today, it is the most viewed painting in the National Gallery. Don't miss it!

8 VOCABULARY BOOSTER

Volunteering in the local community and Responding to a humanitarian crisis

1 PRACTISE Complete the text with the words below.

charity shop   community service   elderly people
learning disabilities   local initiative   one-to-one tuition
refuge   social isolation

Volunteering in the community

There are lots of ways you can make a difference in your community. Here are some volunteering opportunities.

★ Offer to help with cleaning or cooking in a ¹_____ for homeless people.

★ Join a ²_____ to help pick up rubbish in parks and other green spaces in your city.

★ Do some ³_____ like reading to people with learning difficulties.

★ Offer ⁴_____ for children who are having trouble keeping up at school.

★ Visit people in the community who are suffering from ⁵_____ and are very lonely.

★ Volunteer in a ⁶_____, helping to sort out donations of second-hand clothes.

★ Offer to help ⁷_____ living on their own with their shopping and household chores.

★ Join a group of volunteers who take children with ⁸_____ to visit farms near the city.

2 Complete the collocations with the words below.

assess   co-ordinate   distribute   eliminate
encounter   preserve   process   threaten

1 _____ difficulties / challenges / problems
2 _____ the damage / the situation
3 _____ food / new vaccines / emergency supplies
4 _____ information / data / official documents / an application / a payment
5 _____ an animal with extinction / our species / communities with violence / lives / our way of life
6 _____ endangered species / a habitat / seeds for the future / the environment / lives
7 _____ obstacles / diseases / malaria
8 _____ the relief effort / a response / the work / the struggle

3 Complete the sentences with the correct form of the words in Ex 2.

1 We need to make sure that the vaccines are _____ in remote areas as well as cities.
2 It takes time to _____ all the data collected by volunteers on the ground.
3 The situation has to be _____ carefully before sending any aid.
4 Many diseases that used to kill thousands of people every year have now been almost totally _____ worldwide.
5 After the flood, various agencies were involved in _____ the relief effort.
6 The survival of many species, including polar bears, is being _____ by climate change.
7 We need to find more ways to _____ the habitats of endangered species.
8 Volunteers have _____ many difficulties while trying to co-ordinate the relief effort on the ground.

4 EXTEND Choose the correct alternative.

1 After the earthquake it was very difficult to reach remote villages in the mountains, so the inhabitants suffered from **food insecurity / inequality** for many weeks.
2 In some places, if crops fail, there is nothing to eat and people are at serious risk of **persecution / starvation**.
3 One hundred years ago, there was much more **inequality / modern slavery** in the UK than there is today. The difference between the rich and poor was huge.
4 Many people volunteered to clean up the village in the **aftermath / persecution** of the flood.
5 Crop failure and factory closures caused so much unemployment in the country that many young people left their homes and became **asylum seekers / economic migrants**.
6 Victims of **inequality / persecution** often run away from their countries in fear of their lives.
7 Many **asylum seekers / economic migrants** leave their home countries to escape physical danger.
8 **Modern slavery / Starvation** is often very easy to see. However, people don't always know what the signs are, and as a result, victims can go unrecognised while they continue to be exploited by criminals.

5 Imagine there has been a natural disaster in another country, like a flood, earthquake, forest fire, hurricane, severe drought or the outbreak of an infectious disease. What can you as an individual do about it? What can your country's government do to help?

Choose a scenario, write down your ideas and ask friends and family to add theirs. Complete the table below. Prepare to give a presentation to the class.

Scenario: Earthquake

Individual help	Government help
Donate blankets and clothing	Send aid agency help

FUNCTIONS BANK

Unit 1

Restating your ideas p.17

Admit that you didn't say the right thing

Sorry, that didn't come out right.	U1 Speaking
That came out wrong.	U1 Speaking
That isn't what I meant to say.	U1 Speaking

Continue with what you were saying

Let me try that one more time.	U1 Speaking
Let me rephrase that.	U1 Speaking
Let me try that again.	U1 Speaking

Clarify what you meant to say

What I meant was …	U1 Speaking
What I'm trying to say is …	U1 Speaking
Let me put that another way.	U1 Speaking

Comment adverbs p.18

Admittedly, …	U1 Writing
Amazingly, …	U1 Writing
Basically, …	U1 Writing
Consequently, …	U1 Writing
Hopefully, …	U1 Writing
Ideally, …	U1 Writing
Initially, …	U1 Writing
Interestingly, …	U1 Writing
Obviously, …	U1 Writing
Personally, (I think) …	U1 Writing
(Not) Surprisingly, …	U1 Writing
Unfortunately, …	U1 Writing

Unit 2

Talking about photos p.31

Comparing

Both photos show …	U2 Speaking
In both photos, you can see …	U2 Speaking
The common theme in the photos is …	U2 Speaking
The main difference (between the photos) is …	U2 Speaking
In the first photo …, … whereas in the second photo …	U2 Speaking
The second photo shows …	U2 Speaking
Unlike the first photo, …	U2 Speaking

Speculating

I can't be sure, but …	U2 Speaking
It looks like some kind of …	U2 Speaking
It looks to me like a … of some kind.	U2 Speaking
It's / There's a sort of …	U2 Speaking
He / It / They could / might be …, or something like that.	U2 Speaking
I'd say that it's / they're probably …	U2 Speaking

Stating your opinion

In my opinion, …	U2 Speaking
It seems to me that …	U2 Speaking
For me, the main thing / point / consideration is …	U2 Speaking
(Personally,) I would say that …	U2 Speaking
I feel quite strongly that …	U2 Speaking

Opinion essays p.32

Introducing a key point or idea

On the whole, … In terms of …, … When it comes to …	U2 Writing

Expressing an opinion

I personally feel that …	U2 Writing
I firmly believe …	
In my opinion, …	

Sequencing ideas

Firstly, … Secondly, … Finally, … So, in summary, …	U2 Writing

Adding a supporting point

Furthermore, … Moreover, … In addition to this, …	U2 Writing

Introducing a contrasting point

However, … Having said that, … At the same time, … though …	U2 Writing

Introducing an example

For example, … For instance, … such as …	U2 Writing

Unit 3

Discussing ideas p.45

Expressing a preference

Personally, I'd prefer (not) to …	U3 Speaking
It seems to me …	U3 Speaking
For me, the most interesting … is …	U3 Speaking
I feel quite strongly that …	U3 Speaking

Clarifying a point

Sorry if I'm not being clear. The main thing is …	U3 Speaking
OK, let me clarify what I mean.	U3 Speaking
Basically, my point is …	U3 Speaking
What I'm trying to say is …	U3 Speaking

Disagreeing politely

I understand what you're saying, but …	U3 Speaking
I see your point, but …	U3 Speaking
I know you think that, but …	U3 Speaking
I'm sorry, but I don't think (that's a very good idea).	U3 Speaking

Including someone in the discussion

What do you think, George?	U3 Speaking
Bella, do you have any thoughts about that?	U3 Speaking

Signalling you want to speak

Can I say something?	U3 Speaking
Sorry to interrupt, but …	U3 Speaking

Managing an interruption

Just a minute, George, let her finish.	U3 Speaking
Hold on, I haven't finished.	U3 Speaking

Impersonal language p.46

Introducing the subject and aims of a report

The purpose of this report is to …	U3 Writing
This report is based on …	U3 Writing
The objective of the survey was …	U3 Writing
This report is intended to …	U3 Writing

Referring to numbers / data

More / less than …	U3 Writing
The majority of … / Most of …	U3 Writing
Just under / Just over half …	U3 Writing
Nearly / Almost / Approximately …	U3 Writing
The remaining 50% …	U3 Writing

Talking about results

According to the results of …	U3 Writing
The report shows / suggests / indicates that …	U3 Writing
It is clear from the data that …	U3 Writing
Based on the data / numbers / evidence, …	U3 Writing
… supports the idea that …	U3 Writing

Unit 4

Speculating about the future p.59

I think it's quite likely that …	U4 Speaking
There's a strong possibility that …	U4 Speaking
I can see a situation where …	U4 Speaking
I don't think it's realistic to expect that …	U4 Speaking
I can't be the only one who thinks we'll …	U4 Speaking
It's perfectly possible that …	U4 Speaking
I can see myself -ing …	U4 Speaking

Commenting on someone's opinion p.59

The only problem with that is …	U4 Speaking
It's interesting you say that.	U4 Speaking
I hear what you're saying …	U4 Speaking
I think you're right to be …	U4 Speaking
That sounds good.	U4 Speaking
It's a good point.	U4 Speaking
That's what I meant.	U4 Speaking

Enquiring p.60

Explaining your interest

My current situation is that …	U4 Writing
I should also mention that …	U4 Writing

Explaining future plans

It is my intention to …	U4 Writing
What I hope to do is …	U4 Writing
In all probability I will …	U4 Writing

Requesting information

I wonder if you would mind … -ing?	U4 Writing
Could you let me know … ?	U4 Writing
Also, I would like to know …	U4 Writing

Requesting action

I would appreciate -ing …	U4 Writing
Could I ask you to … ?	U4 Writing
I would be extremely grateful if you could …	U4 Writing

Unit 5

Signposting a presentation p.73

Introducing the topic

In this presentation, I'm going to talk about …	U5 Speaking
In my talk today, I'm going to tell you about …	U5 Speaking
The subject of my presentation is …	U5 Speaking
This presentation will be about …	U5 Speaking

Giving an outline of the structure

My talk will be in three parts.	U5 Speaking
I'll be looking at three areas.	U5 Speaking

FUNCTIONS BANK

Firstly, / In the first part, …	U5 Speaking
Second, / Then in the second part …	U5 Speaking
Finally, / In the final section, (I'll talk about) …	U5 Speaking
Introducing a new point / section	
To begin, …	U5 Speaking
I'd like to start by talking about …	U5 Speaking
Let's move on to …	U5 Speaking
Next, I want to discuss / turn to …	U5 Speaking
Finally, let's look at …	U5 Speaking
Summarising / Concluding	
That concludes my talk …	U5 Speaking
To sum up, …	U5 Speaking
So, in conclusion, …	U5 Speaking
I'd like to finish by / with …	U5 Speaking
Reviewing a website p.74	
Introduction and brief description	
One of my favourite websites is …	U5 Writing
A website I really appreciate is …	U5 Writing
(Quintekit) appeals to me because …	U5 Writing
Describing purpose and functions	
(Quintekit) is basically a … site.	U5 Writing
Its main purpose is to allow users to …	U5 Writing
It allows users to …	U5 Writing
Not only that, but …	U5 Writing
It also has a range of … features.	U5 Writing
Positive things about it	
I'm particularly impressed by …	U5 Writing
What I like most about … is …	U5 Writing
The good points include …	U5 Writing
What really stands out is …	U5 Writing
Another positive feature is …	U5 Writing
I especially enjoy …	U5 Writing
Negative things about it	
On the negative side …	U5 Writing
Another slight drawback is …	U5 Writing
I was a bit disappointed by …	U5 Writing
I'm not keen on …	U5 Writing
Recommendations	
I would definitely recommend -ing …	U5 Writing
One way to enhance it would be to …	U5 Writing
I would (perhaps) like to see …	U5 Writing
I can't recommend … highly enough.	U5 Writing

Unit 6

Consumer issues p.87	
Refunds and exchanges	
I'd like to return this / these …	U6 Speaking
I'm afraid I don't have the receipt / proof of purchase.	U6 Speaking
Can I exchange it for another size / colour?	U6 Speaking
I don't really want a store voucher. I'd rather have a refund.	U6 Speaking
It's an unwanted gift. It was given to me for my …	U6 Speaking
I think it's still under warranty / guarantee.	U6 Speaking
Sorry, but I'd rather have a refund.	U6 Speaking
According to your returns policy …	U6 Speaking
I think I have the right to …	U6 Speaking
I should be entitled to …	U6 Speaking
Making a complaint	
I'm afraid I'm not satisfied with the quality / service / solution I've been offered.	U6 Speaking
Can I speak to the manager, please?	U6 Speaking
Please can I speak to a more senior member of staff?	U6 Speaking
I'm disappointed by your customer service.	U6 Speaking
That isn't an acceptable solution.	U6 Speaking
For and against essays p.88	
Introducing the topic	
Everyone / Many (young) people / Most people …	U6 Writing
Presenting a supporting argument	
It cannot be denied …	U6 Writing
It is often said …	U6 Writing
It is true that …	U6 Writing
On the one hand, …	U6 Writing
Presenting an opposing argument	
Having said that, …	U6 Writing
On the other hand, …	U6 Writing
However, …	U6 Writing
In contrast, …	U6 Writing
Making additional points	
… as well as … besides, … furthermore, …	U6 Writing
In addition, … Moreover, … What is more, …	U6 Writing
Presenting your conclusion	
In conclusion, … To sum up, … To conclude, …	U6 Writing

Unit 7

Discussing options p.101	
Talking about advantages and disadvantages	
One major benefit / drawback is …	U7 Speaking
The main (dis)advantage is …	U7 Speaking
For me, it's a plus / minus …	U7 Speaking
What are the pros and cons of that?	U7 Speaking
It would have a positive / negative effect on …	U7 Speaking
Adding an opinion	
Absolutely. Not only that, but …	U7 Speaking
Good point. And I also believe that …	U7 Speaking
Yes, and another thing is, …	U7 Speaking
Making a decision p.101	
Justifying an opinion	
I would definitely opt for …	U7 Speaking
I strongly believe that … is the best.	U7 Speaking
The main reason is because …	U7 Speaking
The reason I think that is …	U7 Speaking
For one thing, …	U7 Speaking
Another thing is …	U7 Speaking
Concluding the discussion	
We need to come to a decision.	U7 Speaking
Which one are we going for?	U7 Speaking
Let's go with …, shall we?	U7 Speaking
So, that's settled, then.	U7 Speaking
Persuasive language p.102	
Presenting a personal viewpoint as fact	
In my opinion / I believe this is the solution to all our problems.	U7 Writing
In our view, this is the worst decision that could have been made.	U7 Writing
Using adjectives and structures emphasising importance	
essential / vital / fundamental / under any circumstances / no matter what / crucial	U7 Writing
Using emotive language	
seriously concerned / terribly upset / extremely disappointed	U7 Writing
Using modal verbs of obligation	
This must not be treated lightly.	U7 Writing
The drama group should not be allowed to …	U7 Writing
Using statistics and figures in a persuasive way	
Seventy-five per cent of people believe … / Eighty per cent of our members agree …	U7 Writing
Using verbs recommending action	
propose / recommend / suggest / urge	U7 Writing

Unit 8

Engaging with ideas p.115	
Acknowledging a different perspective	
I respect your point of view, but …	U8 Speaking
I hadn't considered that aspect.	U8 Speaking
I hear what you're saying, but …	U8 Speaking
That's an interesting perspective, but …	U8 Speaking
Finding common ground	
I think we share the view that …	U8 Speaking
What if we look at it from another angle?	U8 Speaking
Let's try to see it through their eyes.	U8 Speaking
Let's accept that we don't agree about …	U8 Speaking
Emphasising your position	
I'm quite clear about that / this.	U8 Speaking
There's no question about that for me.	U8 Speaking
This is something I feel strongly about.	U8 Speaking
I'm afraid I'm really passionate about this.	U8 Speaking

WRITING BANK

A formal email of enquiry

In a formal email of enquiry, you write to a company, organisation or individual to enquire about something you are interested in and to request information. You usually write an email of enquiry in response to something you have seen, such as an advertisement.

Example task: Write a formal email enquiring about gaining work experience in one of the following:
a local hospital
an animal shelter
a conservation group

Get ideas
- Choose one of the places or organisations and think about what happens there and the work people do.
- Think about the following questions: Why are you interested in working there? How will the experience help you in the future? What information / actions would you like to request?
- Draw a mind map or write a list of your ideas.

Plan
- Choose the best ideas from your notes.
- Think of language to make your email formal and polite.
- Organise your ideas into paragraphs:

Paragraph 1
- Explain why you are writing and what your interest is.

Paragraph 2
- Describe your current situation and any future plans.

Paragraphs 3 and 4
- Request information or action.

Write

Label the email with a clear purpose / topic.	**Piotr Symański:** enquiry about work experience opportunities
Use *Dear Sir or Madam,* or *Dear Sir / Madam,* if you don't have the name of the person you're writing to. If you do have their name, e.g. *Ms Brown*, write *Dear Ms Brown*.	Dear Sir or Madam,
State your reason for writing in the opening paragraph and explain your interest.	I am writing to enquire whether there are any opportunities for work experience within your organisation during the school holidays. I have a passionate interest in the environment, and I truly believe that tackling environmental problems on a local level is vital for the future of our planet.
Use more formal alternatives to everyday words, e.g. *enquire*, not *ask*.	I will enter my final year of secondary school in September and it is my intention to study ecology and conservation at university next year. I understand that there is strong competition to secure a place on a degree course. I would therefore like to gain experience of conservation work since it will demonstrate my interest in nature and strengthen my application for university.
Don't omit *that* in order to sound more formal.	
Use impersonal phrases, e.g. *it is my intention to …* and not *I want to …* or *I plan to …*.	I would be extremely grateful if you could let me know of any positions available for volunteers. I should mention that, in all probability, I will be here for the entire summer, so I am flexible about when I can work.
Use indirect questions, especially to make requests.	If there are currently no opportunities, I wonder if you would mind passing on my details to other conservationists in the area?
	I look forward to hearing from you soon.
If you address the email *Dear Sir or Madam*, end with *Yours faithfully*, and your full name. If you address it *Dear Ms Brown*, use *Yours sincerely*, and your full name.	Yours faithfully, Piotr Symański

Tips for writing a formal email of enquiry
- Use an appropriate formal opening and closing expression.
- Use formal language throughout.
- Use full forms (*I am, I will, I would*), not short forms, to make your email polite and professional.
- Avoid slang and colloquial language, e.g. exclamation marks or emojis / emoticons.

WRITING BANK

A magazine article

In a magazine article, you write to a wider audience about a subject that is personal to you. You use a formal or informal style depending on your target audience and include thoughts, opinions and facts.

Example task: Write a magazine article about the place you love best.

Get ideas

- Think about the places you love and choose your favourite one.
- Think about all the things you know about this place and why you love it.
- Draw a mind map of ideas for each of the topics you want to write about. For example:

Plan

- Choose the best ideas from your notes.
- Think about who your audience is and how to make your article interesting to the readers.
- Organise your ideas into paragraphs, for example:
  Introduction – Introduce the topic and try to grab your readers' attention.
  Main body – Tell your readers all about the place in the second and third paragraphs.
  Conclusion – Bring your article to an end and include an opinion.

Write

Give your article a title.	**The place I love best**
Use a rhetorical question in the introduction to engage your readers.	Who has a happy place like a quiet corner of a room where they can escape the world and relax? I certainly do. Personally, though, mine isn't indoors. It's outdoors in the middle of a wood.
Use comment adverbs to give your opinion of events. They normally come at the beginning of a sentence and we use a comma after them.	Amazingly, I had no idea this place existed until last summer. I was walking through the wood when my brother lost his ball in some thick bushes. I began searching for it and came across a beautiful open space surrounded by tall trees. Consequently, it's completely hidden from view.
Describe the place in detail to help paint a picture in your reader's mind. Include some facts to make your article interesting and engaging.	Interestingly, a few days after discovering this place, I watched a documentary about forest bathing, or *shinrin-yoku* in Japanese. Basically, this is the Japanese practice of spending time among trees, which reduces stress and improves your mood. Initially, I didn't believe this was possible, so I decided to go back to the woods to see for myself.
Finish with some final thoughts about the place and your opinion.	Surprisingly, after spending some time in the hidden space, I left feeling happier and more relaxed. Now I go there regularly, especially when I'm worried or upset. It really is my happy place. Obviously, forest bathing does work!

Tips for writing a magazine article

- Use the language style that is appropriate for your target audience, e.g. informal language for a local / school magazine.
- Make sure you use the same language style throughout.
- Engage your readers with a range of thoughts, opinions and facts.
- Use a variety of comment adverbs to make your writing more interesting.

WRITING BANK

A film review

In a film review, you write a brief description of a film you have seen and give your opinion about it. At the end of the review, you say whether you recommend the film or not.

Example task: Write a film review you have recently seen.

Get ideas

- Think of a film to write about.
- Make notes about the plot, main characters and setting.
- Think of positive and negative things about it. In addition to the plot, consider things like the camerawork, acting, music and how well the film fits its genre.
- Decide whether you would recommend it or not and why.

Plan

- Organise your ideas into paragraphs:

Paragraph 1
- Introduce the film and give a brief summary of what it's about.

Paragraph 2
- Describe some positive points about the film, if any.

Paragraph 3
- Describe some negative points about the film, if any.

Paragraph 4
- Make a recommendation and give your opinion.

Write

Summarise the topic of the film in a few sentences.	**Review of More Than Robots** I recently watched *More Than Robots*. It's basically a documentary about four teams of high-school students who are preparing to compete in the finals of an international robotics competition. The teams from the US, Mexico and Japan have just six weeks to design and build a large robot that can complete a specific task, such as throwing a ball and scoring goals.
Use adverbs to strengthen or emphasise a point.	
Use adverbs to soften a negative point.	What really stands out is the positive effect that the competition has on the teenagers. They learn to work as a team to create something truly amazing. Not only that, but they also learn important life skills, such as communication, co-operation and respect. It is totally game-changing for the competitors.
Use set phrases to make positive points.	
Use set phrases to make negative points.	On the negative side, I think *More Than Robots* is slightly too long for people who aren't technology geeks. Another slight drawback is the music that's played at times.
Use set phrases to make recommendations.	If you're completely into engineering, or only somewhat interested, I would highly recommend watching *More Than Robots*. Overall, it's an absolutely inspirational film and, as the title suggests, it's definitely about more than robots.
Finish with a clear recommendation and explain why.	

Tips for writing a film review

- Keep your summary of the film brief – don't start describing characters.
- Don't spoil the film for the readers by telling them about unexpected events.
- Give honest opinions – the readers want to know what you think.
- Your final recommendation can be positive, negative or mixed.

WRITING BANK

A data-based report

In a data-based report, you look at the results of a survey and summarise the information for the reader. You use impersonal language to present the data and make conclusions.

Example task: Analyse the results of a survey and write a report.

Get ideas
- Think of a topic that interests you, for example, sleep, healthy eating or mental health.
- Go online and find a survey you could base a report on.
- Make notes about the information contained in the survey.

Plan
- Choose the best ideas from your notes.
- Organise your ideas into a paragraph plan, for example:
  Paragraph 1 – Describe the objective of the survey and the participants.
  Paragraph 2 – Include information about what the participants were asked.
  Paragraph 3 – Give the main results of the survey.
  Paragraph 4 – Summarise your conclusions.

Write

Write a title for your report.	**Cyberbullying and teenagers**
Explain the objective of the report.	This report is based on a survey of 10,000 students aged 13–17 at secondary schools in the UK. The objective of the survey was to determine the extent of cyberbullying amongst young people and find out the most common reasons for of it.
Use passive forms rather than active forms where possible.	Students were asked how often they went online every day and whether they had ever experienced cyberbullying. If so, they were then asked what they were bullied about and how it made them feel. According to the results of the survey, the majority of students (92%) go online every day, and just over a quarter of them (27%) have experienced cyberbullying over the last year. Based on the evidence, the two most common reasons for this are appearance (47%) and interests (30%). It is also clear from the data that cyberbullying affected the mental health of more than three quarters of the students (77%).
Use set phrases to present the results.	
Summarise the information, e.g. *nearly all*, and then include the statistic in brackets, e.g. (98%).	
Use impersonal language to present opinions and conclusions.	In summary, the survey indicates that cyberbullying is frequently experienced by 13–17-year-old students in full-time education in the UK and has a negative effect on them. Since cyberbullying takes place online and so much time is spent online by young people, it is not surprising that cyberbullying is proving difficult to stamp out.

Tips for writing a data-based report
- Use formal and impersonal structures (*It was found that* … rather than *I found that* …).
- Use full forms (*It is not* …), not short forms (*It isn't* …).
- Only include the most important information from the survey.
- Present statistics in a variety of ways, e.g. *20%*, *about a fifth* … .

Writing bank 117

WRITING BANK

A story

In a story, you write a description of people and events that you have invented in order to entertain people.

Example task: Write a short story for your school magazine with this ending:
Rita was exhausted when she got home that day, but she would never forget what she had done.

Get ideas
- Think about possible events that could lead to this ending and create a plot outline.
- Imagine what your characters are like (names, appearance, habits, etc.) and think of adjectives or similes to describe them.
- Draw a mind map of the details you want to include in your story. For example:

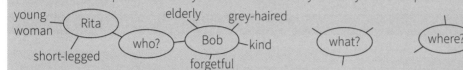 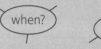

Plan
- Choose the best ideas from your notes.
- Organise your ideas into paragraphs. For example:

Paragraph 1
- Set the scene and introduce your main character(s).

Paragraphs 2 and 3
- Describe the main events in the story.

Paragraph 4
- Bring the story to an end and finish with the sentence provided.

Write

Technique	Example
Engage your readers with an interesting opening paragraph.	Rita knew the day of the race was fast approaching. How could she forget when the date was circled in bright red ink on the kitchen calendar? It jumped out like a warning sign of danger every time she went by and made her feel sick with worry.
Use a rhetorical question for dramatic effect.	
Mix the sequence of events to keep your readers interested.	Six months earlier, Rita had agreed without thinking to take part in the charity event to raise money for cancer research. She wanted to do something to help Bob, the kind, grey-haired, rather forgetful man who lived in the flat below. Little did she know how tough it would be. Running long distances doesn't come naturally to short-legged people like Rita!
Use adjectives, adverbs and similes to bring characters and events to life.	
Use specific structures for dramatic effect.	When the race day dawned, Rita woke with a terrible feeling of fear. She was lying in bed desperately wishing she didn't have to get up when she heard someone on the radio say that 'with courage, nothing is impossible'. With the words swirling around her head, Rita got ready to face her greatest challenge.
Use interesting language where possible, for example, *When the race day dawned* instead of *On the day of the race*.	
Describe feelings to make your story come alive.	She was out of breath as soon as the race started. However, crowds of spectators cheered the runners on, and she didn't stop once. Rita was exhausted when she got home that day, but she would never forget what she had done.
Use linkers and time expressions to connect your ideas.	

Tips for writing a story
- Decide who is narrating the story (first person or third person?).
- Introduce a problem early on that the character(s) must face.
- Show the character(s) fighting for what they want.
- Summarise what happened after the problem is resolved.

WRITING BANK

An opinion essay

In an opinion essay, you express your personal opinion about a topic statement or question. You support your opinion with several reasons and examples and often also include contrasting points.

Example task: Choose a topic below and write an opinion essay.
'The internet does more harm than good.'
'Space exploration is a waste of money.'
'Playing video games improves your intelligence.'

Get ideas
- Choose one of the topics. Think about what you know about the topic and what your opinion of the statement is.
- Make a list of the ideas and arguments that support your opinion. Think of ones that contrast it too.

Plan
- Choose the best ideas and arguments from your notes.
- Organise your ideas and arguments into paragraphs:
  Introduction – Introduce the topic with a general statement. Then state your overall opinion.
  Main body – Use a separate argument to support your opinion in each paragraph. Include examples and a contrasting argument if necessary.
  Conclusion – Summarise your ideas and repeat your overall opinion.

Write

- Start your essay with a general statement about the topic and then state your opinion.
- Use a variety of linkers to connect your ideas.
- Use different phrases to express your opinion.
- Present two or three arguments in the main body of the essay.
- Use a variety of phrases to introduce examples to support your points.
- Briefly mention a contrasting argument, but return to your main argument quickly.
- Restate your opinion in the final paragraph and end with a final comment.

'Space exploration is a waste of money.'

When it comes to space exploration, it isn't cheap. Government agencies spend billions of dollars a year on their space programmes. Many believe this is a waste of money and we should focus on solving problems on Earth instead. However, in my opinion, space exploration is essential in modern society.

Firstly, we need space agencies to operate the satellites that provide the services that are part of today's modern life, such as communication, broadcast entertainment and navigation. In addition to this, satellites make our lives safer by providing data for a wide range of purposes, for instance, climate-change research and defence.

Secondly, space agencies are leaders in research and development in order to ensure safe travel and survival in space. At the same time, though, there are benefits on Earth. For example, air-conditioning systems developed for space are now used in new buildings. Moreover, I firmly believe that research done in space will help to solve problems on Earth, such as scarce food resources. Having said that, space is not the only place where valuable research is carried out. Projects closer to home lead to advances in science too.

So, in summary, space programmes might be expensive, but I personally feel that they are worth it. Throughout history, humans have been on a voyage of exploration and discovery. Why should we stop now?

Tips for writing an opinion essay
- There is no 'right' or 'wrong' opinion, but it is important to support yours with some strong ideas.
- Stick to the point and use ideas and arguments that really support your opinion.
- An opinion essay is a formal piece of writing, but in order to make it personal and interesting, use the first person (*I*, *we*) and facts that your reader will remember.
- Use a rhetorical question as a final thought at the end of your conclusion.

WORDLIST

❶ = in the Oxford 3000 wordlist
All page numbers refer to the Student's Book

Introduction

Saving someone's life p.4

bruise	/bruːz/
bump	/bʌmp/
❶ collapse	/kəˈlæps/
emergency services	/ɪˈmɜːdʒənsi ˈsɜːvɪsɪz/
first aid	/ˌfɜːst ˈeɪd/
❶ recover	/rɪˈkʌvə(r)/
severe injury	/sɪˌvɪər ˈɪndʒəri/
specialist	/ˈspeʃəlɪst/
sprained ankle	/ˌspreɪnd ˈæŋkl/
unconscious	/ʌnˈkɒnʃəs/

Bringing the outside in p.5

biofuel	/ˈbaɪəʊfjuːəl/
carbon dioxide	/ˌkɑːbən daɪˈɒksaɪd/
houseplant	/ˈhaʊsplɑːnt/
leaf (leaves)	/liːf/
❶ modify	/ˈmɒdɪfaɪ/
❶ monitor	/ˈmɒnɪtə(r)/
natural habitat	/ˌnætʃrəl ˈhæbɪtæt/
oxygen	/ˈɒksɪdʒən/
❶ root	/ruːt/
❶ rural	/ˈrʊərəl/
❶ transform	/trænsˈfɔːm/
❶ tropical	/ˈtrɒpɪkl/

Dreams for the future p.6

applicant	/ˈæplɪkənt/
coursework	/ˈkɔːswɜːk/
curriculum	/kəˈrɪkjələm/
full-time	/ˌfʊl ˈtaɪm/
module	/ˈmɒdjuːl/
personal statement	/ˌpɜːsənl ˈsteɪtmənt/
placement	/ˈpleɪsmənt/
recruit	/rɪˈkruːt/
student loan	/ˌstjuːdnt ˈləʊn/
trainee	/ˌtreɪˈniː/
voluntary	/ˈvɒləntri/
well paid	/ˌwel ˈpeɪd/

A different kind of tourism p.7

all-inclusive	/ˌɔːl ɪnˈkluːsɪv/
❶ get away	/ˌget əˈweɪ/
go trekking	/ˌɡəʊ ˈtrekɪŋ/
holidaymaker	/ˈhɒlədeɪmeɪkə(r)/
❶ make a booking	/meɪk ə ˈbʊkɪŋ/
memorable	/ˈmemərəbl/
mountain biking	/ˈmaʊntən baɪkɪŋ/
package holiday	/ˈpækɪdʒ hɒlədeɪ/
❶ resort	/rɪˈzɔːt/

Unit 1

The road to success pp.8–9 and 120

❶ attempt to (do)	/əˈtempt tə duː/
be a boost to someone's confidence	/bi ə ˌbuːst tə ˌsʌmwʌnz ˈkɒnfɪdəns/
be motivated	/bi ˈməʊtɪveɪtɪd/
fulfil a dream	/ˌfʊlfɪl ə ˈdriːm/
❶ master	/ˈmɑːstə(r)/
overcome a problem	/ˌəʊvəˌkʌm ə ˈprɒbləm/
pick up the basics	/ˌpɪk ʌp ðə ˈbeɪsɪks/
watch online tutorials	/ˌwɒtʃ ɒnˌlaɪn tjuːˈtɔːriəlz/
❶ be capable of	/bi ˈkeɪpəbl əv/
be hopeless at	/bi ˈhəʊpləs ət/
❶ focus your attention on	/ˌfəʊkəs jər əˈtenʃn ɒn/
❶ gain experience	/ɡeɪn ɪkˈspɪəriəns/
❶ have the potential to	/ˌhæv ðə pəˈtenʃl tə/
❶ inspire someone to	/ɪnˈspaɪə ˌsʌmwʌn tə/
❶ put the theory into practice	/ˌpʊt ðə ˌθɪəri ɪntə ˈpræktɪs/
❶ be determined to succeed	/bi dɪˌtɜːmɪnd tə səkˈsiːd/
be easy-going	/bi ˌiːzi ˈɡəʊɪŋ/
be open-minded	/bi ˌəʊpən ˈmaɪndɪd/
be self-confident	/bi ˌself ˈkɒnfɪdənt/
be selfish	/bi ˈselfɪʃ/
cope well with stress	/kəʊp ˌwel wɪð ˈstres/
feel awkward in social situations	/fiːl ˌɔːkwəd ɪn ˌsəʊʃl sɪtʃuˈeɪʃnz/
❶ get upset easily	/ˌɡet ʌpˌset ˈiːzəli/
❶ have a positive attitude to life	/hæv ə ˌpɒzətɪv ˈætɪtjuːd tə ˈlaɪf/
❶ have good people skills	/hæv ˌɡʊd ˈpiːpl skɪlz/
❶ tend to complain a lot	/ˌtend tə kəmˈpleɪn ə lɒt/

Real English p.9

❶ come naturally to someone	/kʌm ˈnætʃrəli tə ˌsʌmwʌn/
❶ get the feel of	/ˌɡet ðə ˈfiːl əv/
go downhill	/ˌɡəʊ daʊnˈhɪl/
❶ make all the difference	/meɪk ˌɔːl ðə ˈdɪfrəns/
❶ not getting anywhere	/ˌnɒt ˌɡetɪŋ eniˌweə(r)/
❶ That's always a plus.	/ðæts ˌɔːlweɪz ə ˈplʌs/

Teaching yourself p.11

❶ catch up on	/ˌkætʃ ˈʌp ɒn/
❶ come across	/kʌm əˈkrɒs/
❶ drop out	/ˌdrɒp ˈaʊt/
❶ figure out	/ˌfɪɡər ˈaʊt/
❶ go on to (do something)	/ˌɡəʊ ˌɒn tə ˈduː sʌmθɪŋ/

WORDLIST

❶ go through	/ɡəʊ ˈθruː/	
❶ live up to	/lɪv ˈʌp tə/	
❶ pick up	/pɪk ˈʌp/	

The best age p.12 and p.120

absorb information	/əbˌzɔːb ɪnfəˈmeɪʃn/
❶ acquire a second language	/əˌkwaɪər ə ˌsekənd ˈlæŋɡwɪdʒ/
adolescence	/ædəˈlesns/
adulthood	/ˈædʌlthʊd/
❶ be wise	/ˌbi ˈwaɪz/
distract	/dɪˈstrækt/
have an extensive vocabulary	/hæv ən ɪkˌstensɪv vəˈkæbjələri/
❶ in middle age	/ɪn ˌmɪdl ˈeɪdʒ/
in your late teens	/ɪn jə ˌleɪt ˈtiːnz/
mature	/məˈtʃʊə(r)/
mental arithmetic	/ˌmentl əˈrɪθmətɪk/
❶ recall people's names	/rɪˌkɔːl piːplz ˈneɪmz/
retirement	/rɪˈtaɪəmənt/
the older generation	/ði ˌəʊldə dʒenəˈreɪʃn/
❶ be a natural	/ˌbi ə ˈnætʃrəl/
build rapport	/bɪld ræˈpɔː(r)/
capitalise on something	/ˈkæpɪtəlaɪz ɒn sʌmθɪŋ/
have strict self-control	/hæv ˌstrɪkt self kənˈtrəʊl/
push your boundaries	/pʊʃ jə ˈbaʊndriz/
❶ show leadership	/ˌʃəʊ ˈliːdəʃɪp/
❶ think outside the box	/θɪŋk aʊtˌsaɪd ðə ˈbɒks/

The Outsiders pp.14–15

❶ get hold of someone	/ɡet ˈhəʊld əv sʌmwʌn/
❶ get into something	/ɡet ˈɪntə sʌmθɪŋ/
❶ get off work	/ɡet ɒf ˈwɜːk/
❶ get out	/ɡet ˈaʊt/
❶ get someone	/ˈɡet sʌmwʌn/
❶ get to know	/ɡet tə ˈnəʊ/

Emotional intelligence p.16

assertive	/əˈsɜːtɪv/
❶ be justified	/ˌbi ˈdʒʌstɪfaɪd/
❶ criticism	/ˈkrɪtɪsɪzəm/
❶ judgement	/ˈdʒʌdʒmənt/
lose your temper	/ˌluːz jə ˈtempə(r)/
❶ maintain relationships	/meɪnˌteɪn rɪˈleɪʃnʃɪps/
❶ perspective	/pəˈspektɪv/
state of mind	/ˌsteɪt əv ˈmaɪnd/

An article p.18

Admittedly, …	/ədˈmɪtɪdli/
Amazingly, …	/əˈmeɪzɪŋli/
Basically, …	/ˈbeɪsɪkli/
Consequently, …	/ˈkɒnsɪkwəntli/
Hopefully, …	/ˈhəʊpfəli/
Ideally, …	/aɪˈdiːəli/
Initially, …	/ɪˈnɪʃəli/
Interestingly, …	/ˈɪntrəstɪŋli/
Obviously, …	/ˈɒbviəsli/
Personally, (I think) …	/ˈpɜːsənəli/
(Not) Surprisingly, …	/səˈpraɪzɪŋli/
Unfortunately, …	/ʌnˈfɔːtʃənətli/

Unit 2

It drives me crazy! pp. 22–23 and p.121

astonished	/əˈstɒnɪʃt/
❶ calm down	/kɑːm ˈdaʊn/
❶ drive (someone) crazy	/ˌdraɪv sʌmwʌn ˈkreɪzi/
❶ fall out with (someone)	/fɔːl ˈaʊt wɪð sʌmwʌn/
frustrated	/frʌˈstreɪtɪd/
furious	/ˈfjʊəriəs/
❶ get on (someone's) nerves	/ɡet ɒn sʌmwʌnz ˈnɜːvz/
irritated	/ˈɪrɪteɪtɪd/
❶ make up with (someone)	/ˌmeɪk ˈʌp wɪð sʌmwʌn/
miserable	/ˈmɪzrəbl/
❶ offended	/əˈfendɪd/
puzzled	/ˈpʌzld/
resentful	/rɪˈzentfl/
❶ talk (something) over	/tɔːk sʌmθɪŋ ˈəʊvə(r)/
❶ alarmed	/əˈlɑːmd/
amused	/əˈmjuːzd/
❶ anxious	/ˈæŋkʃəs/
charm	/tʃɑːm/
exasperated	/ɪɡˈzɑːspəreɪtɪd/
❶ grateful	/ˈɡreɪtfl/
stunned	/stʌnd/
upbeat	/ˈʌpbiːt/

Real English p.23

a big deal	/ə ˌbɪɡ ˈdiːl/
❶ be lost for words	/bi ˌlɒst fə ˈwɜːdz/
❶ blow your top	/bləʊ jə ˈtɒp/
❶ give it a rest	/ɡɪv ɪt ə ˈrest/
❶ It's doing my head in.	/ɪts ˌduːɪŋ maɪ ˈhed ɪn/
❶ Tell me about it!	/ˈtel mi əˌbaʊt ɪt/

Be more in control of your life p.25

❶ adapt to the circumstances	/əˌdæpt tə ðə ˈsɜːkəmstænsɪz/
❶ do something positive	/ˌduː sʌmθɪŋ ˈpɒzətɪv/
❶ maintain your focus	/meɪnˌteɪn jə ˈfəʊkəs/
❶ take control of the situation	/teɪk kənˌtrəʊl əv ðə sɪtʃuˈeɪʃn/
❶ take responsibility for your actions	/teɪk rɪspɒnsəˌbɪləti fə jər ˈækʃnz/

WORDLIST

Well-being p.26 and p.121

addiction	/əˈdɪkʃn/
anxiety	/æŋˈzaɪəti/
be mindful	/bi ˈmaɪndfl/
❶ be on the go	/bi ˌɒn ðə ˈɡəʊ/
build self-confidence	/ˌbɪld self ˈkɒnfɪdəns/
burnout	/ˈbɜːnaʊt/
chill out	/tʃɪl ˈaʊt/
depression	/dɪˈpreʃn/
develop a positive mindset	/dɪˌveləp ə ˌpɒzətɪv ˈmaɪndset/
downtime	/ˈdaʊntaɪm/
❶ get on top of someone	/ˌɡet ɒn ˈtɒp əv sʌmwʌn/
mental health	/ˌmentl ˈhelθ/
❶ regret	/rɪˈɡret/
thrive on stress	/ˌθraɪv ɒn ˈstres/
well-being	/ˈwel biːɪŋ/
proactive	/ˌprəʊˈæktɪv/
resilient	/rɪˈzɪliənt/
self-critical	/ˌself ˈkrɪtɪkl/
tactful	/ˈtæktfl/
vulnerable	/ˈvʌlnərəbl/
worthless	/ˈwɜːθləs/

Miracle on the Hudson pp.28–29

❶ evaluate the options	/ɪˌvæljueɪt ði ˈɒpʃnz/
❶ face a challenge	/feɪs ə ˈtʃælɪndʒ/
❶ make a commitment	/ˌmeɪk ə kəˈmɪtmənt/
❶ take account of	/ˌteɪk əˈkaʊnt əv/
trust your instincts	/ˌtrʌst jər ˈɪnstɪŋkts/

Building resilience p.30

❶ accept the fact	/əkˌsept ðə ˌfækt/
build resilience	/ˌbɪld rɪˈzɪliəns/
❶ define	/dɪˈfaɪn/
❶ get through	/ˌɡet ˈθruː/
self-esteem	/ˌself ɪˈstiːm/
setback	/ˈsetbæk/
❶ surround yourself with	/səˌraʊnd jəˌself wɪð/
❶ trust	/trʌst/
unavoidable	/ˌʌnəˈvɔɪdəbl/

Comparing photos p.31

❶ absolutely awful	/ˌæbsəluːtli ˈɔːfl/
completely absorbed	/kəmˌpliːtli əbˈzɔːbd/
❶ extremely useful	/ɪkˌstriːmli ˈjuːsfl/
pretty miserable	/ˌprɪti ˈmɪzrəbl/
❶ quite serious	/ˌkwaɪt ˈsɪəriəs/
❶ totally fascinating	/ˌtəʊtəli ˈfæsɪneɪtɪŋ/

Unit 3

Real English p.37

couch potato	/ˈkaʊtʃ pəteɪtəʊ/
❶ job done	/ˌdʒɒb ˈdʌn/
❶ keep at something	/ˈkiːp ət sʌmθɪŋ/
let off steam	/ˌlet ɒf ˈstiːm/
❶ That's it?	/ˌðæts ˈɪt/
❶ Too much information!	/ˌtuː mʌtʃ ˌɪnfəˈmeɪʃn/

Let's keep fit p.37 and p.122

addictive	/əˈdɪktɪv/
beneficial	/ˌbenɪˈfɪʃl/
❶ challenging	/ˈtʃælɪndʒɪŋ/
❶ complicated	/ˈkɒmplɪkeɪtɪd/
❶ enthusiastic	/ɪnˌθjuːziˈæstɪk/
❶ fit in with your daily routine	/ˌfɪt ɪn wɪð jə ˌdeɪli ruːˈtiːn/
❶ flexible	/ˈfleksəbl/
❶ have a positive impact on	/ˌhæv ə ˌpɒzətɪv ˈɪmpækt ɒn/
❶ increase your heart rate	/ɪnˌkriːs jə ˈhɑːt reɪt/
❶ maintain your physical health	/meɪnˌteɪn jə ˌfɪzɪkl ˈhelθ/
❶ make someone aware of	/ˌmeɪk sʌmwʌn əˈweər əv/
❶ stiff	/stɪf/
❶ stretch your muscles	/ˌstretʃ jə ˈmʌslz/
❶ take up a lot of time	/ˌteɪk ʌp ə ˌlɒt əv ˈtaɪm/
thrilled	/θrɪld/
work up a sweat	/ˌwɜːk ʌp ə ˈswet/
❶ build strength	/ˌbɪld ˈstreŋkθ/
❶ focus on the positives	/ˌfəʊkəs ɒn ðə ˈpɒzətɪvz/
❶ get fit	/ˌɡet ˈfɪt/
❶ hate losing	/ˌheɪt ˈluːzɪŋ/
increase your stamina	/ɪnˌkriːs jə ˈstæmɪnə/
individual sport	/ˌɪndɪˈvɪdʒuəl spɔːt/
❶ take on a challenge	/ˌteɪk ɒn ə ˈtʃælɪndʒ/
team sport	/ˈtiːm spɔːt/

The origins of sport p.39

dispute	/dɪˈspjuːt/
originate	/əˈrɪdʒɪneɪt/
recreation	/ˌrekriˈeɪʃn/
survival	/səˈvaɪvl/
tribe	/traɪb/
warfare	/ˈwɔːfeə(r)/

Transferable skills p.40 and p.122

❶ accept the consequences of	/əkˌsept ðə ˈkɒnsɪkwənsɪz əv/
❶ adapt to	/əˈdæpt tə/
❶ be willing to	/ˌbi ˈwɪlɪŋ tə/
collaboration	/kəˌlæbəˈreɪʃn/
❶ commitment	/kəˈmɪtmənt/
contribute to	/kənˈtrɪbjuːt tə/

WORDLIST

cope under pressure	/ˌkəʊp ˌʌndə ˈpreʃə(r)/
❶ demand	/dɪˈmɑːnd/
❶ demonstrate	/ˈdemənstreɪt/
❶ failure	/ˈfeɪljə(r)/
❶ leadership	/ˈliːdəʃɪp/
organisational skills	/ɔːgənaɪˈzeɪʃənl skɪlz/
self-confidence	/ˌself ˈkɒnfɪdəns/
❶ take responsibility for	/ˌteɪk rɪspɒnsəˈbɪləti fə(r)/
teamwork	/ˈtiːmwɜːk/
devote time to something	/dɪˌvəʊt ˈtaɪm tə sʌmθɪŋ/
❶ do yourself proud	/ˌduː jəself ˈpraʊd/
❶ know something like the back of your hand	/ˌnəʊ sʌmθɪŋ laɪk ðə ˌbæk əv jə ˈhænd/
❶ leave your comfort zone	/ˌliːv jə ˈkʌmfət zəʊn/
mutual respect	/ˌmjuːtʃuəl rɪˈspekt/
❶ pursue your dream(s)	/pəˌsjuː jə ˈdriːm(z)/

Review: *Rising Phoenix* pp.42–43

excel	/ɪkˈsel/
fulfil your potential	/fʊlˌfɪl jə pəˈtenʃl/
overcome obstacles	/ˌəʊvəkʌm ˈɒbstəklz/
psychological barrier	/ˌsaɪkəˌlɒdʒɪkl ˈbæriə(r)/
specialise in	/ˈspeʃəlaɪz ɪn/

Managing your reaction p.44

❶ challenge	/ˈtʃælɪndʒ/
❶ conflict	/ˈkɒnflɪkt/
❶ get emotional about	/ˌget ɪˈməʊʃənl əbaʊt/
❶ hesitate	/ˈhezɪteɪt/
make a fuss	/ˌmeɪk ə ˈfʌs/
overreact	/ˌəʊvəriˈækt/
❶ propose	/prəˈpəʊz/
❶ take it personally	/ˌteɪk ɪt ˈpɜːsənəli/

Unit 4

Real English p.51

a trade-off	/ə ˈtreɪd ɒf/
all mod cons	/ˌɔːl mɒd ˈkɒnz/
❶ Don't get me wrong …	/ˌdəʊnt get mi ˈrɒŋ/
❶ miss the boat	/ˌmɪs ðə ˈbəʊt/
❶ Now you're talking!	/ˌnaʊ jɔː ˌtɔːkɪŋ/
❶ over the top	/ˌəʊvə ðə ˈtɒp/

Alternative living spaces p.51 and p.123

affordable	/əˈfɔːdəbl/
central heating	/ˌsentrəl ˈhiːtɪŋ/
energy-efficient	/ˈenədʒi ɪˌfɪʃnt/
❶ facilities	/fəˈsɪlətiz/
ingenious	/ɪnˈdʒiːniəs/
open-plan	/ˌəʊpən ˈplæn/
proportions	/prəˈpɔːʃnz/
remote control	/rɪˌməʊt kənˈtrəʊl/
restricted	/rɪˈstrɪktɪd/
smart appliance	/ˌsmɑːt əˈplaɪəns/
spacious	/ˈspeɪʃəs/
staircase	/ˈsteəkeɪs/
storage	/ˈstɔːrɪdʒ/
❶ urban	/ˈɜːbən/
well equipped	/ˌwel ɪˈkwɪpt/
work surface	/ˈwɜːk sɜːfɪs/
block of flats	/ˌblɒk əv ˈflæts/
❶ cottage	/ˈkɒtɪdʒ/
semi-detached house	/ˌsemi dɪˌtætʃt ˈhaʊs/
skyscraper	/ˈskaɪskreɪpə(r)/
terraced house	/ˌterəst ˈhaʊs/
three-storey building	/ˌθriː stɔːri ˈbɪldɪŋ/

The future of city centres p.53

❶ go out of business	/ˌgəʊ aʊt əv ˈbɪznəs/
home office	/ˌhəʊm ˈɒfɪs/
part-time job	/ˌpɑːt taɪm ˈdʒɒb/
self-employed	/ˌself ɪmˈplɔɪd/
work remotely	/ˌwɜːk rɪˈməʊtli/
workplace	/ˈwɜːkpleɪs/

Nomads p.54 and p.123

appeal to	/əˈpiːl tə/
assistance	/əˈsɪstəns/
communal	/kəˈmjuːnl/
dependent	/dɪˈpendənt/
emigrate	/ˈemɪgreɪt/
extended family	/ɪkˌstendɪd ˈfæməli/
lifestyle choice	/ˈlaɪfstaɪl tʃɔɪs/
nomadic existence	/nəʊˌmædɪk ɪgˈzɪstəns/
❶ permanent	/ˈpɜːmənənt/
❶ possession	/pəˈzeʃn/
❶ settle	/ˈsetl/
settlement	/ˈsetlmənt/
❶ shelter	/ˈʃeltə(r)/
support network	/səˈpɔːt netwɜːk/
❶ temporary	/ˈtemprəri/
wander	/ˈwɒndə(r)/
assumption	/əˈsʌmpʃn/
basic necessities	/ˌbeɪsɪk nəˈsesətiz/
disadvantaged	/ˌdɪsədˈvɑːntɪdʒd/
hardship	/ˈhɑːdʃɪp/
social housing	/ˌsəʊʃl ˈhaʊzɪŋ/
stereotype	/ˈsteriətaɪp/

A short history of migration p.57

drought	/draʊt/
extreme weather event	/ɪkˌstriːm ˈweðər ɪvent/

WORDLIST

❶ flooding	/ˈflʌdɪŋ/	hardware	/ˈhɑːdweə(r)/
food insecurity	/ˈfuːd ɪnsɪˈkjʊərəti/	hydroelectric power	/ˌhaɪdrəʊɪˌlektrɪk ˈpaʊə(r)/
habitable	/ˈhæbɪtəbl/	❶ network	/ˈnetwɜːk/
❶ pressure on resources	/ˌpreʃə ɒn rɪˈsɔːsɪz/	❶ recycling waste	/riːˌsaɪklɪŋ ˈweɪst/
❶ rising sea level	/ˌraɪzɪŋ ˈsiː levl/	❶ software	/ˈsɒftweə(r)/
uninhabitable	/ˌʌnɪnˈhæbɪtəbl/	wind turbine	/ˈwɪnd tɜːbaɪn/
		wireless mouse	/ˌwaɪələs ˈmaʊs/

Identifying and analysing trends p.58

a downturn	/ə ˈdaʊntɜːn/	**Real English p.65**	
an upward trend	/ən ˌʌpwəd ˈtrend/	a no-brainer	/ə ˌnəʊ ˈbreɪnə/
❶ decrease (n)	/ˈdiːkriːs/	❶ get your head around	/ˌget jə ˈhed əraʊnd/
❶ decrease (v)	/dɪˈkriːs/	it's not rocket science	/ɪts ˌnɒt ˈrɒkɪt saɪəns/
❶ dramatic	/drəˈmætɪk/	piece of kit	/ˌpiːs əv ˈkɪt/
dramatically	/drəˈmætɪkli/	❶ take for granted	/ˌteɪk fə ˈɡrɑːntɪd/
❶ fall	/fɔːl/		
❶ go down	/ɡəʊ ˈdaʊn/	**Streaming p.67**	
❶ go up	/ɡəʊ ˈʌp/	digital revolution	/ˌdɪdʒɪtl revəˈluːʃn/
❶ increase (n)	/ˈɪŋkriːs/	distance learning	/ˌdɪstəns ˈlɜːnɪŋ/
❶ increase (v)	/ɪnˈkriːs/	on-demand content	/ˌɒn dɪˌmɑːnd ˈkɒntent/
❶ rise	/raɪz/	social interaction	/ˌsəʊʃl ɪntərˈækʃn/
❶ sharp	/ʃɑːp/	subscription service	/səbˈskrɪpʃn ˌsɜːvɪs/
sharply	/ˈʃɑːpli/		
❶ slight	/slaɪt/	**Technology and the environment p.68 and p.124**	
❶ slightly	/ˈslaɪtli/	alternative energy	/ɔːlˌtɜːnətɪv ˈenədʒi/
steadily	/ˈstedəli/	carbon footprint	/ˌkɑːbən ˈfʊtprɪnt/
❶ steady	/ˈstedi/	consumption	/kənˈsʌmpʃn/
		deforestation	/ˌdiːfɒrɪˈsteɪʃn/

Unit 5

What gadget couldn't you live without? pp.64–65 and p.124

		dispose of	/dɪˈspəʊz əv/
		endanger	/ɪnˈdeɪndʒə(r)/
		environmentally friendly	/ɪnˌvaɪrənmentəli ˈfrendli/
❶ advances in technology	/ədˌvɑːnsɪz ɪn tekˈnɒlədʒi/	❶ generate	/ˈdʒenəreɪt/
artificial intelligence	/ˌɑːtɪfɪʃl ɪnˈtelɪdʒəns/	global warming	/ˌɡləʊbl ˈwɔːmɪŋ/
browse	/braʊz/	landfill site	/ˈlændfɪl saɪt/
gadget	/ˈɡædʒɪt/	natural resources	/ˌnætʃrəl rɪˈsɔːsɪz/
game-changing	/ˈɡeɪm tʃeɪndʒɪŋ/	raw material	/ˌrɔː məˈtɪəriəl/
geek	/ɡiːk/	renewable	/rɪˈnjuːəbl/
high-tech	/ˌhaɪ ˈtek/	reuse	/ˌriːˈjuːz/
innovative	/ˈɪnəveɪtɪv/	viable	/ˈvaɪəbl/
input	/ˈɪnpʊt/	carbon capture	/ˌkɑːbən ˈkæptʃə(r)/
❶ significant	/sɪɡˈnɪfɪkənt/	carbon storage	/ˌkɑːbən ˈstɔːrɪdʒ/
sophisticated	/səˈfɪstɪkeɪtɪd/	climate change denial	/ˈklaɪmət tʃeɪndʒ dɪnaɪəl/
streaming	/ˈstriːmɪŋ/	conservationist	/ˌkɒnsəˈveɪʃənɪst/
technophobe	/ˈteknəʊfəʊb/	eco-anxiety	/ˌiːkəʊ æŋˈzaɪəti/
❶ update	/ˈʌpdeɪt/	ecology	/ɪˈkɒlədʒi/
user-friendly	/ˌjuːzə ˈfrendli/	monoculture	/ˈmɒnəkʌltʃə(r)/
wearable technology	/ˌweərəbl tekˈnɒlədʒi/	wildfires	/ˈwaɪldfaɪə(r)z/
biodegradable	/ˌbaɪəʊdɪˈɡreɪdəbl/	zero-emissions	/ˌzɪərəʊ ɪˈmɪʃnz/
click on an icon	/ˌklɪk ɒn ən ˈaɪkɒn/		
climate change	/ˈklaɪmət tʃeɪndʒ/	**Quitting social media pp.70–71**	
		❶ adapt to	/əˈdæpt tə/
		obsessed with	/əbˈsest wɪð/

124 Wordlist

WORDLIST

peer group	/ˈpɪə gruːp/
scroll through	/ˌskrəʊl ˈθruː/
❶ target	/ˈtɑːgɪt/
❶ update	/ˈʌpdeɪt/

Your digital footprint p.72

background check	/ˈbækgraʊnd tʃek/
hacking	/ˈhækɪŋ/
inactive	/ɪnˈæktɪv/
privacy settings	/ˈprɪvəsi ˌsetɪŋz/
required information	/rɪˌkwaɪəd ɪnfəˈmeɪʃn/
respectful	/rɪˈspektfl/
tag	/tæg/
trace	/treɪs/
untag	/ʌnˈtæg/

Unit 6

Real English p.79

❶ have your eye on something	/ˌhæv jər ˈaɪ ɒn ˈsʌmθɪŋ/
❶ it all adds up	/ɪt ˌɔːl ædz ˈʌp/
❶ not break the bank	/nɒt ˌbreɪk ðə ˈbæŋk/
save money for a rainy day	/seɪv ˌmʌni fər ə ˌreɪni ˈdeɪ/
❶ spend money like water	/spend ˌmʌni laɪk ˈwɔːtə(r)/
strapped for cash	/stræpt fə ˈkæʃ/

No-spend challenge p.79 and p.125

accessories	/əkˈsesəriz/
❶ be on a limited budget	/bi ɒn ə ˌlɪmɪtɪd ˈbʌdʒɪt/
❶ build up your savings account	/ˌbɪld ʌp jə ˈseɪvɪŋz əkaʊnt/
bus fares	/ˈbʌs feəz/
charity donations	/ˈtʃærəti dəʊneɪʃnz/
cut out non-essentials	/ˌkʌt aʊt ˌnɒn ɪˈsenʃlz/
everyday expenses	/ˌevrideɪ ɪkˈspensɪz/
gaming	/ˈgeɪmɪŋ/
❶ get your spending under control	/ˌget jə ˌspendɪŋ ʌndə kənˈtrəʊl/
gym membership	/ˈdʒɪm membəʃɪp/
keep track of your finances	/kiːp ˌtræk əv jə ˈfaɪnænsɪz/
owe someone money	/əʊ ˌsʌmwʌn ˈmʌni/
second-hand stuff	/ˌsekənd ˈhænd stʌf/
spend (your) money wisely	/ˌspend jə ˌmʌni ˈwaɪzli/
takeaways	/ˈteɪkəweɪz/
tuition fees	/tjuˈɪʃn fiːz/
❶ use up the things I already have	/ˌjuːz ʌp ðə ˌθɪŋz aɪ ɔːlˌredi ˈhæv/
make a deposit	/ˌmeɪk ə dɪˈpɒzɪt/
❶ make a loss	/ˌmeɪk ə ˈlɒs/
make sacrifices	/ˌmeɪk ˈsækrɪfaɪsɪz/
❶ put money towards	/ˌpʊt ˈmʌni təwɔːdz/
❶ run out of money	/ˌrʌn aʊt əv ˈmʌni/
❶ take control of your finances	/ˌteɪk kənˌtrəʊl əv jə ˈfaɪnænsɪz/

Less is more p.81

consumerism	/kənˈsjuːmərɪzəm/
❶ do without	/duː wɪˈðaʊt/
❶ get rid of	/ˌget ˈrɪd əv/
lead a more meaningful life	/liːd ə mɔː ˌmiːnɪŋfl ˈlaɪf/
material possession	/məˌtɪəriəl pəˈzeʃn/
❶ pursue your passion	/pəˌsjuː jə ˈpæʃn/

Social commerce p.82 and p.125

carry out a transaction	/ˌkæri ˌaʊt ə trænˈzækʃn/
❶ choose a delivery option	/ˌtʃuːz ə dɪˈlɪvəri ɒpʃn/
confirmation email	/ˌkɒnfəˌmeɪʃn ˈiːmeɪl/
pick up a bargain	/ˌpɪk ʌp ə ˈbɑːgən/
potential customer	/pəˌtenʃl ˈkʌstəmə(r)/
proceed to the checkout	/prəˌsiːd tə ðə ˈtʃekaʊt/
❶ purchase a product	/ˌpɜːtʃəs ə ˈprɒdʌkt/
reference number	/ˈrefrəns nʌmbə(r)/
retail price	/ˈriːteɪl praɪs/
❶ select the right quantity	/sɪˌlekt ðə ˌraɪt ˈkwɒntəti/
shipping costs	/ˈʃɪpɪŋ kɒsts/
special offer	/ˌspeʃl ˈɒfə(r)/
contactless	/ˈkɒntæktləs/
cost-cutting	/ˈkɒst kʌtɪŋ/
impulse buy	/ˈɪmpʌls baɪ/
overdrawn	/ˌəʊvəˈdrɔːn/
❶ pay your way	/ˌpeɪ jə ˈweɪ/
tighten your belt	/ˌtaɪtn jə ˈbelt/

Fast fashion pp.84–85

designer label	/dɪˌzaɪnə ˈleɪbl/
fashion-conscious	/ˈfæʃn kɒnʃəs/
garment	/ˈgɑːmənt/
❶ get dressed up	/ˌget ˌdrest ˈʌp/
kit	/kɪt/
❶ mix and match	/ˌmɪks ən ˈmætʃ/
outfit	/ˈaʊtfɪt/
stylish	/ˈstaɪlɪʃ/

The small print p.86

faulty	/ˈfɔːlti/
genuine	/ˈdʒenjuɪn/
interest rate	/ˈɪntrest reɪt/
proof of purchase	/ˌpruːf əv ˈpɜːtʃəs/
❶ prove	/pruːv/
❶ receipt	/rɪˈsiːt/
refund	/ˈriːfʌnd/
returns policy	/rɪˈtɜːnz pɒləsi/

Wordlist 125

WORDLIST

short-term loan /ˌʃɔːt tɜːm 'ləʊn/
🔊 terms and conditions /ˌtɜːmz ən kən'dɪʃnz/
warranty information /'wɒrənti ɪnfəmeɪʃn/

Asserting your rights as a customer p.87

🔊 It shows an error message. /ɪt ʃəʊz ən 'erə mesɪdʒ/
🔊 It won't switch on. /ɪt ˌwəʊnt swɪtʃ 'ɒn/
It's ripped. /ɪts 'rɪpt/
The screen is cracked. /ðə ˌskriːn ɪz 'krækt/
The sleeves are too long. /ðə ˌsliːvz ə tuː 'lɒŋ/
🔊 There's a mark on it. /ðeərz ə 'mɑːk ɒn ɪt/

Unit 7

That sounds amazing! p.92 and p.126

a live gig /ə ˌlaɪv 'gɪg/
a masterpiece /ə 'mɑːstəpiːs/
a musical production /ə ˌmjuːzɪkl prə'dʌkʃn/
a new stage adaptation /ə ˌnjuː 'steɪdʒ ædæpˌteɪʃn/
a spectacular piece of work /ə spek ˌtækjələ ˌpiːs əv 'wɜːk/
a VR headset /ə ˌviː ɑː 'hedset/
abstract art /ˌæbstrækt 'ɑːt/
art critic /'ɑːt krɪtɪk/
contemporary dance /kənˌtemprəri 'dɑːns/
give an outstanding performance /gɪv ən aʊtˌstændɪŋ pəˈfɔːməns/
gorgeous colours /ˌgɔːdʒəs 'kʌləz/
🔊 on display /ɒn dɪ'spleɪ/
stunning artwork /ˌstʌnɪŋ 'ɑːtwɜːk/
the performing arts /ðə pəˌfɔːmɪŋ 'ɑːts/
view the exhibits /ˌvjuː ði ɪg'zɪbɪts/
visual arts /ˌvɪʒuəl 'ɑːts/
clay /kleɪ/
🔊 drawing /'drɔːɪŋ/
🔊 frame /freɪm/
metaphor /'metəfə(r)/
oil painting /'ɔɪl peɪntɪŋ/
🔊 portrait /'pɔːtreɪt/
pottery /'pɒtəri/
🔊 sculpture /'skʌlptʃə(r)/

Real English p.93

🔊 I don't get it. /aɪ ˌdəʊnt 'get ɪt/
🔊 I was blown away. /aɪ wəz ˌbləʊn ə'weɪ/
🔊 It does nothing for me. /ɪt dʌz 'nʌθɪŋ fə ˌmiː/
🔊 That's my kind of thing. /'ðæts maɪ ˌkaɪnd əv ˌθɪŋ/
🔊 well worth seeing /ˌwel wɜːθ 'siːɪŋ/

What a great score! p.95

🔊 artist /'ɑːtɪst/
🔊 blues /bluːz/
🔊 classical /'klæsɪkl/
🔊 country /'kʌntri/
🔊 electronic /ɪˌlek'trɒnɪk/
hard rock /ˌhɑːd 'rɒk/
hip-hop /'hɪp hɒp/
🔊 mix /mɪks/
🔊 note /nəʊt/
🔊 pop /pɒp/
rap /ræp/
reggae /'regeɪ/
🔊 release /rɪ'liːs/
salsa /'sælsə/
🔊 shoot /ʃuːt/
🔊 soul /səʊl/
🔊 track /træk/

Updated masterpieces p.96 and p.126

add a new dimension /ˌæd ə ˌnjuː daɪ'menʃn/
🔊 be inspired by /bi ɪn'spaɪəd baɪ/
be passionate about /bi 'pæʃənət əbaʊt/
🔊 capture /'kæptʃə(r)/
colourful /'kʌləfl/
convey a sense of /kənˌveɪ ə 'sens əv/
🔊 detailed /'diːteɪld/
🔊 dramatic /drə'mætɪk/
🔊 draw attention to /ˌdrɔː ə'tenʃn tə/
🔊 humorous /'hjuːmərəs/
portray /pɔː'treɪ/
🔊 realistic /ˌriːə'lɪstɪk/
🔊 striking /'straɪkɪŋ/
thought-provoking /'θɔːt prəvəʊkɪŋ/
vivid /'vɪvɪd/
canvas /'kænvəs/
🔊 landscape /'lændskeɪp/
line drawing /'laɪn drɔːɪŋ/
performance art /pə'fɔːməns ɑːt/
shading /'ʃeɪdɪŋ/
spray paint /'spreɪ peɪnt/
surrealism /sə'riːəlɪzəm/
watercolour /'wɔːtəkʌlə(r)/

Art and travel pp.98–99

🔊 get away from it all /get ə'weɪ frəm ɪt ˌɔːl/
get itchy feet /get ˌɪtʃi 'fiːt/
🔊 hit the road /ˌhɪt ðə 'rəʊd/
🔊 off the beaten track /ˌɒf ðə ˌbiːtn 'træk/
🔊 see the world /ˌsiː ðə 'wɜːld/
🔊 the four corners of the world /ðə ˌfɔː ˌkɔːnəz əv ðə 'wɜːld/

WORDLIST

Copyright and plagiarism p.100

attribution	/ˌætrɪˈbjuːʃn/
citation	/saɪˈteɪʃn/
copyright	/ˈkɒpiraɪt/
direct quotation	/dəˌrekt kwəʊˈteɪʃn/
❶ licence	/ˈlaɪsns/
logo	/ˈləʊgəʊ/
paraphrase	/ˈpærəfreɪz/
piracy	/ˈpaɪrəsi/
plagiarism	/ˈpleɪdʒərɪzəm/
❶ reference an idea	/ˌrefrəns ən aɪˈdɪə/
slogan	/ˈsləʊgən/
trademark	/ˈtreɪdmɑːk/

Unit 8

Lending a helping hand p.107 and p.127

become homeless	/bɪˌkʌm ˈhəʊmləs/
charity shop	/ˈtʃærəti ʃɒp/
community service	/kəˌmjuːnəti ˈsɜːvɪs/
elderly people	/ˌeldəli ˈpiːpl/
❶ engage with the issues	/ɪnˌgeɪdʒ wɪð ði ˈɪʃuːz/
❶ lack confidence	/ˌlæk ˈkɒnfɪdəns/
learning disability	/ˈlɜːnɪŋ dɪsəbɪləti/
local initiative	/ˌləʊkl ɪˈnɪʃətɪv/
❶ make a contribution	/ˌmeɪk ə kɒntrɪˈbjuːʃn/
one-to-one tuition	/ˌwʌn tə ˌwʌn tjuˈɪʃn/
provide assistance	/prəˌvaɪd əˈsɪstəns/
❶ raise funds	/ˌreɪz ˈfʌndz/
refuge	/ˈrefjuːdʒ/
retain your independence	/rɪˌteɪn jər ɪndɪˈpendəns/
social isolation	/ˌsəʊʃl aɪsəˈleɪʃn/
suffer hardship	/ˌsʌfə ˈhɑːdʃɪp/
❶ collapse	/kəˈlæps/
❶ disaster relief	/dɪˈzɑːstə rɪliːf/
famine	/ˈfæmɪn/
❶ good cause	/ˌgʊd ˈkɔːz/
❶ loss	/lɒs/
obstacle	/ˈɒbstəkl/
❶ poverty	/ˈpɒvəti/
❶ struggle	/ˈstrʌgl/

Real English p.107

❶ for a good cause	/fər ə ˌgʊd ˈkɔːz/
❶ give something back	/ˌgɪv sʌmθɪŋ ˈbæk/
❶ keep an eye on	/ˌkiːp ən ˈaɪ ɒn/
❶ lend a hand	/ˌlend ə ˈhænd/
real eye-opener	/ˌriːəl ˈaɪ əʊpənə(r)/
safety net	/ˈseɪfti net/

Different kinds of volunteering p.109

❶ a real laugh	/ə ˌriːəl ˈlɑːf/
not that hard	/ˌnɒt ðæt ˈhɑːd/
❶ check out	/ˌtʃek ˈaʊt/
❶ have a go at	/ˌhæv ə ˈgəʊ ət/
❶ said to myself	/ˌsed tə maɪˈself/

Crisis mapping p.110 and p.127

aid agency	/ˈeɪd eɪdʒənsi/
armed conflict	/ˌɑːmd ˈkɒnflɪkt/
❶ assess	/əˈses/
co-ordinate	/kəʊˈɔːdɪneɪt/
❶ distribute	/dɪˈstrɪbjuːt/
eliminate	/ɪˈlɪmɪneɪt/
❶ encounter	/ɪnˈkaʊntə(r)/
infrastructure	/ˈɪnfrəstrʌktʃə(r)/
❶ preserve	/prɪˈzɜːv/
❶ priority	/praɪˈɒrəti/
❶ process	/ˈprəʊses/
refugee	/ˌrefjuˈdʒiː/
relief effort	/rɪˈliːf efət/
❶ suffering	/ˈsʌfərɪŋ/
survivor	/səˈvaɪvə(r)/
❶ threaten	/ˈθretn/
aftermath of	/ˈɑːftəmɑːθ əv/
asylum seeker	/əˈsaɪləm siːkə(r)/
economic migrant	/ˌiːkənɒmɪk ˈmaɪgrənt/
inequality	/ˌɪnɪˈkwɒləti/
persecution	/ˌpɜːsɪˈkjuːʃn/
starvation	/stɑːˈveɪʃn/

Future-proofing the world pp.112–113

acidity	/əˈsɪdəti/
biodiversity	/ˌbaɪəʊdaɪˈvɜːsəti/
eradicate	/ɪˈrædɪkeɪt/
extinction	/ɪkˈstɪŋkʃn/
parasite	/ˈpærəsaɪt/
resistant	/rɪˈzɪstənt/

Disagreeing diplomatically p.114

acknowledge different perspectives	/əkˌnɒlɪdʒ ˌdɪfrənt pəˈspektɪvz/
avoid confrontation	/əˌvɔɪd kɒnfrʌnˈteɪʃn/
challenge prejudice or discrimination	/ˌtʃælɪndʒ ˌpredʒədɪs ɔː dɪskrɪmɪˈneɪʃn/
find a compromise	/ˌfaɪnd ə ˈkɒmprəmaɪz/
❶ go against your values	/ˌgəʊ əgenst jə ˈvæljuːz/
❶ make judgements	/ˌmeɪk ˈdʒʌdʒmənts/
set aside your differences	/ˌset əˌsaɪd jə ˈdɪfrənsɪz/
❶ show respect	/ˌʃəʊ rɪˈspekt/
❶ speak from an informed position	/ˌspiːk frəm ən ɪnˌfɔːmd pəˈzɪʃn/

OXFORD
UNIVERSITY PRESS

Great Clarendon Street, Oxford, OX2 6DP, United Kingdom

Oxford University Press is a department of the University of Oxford. It furthers the University's objective of excellence in research, scholarship, and education by publishing worldwide. Oxford is a registered trade mark of Oxford University Press in the UK and in certain other countries

© Oxford University Press 2022

The moral rights of the author have been asserted

First published in 2022

2026 2025 2024

10 9 8 7 6 5

No unauthorized photocopying

All rights reserved. No part of this publication may be reproduced, stored in a retrieval system, or transmitted, in any form or by any means, without the prior permission in writing of Oxford University Press, or as expressly permitted by law, by licence or under terms agreed with the appropriate reprographics rights organization. Enquiries concerning reproduction outside the scope of the above should be sent to the ELT Rights Department, Oxford University Press, at the address above

You must not circulate this work in any other form and you must impose this same condition on any acquirer

Links to third party websites are provided by Oxford in good faith and for information only. Oxford disclaims any responsibility for the materials contained in any third party website referenced in this work

ISBN: 978 0 19 406415 6

Printed in China

This book is printed on paper from certified and well-managed sources

ACKNOWLEDGEMENTS

The authors and publisher are grateful to those who have given permission to reproduce the following extracts and adaptations of copyright material: p.13 Adapted and abridged from 'Connectivism: A Theory of Learning for a Digital Age', by Thomas Baker, March 2011, https://oupeltglobalblog.com/. Reproduced by permission of Oxford University Press and Prof. George Siemens; p.23 Text about Georgia and Melissa Laurie is included with permission (and the image was supplied by Hana Laurie, © Hana Laurie); p.46 Graph in exercise 5 is adapted from Figure 1 'Filipino Professional Nurses Deployed Overseas, 2000–2015' (data calculated by the author from source: Philippine Overseas Employment Agency, 2015) from 'Learning to Fill the Labor Niche: Filipino Nursing Graduates and the Risk of the Migration Trap' by Yasmin Y Ortiga in *The Russell Sage Foundation Journal of the Social Sciences*, Jan 2018, 4 (1) 172–187. Reproduced by permission of The Russell Sage Foundation, permission conveyed through Copyright Clearance Center, Inc; p.58 Texts about WildEarth safaris, Be My Eyes, and Eric Whitacre's Virtual Choir are included with permission of the organisations named; p.88 Text about the Walrus From Space project is included with permission and is a project co-led by WWF and British Antarctic Survey (BAS).

Sources: p.19 https://misophoniainstitute.org/; p.23 'Brit saves twin sister by punching crocodile in the face', BBC News, June 2021; p.45 HESA destination of leavers survey, Philippine Nurses Association, www.nursingcentre.com; p.46 OECD/Health Workforce Migration/Foreign-trained doctors by country of origin, stats.oecd.org; p.50 'Finland ends homelessness and provides shelter for all in need', Kontrast.at, Nov. 2020, https://scoop.me; p.63 The National Financial Educators Council, Dec 2019; p.77 some information for this text supplied by Nada Badran; p.83 'Some people feel threatened': face to face with Ai-Da the robot artist' by Mark Brown, *The Guardian*, May 2021; p.87 www.msf.org.uk; p.92 www.seashepherdglobal.org, www.fao.org, www.msc.org, www.cbd.int;p.95 'Space research can save the planet – again' by Grey Autry, July 2019, https://foreignpolicy.com.

Cover images by: Getty Images (Alexander Spatari, TorriPhoto, Stevica Mrdja/EyeEm); Shutterstock (lzf)

The publisher would like to thank the following for the permission to reproduce photographs: 123RF (Dean Drobot); Alamy Stock Photo (Album, Archivart, Carolyn Jenkins, Cavan Images, dpa picture alliance, Eric Hui, Geoffrey Robinson, IanDagnall Computing, Image Source, imageBROKER, Iuliia Mazur, Mim Friday, Oleksandr Prykhodko, PA Images, R.M. Nunes, Robert Harding World Imagery, Sam Oaksey, Stefano Paterna, Susan E. Degginger, WENN Rights Ltd, World History Archive, Yurii Zushchyk, ZUMA Press, Inc.); Nada Badran; João Carvalho; Getty Images (Andrew Paterson, Dan Kitwood, frantic00, Justin Lambert, Moritz Winde, Neilson Barnard, SDI Productions, wundervisuals); Hana Laurie; Ema Klucovska; Shutterstock (abramsdesign, acharyahargreaves, Africa Studio, alazur, Alex Hinds, Alex Kravtsov, AlexMaster, Ali Babashzade, Anansing, Andrii Spy_k, Andrii Yalanskyi, Andy Glenn, ANL, Anna Andersson Fotografi, Anton Havelaar, Artem Varnitsin, Audrius Venclova, Bana Balleh, Blue Planet Studio, Bunditinay, Dean Drobot, Diana Rui, Dirima, Elena_Alex_Ferns, Erni, ESB Professional, fizkes, Glinskaja Olga, GoodStudio, Gorodenkoff, IhorZigor, imnoom, Ingo Bartussek, Ingus Kruklitis, Ira Lichi, Ivan Sarenas, James Aloysius Mahan V, KatePhotographer, KellySHUTSTOC, Kevin Wells Photography, Macrovector, Martha Kraft, Mateusz Kuca, Max Earey, Media Guru, Michael715, miker, Modvector, monticello, Moviestore, Nadia Snopek, NotionPic, nullplus, Ollivka, Paper Trident, Phanu D Pongvanit, pio3, Poprugin Aleksey, Poring Studio, Prathankarnpap, Prostock-studio, Pul Kock Lee, Rawpixel.com, Rich Carey, Richard Oldroyd, Robert Plociennik, rook76, Sanchik, SewCream, Sky Designs, Slavun, Smolina Marianna, SofikoS, SpeedKingz, Stakes, Stiva Urban, Strahil Dimitrov, Sunbeam_ks, suriya yapin, svitlini, Ted Shaffrey/AP, thaikrit, Theastock, Torwaistudio, Vector A, Wachiwit, Wolfgang Zwanzger, XArtProduction, Zaruba Ondrej).

Commissioned photography by: MTJ Media pp.8, 18, 30, 40, 52, 62, 74, 84.

Videos filmed and produced by: MTJ Media.

The publisher would like to thank the following reviewers for their helpful comments: Maria Fernanda Puertas, José Luis Rivero, Daniela Kavecká, Ferenc Kelemen and Anita Prol Pato.